COYKENDALL'S
SPORTING
COLLECTIBLES
PRICE GUIDE

COYKENDALL'S SPORTING COLLECTIBLES PRICE GUIDE

Ralf Coykendall, Jr.

Lyons & Burford, Publishers

This one is for five children
who aren't children anymore:
the finest collectibles of all.

Printed in the United States of America

10 9 8 7 6 5 4 3 2 1

Library of Congress Cataloging-in-Publication Data

Coykendall, Ralf W. (Ralf Wales), 1929–
    Coykendall's sporting collectibles price guide / Ralf Coykendall,
Jr.
        p.   cm.
    ISBN 1-55821-101-2
    1. Sports—Collectibles—United States—Catalogs.   I. Title.
II. Title: Sporting collectibles price guide.
GV568.5.C69   1991
796'.075—dc20   91-4163
                                                        CIP

Contents

Acknowledgments

A great many people helped make this book possible and each has my very warmest appreciation. They are, in no particular order, as follows: Beverly and Bob Strauss of Circus Promotions; the entire crew at the Richard Oliver auction galleries; Ken and Diane Callahan; Tom Daly; Greg Hamilton; Robert Hanafee; and everyone at the Richard A. Bourne auction galleries in Hyannis. Others are Judy Bowman; Jack Ordeman; Tim Stevenson; Andy Avery; Arthur Chesmore; and James Julia and Gary Guyette and their staff at Julia's auction galleries. Martin Keane helped, as did Richard Oinonen, Jim Tillinghast, Skip Woodruff, Russell Fink, William Webster and Michael Lidgerding at Wild Wings; John Shoffner; the people at the National Wildlife Galleries in Fort Myers; and Alanna Fisher at the American Museum of Fly Fishing. To each and every one of you my deepfelt thank you. And to my publisher, Nick Lyons, a special appreciation for the time and effort he expended to make my manuscript a worthwhile book.

Introduction

It was my good fortune to grow up in the afterglow of the golden age of American sport in a home where fine firearms, fishing tackle, and decoys were considered tools to be used, sporting art was hung and enjoyed, and fine books were read and reread in the seasons between hunting and fishing with little thought to their monetary worth. Times change. The tools and trappings of my youth have become the sporting antiques and collectibles of today, and the golden afterglow has turned to a gleam in the eyes of an increasing number of dealers and collectors. It is my hope that my small contribution here will satisfy the gleam and rekindle the warm afterglow.

There are thousands upon thousands of sporting antiques and collectibles in myriad sorts and sizes to consider, and no single volume can even begin to cover them fully. The material included here is incomplete and often inconclusive. There are other decoys, other sporting books and prints, and other everything else as well. If what you are looking for is not here, I have attempted to provide guidelines to its probable worth. This book is the first in a series, and future issues will cover additional sporting antiques and collectibles as well as important price changes. If I sound as though I am apologizing, I am not. This is a useful volume and will work wonders for its readers.

—RALF COYKENDALL
April 1991

PUBLISHER'S NOTE

A book of this kind, especially the first in a prospective series, is invariably incomplete. The number of books, guns, decoys, collectibles of all kinds is such that even a book on one of the categories here would be limited in what it could do. All items do not come up for sale in a given year, of course, and prices among dealers vary. There is no substitute for an astute, reliable, and specialist dealer!

But Coykendall's Sporting Collectibles Price Guide *makes a first step toward what we hope we will become a full library of valuable guidelines to current prices received during the previous two years. It can, we think, be of great help to anyone who randomly finds or seriously collects in the sporting field. We offer it with that spirit, and with the hope that the* Guide *will become more and more valuable in forthcoming editions.*

COYKENDALL'S
SPORTING
COLLECTIBLES
PRICE GUIDE

SPORTING PRINTS

Every book has a beginning and I can think of no more fitting subject for this one than sporting art, which has been around since primitive man sketched pictures of the hunt on the walls of caves. Collectible sporting art dates from the early hunt scenes of England and France, but for our purposes here begins and ends with the so-called sporting prints of Henry Alken of England and John James Audubon of Paris and Philadelphia, both of whom, oddly enough, were born in 1785 and died in 1851. The reader will note two seemingly contradictory statements in the previous sentence: the limiting words "sporting art," and the phrase "so-called sporting prints." A book of this scope cannot begin to do justice to the subject of original art by sporting artists, and I will not try to do so. It would be an easy matter to state that this or that painting by this or that artist sold for a given amount, but it would not reflect the true worth of other works by the same artist. Collectors of original art will be better served by one or more of the galleries listed in the appendix. These individuals deal with original art on a day-to-day basis and are in the business of serving you, so do not hesitate to inquire about original work.

And as for "so-called sporting art," I sometimes wonder if the fine western art of today and yesterday and the bird studies by a variety of artists are truly "sporting art" as I understand it. The final answer is, of course, up to the collector, and that is as it should be. Let's face it: Portraits by Frank W. Benson and Churchill Ettinger are worth a good deal more than their average sporting paintings. A number of years ago Church Ettinger and I had a two-man show together in a swanky Vermont community—his paintings and my bird carvings—and we were both successful. I sold all of my carvings the very first day and Church sold nothing, but received three portrait commissions. I think I'll let you decide who made the most money.

The earliest sporting prints were woodcuts and steel engravings that were sometimes hand-colored. Included among these are the wonderful early hand-colored plates of trout and salmon flies that many a collector has defaced a fine book to frame. Add to this the hand-colored prints of Alken and Audubon and the many hand-colored lithographs produced by Currier and Ives beginning before the Civil War, and you need look no further for enough material to please any collector—but the list goes on. *Harpers Weekly* did a great deal to advance sporting art in America, and the works of A. B. Frost and others that appeared in its pages are eagerly sought after today. In 1895 and again in 1903, the publishing company Scribners produced portfolios of Frost's shooting scenes, and these portfolios and the prints from them are among the finest of sporting Americana, and are priced accordingly. During the first forty years of this century, many, many sporting artists had their beginnings in the pages or on the covers of America's sporting magazines. In fact, many of the artists we now call "sporting artists" were illustrators first, last, and always.

World War II saw photography come into its own and, for better or worse, take over as the preferred method of illustration for many publications. It may be stretching a point to say the rapid advance of photography killed the golden age of sporting art, but it certainly changed it forever. Only recently have we seen a return to fine sporting art that does not look photographic, and the artists and galleries that are responsible for this renaissance are to be congratulated. I am particularly taken with the delicate, thoughtful watercolors of Thomas Aquinas Daly, the soft touch of Robert Abbett and Rod Crossman, and the "weatherwise" feel of Chet Reneson's large watercolors.

Etchings and drypoints are their own category of collectibles, and sporting artists are very well represented in this medium. Frank W. Benson is considered by many to be the finest of the lot, as evidenced by John T. Ordeman's *Frank Benson—Master of the Sporting Print,* and he is followed, not necessarily in this order, by Roland Clark, Richard Bishop, William Schaldach, and many others. Serious collectors of etchings and other prints

The Gunner, a 1915 etching by Frank W. Benson. (Courtesy of John T. Ordeman)

are serious about condition and original image and impression, and you should be too. Deal only with knowledgeable and honest dealers and ask for written receipts.

Since the end of World War II, full-color prints in limited editions have become increasingly popular with collectors, and artists and galleries are eager to fill this heretofore limited market. Evaluation of any of these various and varied prints is based upon two things: the popularity of the artist, and the number of prints produced. If you will look at the various prints listed in the chapter Duck Stamps and Duck-Stamp Prints, you will note that an oversupply can virtually kill a market, and the same is true of any given sporting print. A good example of limitation limiting price is the four-print "Misty Morning" series of excellent prints by David Maass. The first print in the series, "Misty Morning—Woodcock" was produced in an edition of 450 prints and sells today for $1,000. The next three were produced in editions of 580 prints each that sell for $500 each. One hundred and thirty owners of the last three prints want the first one too. An interesting sidenote is the recent issue of the first in a series of "Misty Morning Revisited" prints by Wild Wings of Lake City, Minnesota: "Misty Morning Revisited—Ruffed Grouse" by Maass in an edition of 1,200 prints. Is it an investment? Only time will tell.

No discussion of sporting prints is any more important than that of their proper care and framing once they are yours. Too many prints are ruined in shipping, storing, or by improper framing. Fine prints should be shipped and stored flat, and, if you have an extensive collection, an artist's or architect's cabinet with multiple drawers is an ideal safe for them. When prints are framed they should always be matted and backed with acid free papers and then sealed against air and moisture. This is best accomplished by an accredited framing gallery. Direct sunlight can fade a print rather quickly, and prints should be displayed away from such contact. A given print may or may not be worth more than you paid for some time in the future, but it certainly will be worth less if you fail to care for it properly.

The following old or collectible sporting prints are listed alphabetically by artist, and the prices shown were asked in 1990. The number in parentheses signifies the amount produced, and it should be noted that values are for prints in fine, as-issued, condition. Future issues of this guide will list additional sporting prints and changes that affect those shown here.

ROBERT ABBETT

Autumn Pools (600)	100.00
Black Lab Family (850)	150.00
Brittany Head II (750)	250.00
Close Honor (1,000)	750.00
Fishing at the Bitterroot (500)	300.00
Hillside Woodcock (850)	125.00
Hunting the Edges (500)	450.00
Irish Setter Family (1,000)	600.00
Old Road Cover (900)	200.00
Ready To Go (750)	400.00
Second Season (750)	900.00
Setter and Woodcock (500)	450.00
Upwind Setter and Grouse (850)	400.00
Wood Ducks (850)	125.00

HARRY ADAMSON

After the Storm—Pintails (850)	125.00
Arctic Citadel—Dall Sheep (580)	400.00
California Pintails (950)	200.00
The Loafing Bar—Mallards (580)	200.00
Swamp Mist—Mallards (580)	250.00
Whispering Wings—Pintails (600)	500.00
Winging In—Pintails (540)	325.00
Winter Quarters—Widgeon (580)	125.00

BARNEY ANDERSON

Mallards (580)	125.00
Bluebills (580)	125.00

JOHN J. AUDUBON

Birds of America—Havell Edition 1827–38	to 10,000.00

ROBERT BATEMAN

The Challenge 400.00
High Kingdom—Snow Leopard 600.00
Midnight Black Wolf 1,000.00
Others from . . . .   250.00 to 1,500.00

FRANK W. BENSON

Etchings and drypoints:
The Gunner (150) 2,250.00
Marsh Gunner (150) 1,800.00
Cloudy Dawn (150) 700.00
Ducks Alighting (369) 550.00
Essex Marshes (150) 650.00
Flying Brant (150) 575.00
On Swift Wings (150) 600.00
Over Sunk Marsh (150) 750.00
Two Canoes (150) 975.00
Wild Geese (150) 650.00

RICHARD E. BISHOP

Etchings and drypoints:
Blue Wing Teal 150.00
Flooded Timber—Mallards 200.00
Good Calling—Mallards 300.00
In The Bag—Mallards 150.00
In The Stocks—Mallards 200.00
Overflow Mallards 200.00

Note: Richard Bishop was a special talent: Unfortunately, he did not limit his prints, and their values are therefore diminished. Some dealers mark his prints as much as twice the price listed, number the prints, and otherwise qualify unreal prices. Beware!

HERB BOOTH

Callin 'Em (600) 150.00
The Home Place (600) 250.00

Marsh Gunner, a 1918 etching by Frank W. Benson, is, according to John T. Ordeman, Michelangelo's *David* in hip boots standing in an Essex, Massachusetts, marsh. (Courtesy of John T. Ordeman)

September (600) 300.00
Split Covey (600) 125.00

KEN CARLSON

Bald Eagle (580) 125.00
Pintails (580) 150.00
Rainbow Trout (300) 85.00
Woodcock (600) 150.00

ROLAND CLARK

Aquatints:
Down Wind (250) 900.00

The Last Round, a drypoint engraving by Roland Clark. (Courtesy of John T. Ordeman)

Sanctuary (250) 900.00
The Scout (250) 850.00

Other Derrydale prints
(See Derrydale listing) . . . .   800.00 to 2,000.00
Other Frank J. Lowe aquatints . . . .   650.00 to 1,000.00
Etchings:
Bobwhite Quail (535) 300.00
Hawks and Ducks 550.00
Ice Hole 450.00
Trio (75) 500.00
Woodcock (535) 300.00
Other etchings and drypoints . . . .   300.00 to 750.00

GUY COHELEACH

Golden Eagle 100.00
Coheleach's big-game prints . . . .   300.00 to 800.00

ARTHUR COOK

After The Storm (350) 150.00
The Traveler Rests—Arctic Tern (450) 125.00

JOHN COWAN

Boat Blind (600) 250.00
Creek Bottoms (600) 225.00
Fast Water (600) 250.00
In The Broomweed—Quail (750) 650.00
Magic Minutes (600) 650.00
Mallards High (600) 650.00
Off Base (600) 750.00
Too Soon (600) 700.00
Releasing A Spawner (800) 225.00
Two Down (600) 650.00

Two of three small folio prints entitled *Wild Duck Shooting*, by Currier and Ives.

CURRIER AND IVES

Small folio . . . . to 1,000.00
Medium folio . . . . to 5,000.00
Large folio . . . . to 10,000.00

Currier and Ives prints are a specialty unto themselves, and no one should undertake their purchase without knowing much about them. Many fine guides to Currier and Ives prints are available. An especially helpful book, *Currier and Ives Sporting Prints,* is hard to find, but worth the trouble to try.

THOMAS AQUINAS DALY

Aquatints . . . . to 500.00

Georgia Pines, an aquatint by Thomas A. Daly.
(Courtesy of the artist)

Limestone, an aquatint by Thomas A. Daly. (Courtesy of the artist)

DERRYDALE PRINTS

E. Phillips Williamson, writing in *The Sporting Connection* in 1984, stated: "The Derrydale Press not only published the works of a number of celebrated sporting writers, but from the beginning, issued what has become the finest lot of sporting prints every produced in America." High praise from a leading collector and acknowledged authority, and his pick of the "very best" of the ninety-five Derrydale sporting prints is worthy of serious consideration by any and all collectors. His choices, together with retail prices, follow. All the listed prints are aquatints unless otherwise noted, and edition sizes are noted as available.

Ralph Boyer

At The Riffle (drypoint—edition of 60)	800.00
The Lip of the Pool (drypoint—edition of 60)	800.00
Fathers of American Sport (edition of 250 sets of 6)	1,200.00
After A Big One (edition of 200)	500.00
An Anxious Moment (edition of 250)	500.00

Paul Brown

Polo Scenes—set of 4 (edition of 175)	5,000.00
The Meadowbrook Cup (edition of 250)	2,500.00
Fox Hunting Scenes—set of 4 (edition of 250 sets) . . .	8,000.00

Roland Clark

The Alarm (edition of 250)	2,000.00
Winter Marsh (edition of 250)	1,000.00
Calm Weather (edition of 250)	1,000.00
A Straggler (edition of 250)	1,000.00
Mallards Rising (edition of 250)	2,000.00

A. B. Frost

Coming Ashore (edition of 200)	2,000.00
Grouse Shooting in the Rhododendrons	

(edition of 200) 2,000.00
A Chance Shot While Setting Out Decoys
(edition of 200) 2,000.00
October Woodcock Shooting (edition of 200) 4,000.00

Edwin Megargee
Cock Fighting Scenes—set of 4 (edition of 250 sets) . .   2,000.00
Closing In (edition of 250) 500.00
Staunch (edition of 250) 500.00
Steady (edition of 250) 500.00
November Morn (edition of 250) 2,000.00

William Schaldach
Woodcock (edition of 250) 1,500.00

Joseph P. Sims
The Rose Tree Fox Hunting Club (edition of 150) 2,500.00

Franklin B. Voss
Foxhunting in America—set of 3
(edition of 250 sets) 3,600.00

Various Artists
William Woodward's horse prints (8 separate
prints), value each 800.00

There are, of course, other Derrydale prints, but I bow to Phil Williamson and draw the line here. The next issue of this guide will list all the Derrydale Press books and all the Derrydale Press prints, together with the latest values for each of these treasures that Gene Connett produced more than half a century ago.

CHURCHILL ETTINGER
Worn Rock Pool 275.00
Etchings . . . .   to 250.00

AQUATINTS

An aquatint is a work in oil or watercolor that is then reproduced in a single color (usually sepia), then hand-colored by commercial artists working either with the original or an artist-colored print as a guide. The quality of a given print is dependent upon the colorist's skill.

JAMES P. FISHER

American Goldeneyes (450) 60.00
Canvasback Decoy (950) 125.00
Mallard Decoy (450) 60.00
Primitive Mallard (450) 50.00

A. B. FROST

Scribner's Shooting Scenes (set of 12) 10,000.00
   Individual prints . . . .   400.00 to 800.00
Scribner's—A Day's Shooting (set of 6) 5,000.00
   Individual prints . . . .   350.00 to 800.00
Derrydale prints (See Derrydale prints)
Harpers Weekly prints . . . .   25.00 to 100.00

SIGNED PRINTS

A signed print is a signed print, and a signed-and-numbered print is a signed-and-numbered print! Be sure you understand that a print "signed in the plate" means nothing. A print is produced and then signed or signed and numbered by the artist after he or she approves it. This, invariably, is done in pencil. And, having said this, I will tell you that A. B. Frost's prints are the only prints listed here that are worth anything without the artist's signature. He is the exception that proves the rule.

JOHN FROST

Maryland Marsh (150) 500.00

NANCY GLAZIER

The Americans (600) 400.00
King's Crossing—Elk (600) 135.00
The Matriarch (750) 200.00
Morning Glory—Mule Deer (600) 450.00
Royalty (600) 135.00

FRANCIS GOLDEN

Angus Pool (100) 300.00
Canadas and Young (850) 125.00

OWEN GROMME

Back to Cover—Pheasants (450) 575.00
Brittany on Point—Woodcock (450) 900.00
Canvasbacks (850) 300.00
Early Autumn (850) 850.00
Early Spring Drummer (850) 500.00
English Setter (850) 475.00
Midday Retreat—Bobwhites (580) 800.00
Morning Frost—Ruffed Grouse (580) 450.00
Sawbuck Bobwhites (950) 450.00
Sunlit Glade—Ruffed Grouse (450) 1,200.00
Whistling Swans (580) 1,000.00

JOHN GROTH

Etchings . . . .   100.00 to 500.00

DAVID HAGERBAUMER

Afternoon Squall—Canada Geese (450) 150.00
Double Rise (450) 300.00
Green Wing Flurry (600) 400.00
Hickory Grove—Bobwhites (450) 250.00

Home Place Covey (950) 185.00
The Old Duck Camp (450) 150.00
Indian Summer—Ruffed Grouse (450) 250.00
The Shanty (450) 50.00
Through the Pines—Doves (450) 250.00
Etchings . . . . to 125.00

WINSLOW HOMER

Leaping Trout (Angler's Club print) 500.00
Canoe in the Rapids (Colliers) 100.00

Homer did not sign his prints.

LYNN BOGUE HUNT

Set of 18 game-bird prints for du Pont 2,000.00
Individual prints 250.00

Note: these are unsigned. Signed prints are worth much more.

Field & Stream portfolios:
Game birds 100.00
Game Fishing 150.00
Etchings . . . .   250.00 to 400.00

JAMES KILLEN

In the Feed—Canada Geese (500) 125.00
After the Snowfall (850) 125.00
Black Lab with Ringneck Duck (850) 300.00
On the High Plains (990) 125.00
That's My Dog (various breeds—unlimited editions) . .   30.00

EDWARD KING

Woodcock Shooting—In the Birches (350) 300.00
Quail Shooting—In the Briar Patch (350) 300.00
Other Derrydale prints . . . . to 1,000.00

S. A. KILBOURNE

Portfolio of fish prints 1,000.00
Individual prints . . . .   100.00 to 350.00

MARGUERITE KIRMSE

The Fox (250) 500.00
The Hounds (250) 500.00
Etchings . . . .   50.00 to 350.00

HANS KLEIBER

Etchings:
Fall in the Rockies 375.00
Lake Geneva Bighorn 150.00
Two Mallards 150.00

J. D. KNAP

Daybreak 375.00
All Clear 375.00

LEE LEBLANC

Arkansas Mallards (400) 250.00
Busted Covey (800) 125.00
Cache River Memory (800) 100.00
Honkers at Horicon (400) 120.00
A Noble Pair—Wild Turkeys (580) 120.00
Stately Pair—Mallards (580) 120.00

DAVID LOCKHART

Autumn Calm—Black Ducks (850) 125.00
Puddle Jumpers (490) 125.00
Covey Point—Quail (480) 125.00
Dove Club at Weber's (600) 125.00

DAVID MAASS

Autumn Birch—Woodcock (580) 500.00

REMARQUED PRINTS

A remarqued *print is one in which the artist has added to the border a small original sketch in black-and-white or color. Remarques tend to add value, but you can't always count on this.*

Autumn Marsh—Mallards (580)	500.00
Back Bay—Mallards (600)	325.00
Canada Geese Coming In (400)	400.00
Covey Break—Quail (580)	125.00
Canvasbacks on Delta Marsh (750)	175.00
Early Winter Morning—Bobwhite (850)	300.00
Early Winter Morning—Pheasant (950)	350.00
Early Winter Morning—Ruffed Grouse (950)	250.00
Early Winter Morning—Turkey (950)	175.00
Mallards (600)	500.00
Mallards In Autumn (950)	150.00
Misty Morning—Green Wing Teal (580)	350.00
Misty Morning—Mallards (580)	500.00
Misty Morning—Quail (580)	500.00
Misty Morning—Woodcock (450)	1,000.00
Misty Morning—Woodcock, remarqued	1,125.00
Touch of Winter (850)	250.00
Willow Point—Redheads (950)	125.00

ALDERSON MAGEE

Bobcat (600)	125.00
Coachman's Conquest—Brook Trout (450)	200.00
First Hatched—Canada Geese (580)	175.00
Professor's Prize—Rainbow Trout (600)	100.00
Jumping Mallards (600)	225.00

HENRY McDANIELS

An Unnamed Pool (325)	250.00

Anticipation (300) 150.00
Morning on Taylor's Shore (150) 400.00
Fishing the Dry Fly on the Upper Connecticut (400) . .   1,200.00
The Best Time of Day (550) 175.00
The Return (300) 150.00

EDWIN MEGARGEE

(See Derrydale Prints)

WAYNE MEINEKE

Harvest—Canada Geese (800) 150.00
Oak Ridge—Whitetail Deer (800) 200.00
Winter Retreat—Mule Deer (1,500) 125.00

ROSEMARY MILLETTE

Abandoned Homestead—Pheasants (580) 250.00
Autumn Encounter—Pheasants (1,200) 375.00
Evening Passage (950) 150.00
Golden Glow (950) 150.00
October Mist—Whitetail Deer (850) 200.00
Winter Repose (580) 350.00

GARY MOSS

Canadas on the Coast (850) 350.00
Family of Swans (850) 150.00
On the Prowl—Ruffed Grouse (580) 125.00
Trio of Canadas (850) 250.00
Trio of Canvasbacks (580) 125.00
Northwoods Grouse (650) 125.00

RICHARD PLASSCHAERT

Autumn Retreat—Wood Ducks (580) 275.00
Broken Covey (580) 150.00
Moonam Marsh—Mallards (580) 250.00
Moonam Marsh—Wood Ducks (580) 300.00

DUCK-STAMP PRINTS

Many of the artists listed here also designed state or federal duck-stamp prints, and you should refer to the chapter Duck Stamps and Duck-Stamp Prints for additional material.

Moonam Marsh—Green Wing Teal (580) 175.00
Winter Habitat—Pheasants (750) 300.00
Woodlot Feeding—Pheasants (750) 250.00

OGDEN PLEISSNER

The Battenkill at Benedict's Crossing (270) 1,200.00
Dawn on the Duck Marsh (270) 600.00
The Head of the Pool (280) 1,200.00
Hendrickson's Pool—Beaverkill (290) 1,200.00
Hillside Orchard—Grouse Shooting (275) 1,400.00
The Quail Hunters (425) 600.00
Setting up on Horseshoe Pond (275) 500.00
Woodcock Cover (270) 1,500.00
Marshgunners (300) 375.00

It was my very good fortune to have conducted the last interview with Ogden Pleissner before he died in 1983. He is missed, but his art is eternal and a fine long-term investment.

ALEXANDER POPE

1878 chromolithographs of game birds . . . . . . 150.00 to 350.00

MAYNARD REECE

Against the Wind—Canvasbacks (550) 450.00
Autumn Trio—Pheasants (950) 225.00
Cold Moring—Mallards (950) 175.00
Dark Sky—Bobwhites (950) 375.00
Dark Sky—Ruffed Grouse (950) 350.00

Dark Sky—Snow Geese (950) 175.00
Wood Ducks (550) 250.00
Quail Cover (750) 300.00

CHET RENESON

Ambush (200) 200.00
Caught in the Open (400) 300.00
Early Season (400) 160.00
Flight Birds (400) 300.00
Good Luck Wind (500) 400.00
Opening Day (400) 250.00
Season's Best (400) 100.00
Well Hooked (500) 200.00
Winter Grouse (400) 110.00

A. LASSELL RIPLEY

Late Season Grouse 750.00
Turkey Blind 750.00
Turkey Drive 750.00
Woodcock Hunt (300) 1,000.00
Etchings . . . .   250.00 to 750.00

CARL RUNGIUS

Etchings . . . .   500.00 to 1,000.00

WILLIAM J. SCHALDACH

Eastern Brook Trout (300) 500.00
Brook Trout 150.00
Etchings and drypoints . . . .   250.00 to 750.00

Note: I may be opinionated, but to me, no artist has captured the elusive woodcock on plate and paper as did this fine sportsman, author, and artist.

MANFRED SCHATZ

Feathered Magic (750) 200.00
Grey Ghost (850) 575.00

Leaping Quananiche, an etching by William J. Schaldach. (Courtesy of John T. Ordeman)

Julie's Pond—Mallards (750) 225.00
Out of Marshgrass (750) 400.00
Out of the Mist (500) 225.00
Wolf Pack (500) 900.00

PETER SCOTT

Canada Geese Coming to the Marsh (950) 125.00
Pintails on a Hazy Day 300.00

MICHAEL SIEVE

Alaskan Classic—Dall Sheep (850) 125.00
Alpine Meadow—Elk (850) 200.00
Cattail Swamp—Red Fox (750) 200.00
Cautious Approach—Whitetail Deer (850) 350.00
Evening Stand Whitetail Deer (950) 400.00
Fast Break—Whitetail Deer (850) 500.00
Last Chance At Trail's End (950) 500.00
Wapiti Ridge (650) 125.00

GARY SORRELS

Early Winter—Whitetail Deer (600) 300.00
In the Clearing—Elk (850) 75.00
Pronghorn Range (600) 120.00
Winter Rendezvous—Whitetail Deer (600) 100.00

MILTON C. WEILER

Virgin Water (500) 150.00
Shang Wheeler's Decoys (400) 250.00
Matapedia Mist (250) 150.00
Upper Twin Pool—Henryville (125) 750.00
Atlantic Salmon Fishing on the Matapedia (375) 500.00
Classic Decoy portfolio 1,000.00
Classic Shorebird Decoy portfolio 750.00
Signed individual prints from the portfolios . . . . to 100.00

FURTHER READING AND STUDY

No serious collector or potential collector should be satisfied with the limited presentation I have provided here, not when the shelves of libraries and book stores are crowded with more information. Pick an artist or artists, and chances are good to excellent that someone somewhere has written about them. John T. Ordeman's books on Benson, Clark, and Schaldach are of great merit, as are *A. B. Frost* by Lanier, and the Pleissner book by Bergh. Abbett, Bateman, Coheleach, and many others are treated in one or more books, and a new series, "Masters of the Wild," is now being issued one volume every two months and will cover most, if not all, sporting artists. You can find these books through your local book store or one of the book and art dealers listed in the appendix of this volume. If you plan to collect sporting art, you will need all the help and knowledge you can acquire.

SPORTING BOOKS

Sporting books have always been an important part of my life. In my "growing-up years" I learned about trout from Ray Bergman, ruffed grouse and woodcock from John Alden Knight, and ducks from Van Campen Heilner. Books were a sporting season that never ended, a tonic for all ills, and a warmth against the cold. In my sixteenth year I carried an author-signed copy of Bill Schaldach's book, *Carl Rungius—Big Game Painter*, to the Canadian Rockies for the old artist's signature.

And now, writing this, I am reminded of the one and only time I ever knew exactly what to get my father for his birthday. Dad and Joel Barber had been friends for years but it was not until after Joel's death that I discovered my father had always wanted a copy of his book *Long Shore*, published by the Derrydale Press. Ralph Terrill of New York's Crossroads of Sport found a copy of the book for me, and I presented it to my father for his seventieth birthday. That little book of prose stayed on Dad's bedside table until he died five years later, and I don't think a night went by when he didn't read a page or two and smile.

Collecting books can be as expensive as you want to make it, or it can be something you approach with a very strict budget; either way, it is enjoyable and, on occasion, profitable. I cannot tell you what to collect, but I can give you an outline of the possibilities. If you purchase fine sporting books only for their value in the future marketplace, you will miss the true enjoyment of these fine volumes, and may be disappointed in their monetary appreciation as well. Buy books you like about sporting subjects that interest you, and take care of them and let their value take care of itself.

Many writers and many more booksellers have tried to put sporting books into the either-or categories of fishing books and hunting or shooting books, but it just doesn't work that way. Many, if not most, sporting authors who penned more than a book or two wrote about both fishing and hunting, and many did so in a single volume. For this reason, all books referred to and listed here are "sporting books," without reference to their specific contents. If you are a serious collector of a given subject, this listing will require some patience, but for the average collector the alphabetical listings should prove completely satisfactory and form a valuable reference you can refer to again and again.

CONDITION AND CONDITION

I have a good friend who is in the restaurant business and enjoys considerable success. When I asked him about it he said there were three things that were important to anyone considering a business such as his: location, location, and location. When it comes to books, the three things that are of importance are condition, condition, and condition. Make no mistake about it, even the scarcest volume can be next to worthless in poor condition. By the same token, a book of just average value in very fine condition in a fine dust jacket can be worth considerably more than the same book in so-so condition. Learn about condition and how to recognize the seemingly infinite differences between good and very good and fine and very fine, and you will have taken a big step in the right direction. Generally speaking, booksellers all use the terms *poor, good, very good, fine, very fine,* and *mint* to describe the books they sell, and all stand behind their descriptions and their sales. With rare exceptions, book dealers are the most honest of all sporting antiques and collectibles dealers, but it is up to you to know what you are buying and the condition it is in when you do so.

First and *limited* editions are both worthy of your attention, although these terms, in themselves, mean little or nothing. Serious book collectors

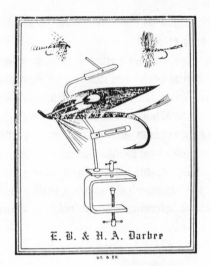

E. B. & H. A. Darbee

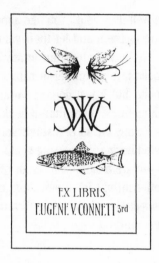

EX LIBRIS
EUGENE V. CONNETT 3rd

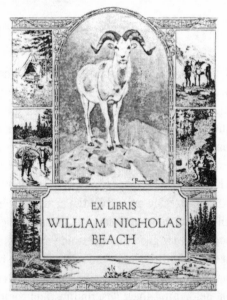

EX LIBRIS
WILLIAM NICHOLAS
BEACH

Many things can add value to a collectible book; for instance, the bookplate of a famous craftsman, publisher, or writer. The fly-tying art of Harry and Elsie Darbee's bookplate, the fishing art on that of Eugene Connett, and the extraordinary etching by Carl Rungius for William Beach are rare and increase the worth of any volume on which they appear.

want only first editions in as near to "as issued" condition as possible, but you must offset this with the often overlooked fact that every book printed was a "first edition" or "first printing" when it was issued for the first time. Some of these books are priceless and others are next to worthless. An author I know said that others could have all the first editions of his books, and he'd settle for second and later printings. He, of course was talking about his earnings and not about book values, but his feelings do point out that scarcity is a two-way street: bad for the author and a boon to the collector. A given book by a well-known author is worth more when it is a first edition or the only edition of the work. And the same book in very fine condition with a fine dust jacket is worth just that much more. Popularity, scarcity, and condition all contribute to a book's value.

Limited-edition sporting books can confuse beginning sporting book collectors simply because the words are often misused. Today's "limited edition" offerings of previously printed books in editions of 2,500 or 3,000 are not particularly collectable, nor are they apt to increase in value as the years go by. Original books published in limited editions of 1,000 and fewer copies have proved good investments in some instances, but too many publishers have followed their limited printings with "trade editions" and thereby limited the original potential. Truly valuable limited editions are those that were privately printed in *very* small numbers: deluxe printings such as the Derrydale Press editions of 35 to 50 copies, and elaborate and truly limited editions of popular books such as John Alden Knight's *Ruffed Grouse,* published by Borzoi Books/Alfred A. Knopf in an edition of only 210 copies. Another important consideration when evaluating a limited edition book is its overall condition. Unlike regular editions, limited editions must be in fine to very fine or better condition to command attention. Book collectors are a fussy lot, and you should be too.

The best way to acquire fine sporting books is through one or another of the many reputable dealers who you will find in the appendix at the end of this book, but there are other methods, and if you are willing to spend the time and energy required, they can be very rewarding. Flea markets are often sources for books of all kinds, as are antique shops and yard sales. Books turn up just about everywhere and anywhere, and I will end this section with a true story about an estate sale in Vermont that proves everybody makes mistakes.

The sale was at the elaborate home of a local sportsman who had passed away, and was run by a well-established antique appraiser who, for reasons I can only wonder about, decided to sell the extensive library at five dollars per book. That library contained thirty-eight Derrydale Press books, more than one hundred golf books, hunting and fishing books beyond counting, as well as three illuminated manuscripts from the fourteenth century. Five bucks a book only five miles from home, and I never heard about it until the week after the sale. As I said, everybody makes mistakes, and it is up to you to capitalize on these errors and do as I say and not as I did. Books are out there for the picking if you keep your eyes and ears open.

The following listing of books is arranged alphabetically by author and should give you a good idea of the scope of sporting books sold and offered for sale each year. The list is far from complete and will be updated in future issues of this guide.

ABBOTT, HENRY

The Birch Bark Books of Henry Abbott: 1980 reprint of
all 19 of these rarities 22.50

ACKLEY, PARKER O.

Handbook for Shooters and Reloaders: Salt Lake City
1962 (first edition) 45.00

AKELEY, CARL E.

In Brightest Africa: Garden City 1923 (first edition) . . .   35.00

Another copy (later date) 15.00

AKELEY, MARY L. J.

Carl Akeley's Africa: New York. With map and
map end papers 32.50

The Wilderness Lives Again: New York 1940. A scarce
title about Carl Akeley's work 45.00

ALLERTON, R. G.

Brook Trout Fishing: New York 1869. Includes the scarce
plate. Library markings 650.00

AMERICAN SPORTSMAN

The American Sportsman: New York 1968–70. A
complete 12-volume set 80.00

ANGLERS' CLUB OF NEW YORK

The Anglers' Club Story: One of 750 copies printed at
the Peter Pauper Press 150.00

The Best of the Anglers' Club Bulletin: One of 1,000
copies. First edition 100.00

Well-Dressed Lines: New York 1962. One
of 500 copies 160.00

ANNABEL, RUSSELL

Hunting and Fishing In Alaska: Borzoi/Knopf 1948. First
edition in a chipped dust jacket (dj) 140.00

Another copy: No dj 100.00

Tales of a Big Game Guide: Derrydale 1938. One of 950
copies. A fine copy 475.00

Another copy 375.00

DJ's

*No, dj's are not people who play recordings on the radio—at least not
here. Dust jackets (dj's) are the paper covers that protect books and can
add greatly to a volume's value. The true collector wants a first edition in
very fine or better shape, and wants it with a dust jacket.*

ARMS, DOROTHY N.

Fishing Memories: New York 1938. Illustrated by William
Schaldach. First edition with dj 35.00

ASH, EDWARD

The Practical Dog Book: Derrydale Press 1931. One of
500 copies 350.00

ASHLEY-COOPER, JOHN

The Great Salmon Rivers of Scotland: London 1980. One
of 30 signed and numbered copies 900.00

Trade edition 50.00

A Line on Salmon: London 1983. One of 35 signed and
numbered copies 800.00

Trade edition 50.00

A Salmon Fisher's Odyssey: London 1982. One of 20
signed and numbered copies 1,100.00

Trade edition 50.00

ATHERTON, JOHN

The Fly and The Fish: Anglers' Club 1951. One of 222
copies. Slipcase 400.00

Another copy: 1971 reprint of the above 35.00

BABCOCK, HAVILAH

I Don't Want To Shoot An Elephant: New York 1958.
First edition, dj 150.00

Another copy: No dj 90.00

Another copy: 1985 reprint 20.00

My Health Is Better in November: Columbia, SC 1947.
First edition, moderate wear, dj 80.00

Tales of Quails 'n Such: New York 1951. One of 299
copies signed and numbered by author 200.00

Another copy: 1951 first trade edition 100.00

Another copy: 1985 reprint 20.00

BARBER, JOEL

'Long Shore: Derrydale Press 1939. One of 750 signed
and numbered copies. Binding worn 375.00

Wild Fowl Decoys: Derrydale Press 1934. One of 55
signed and numbered copies. Has been rebacked 1,800.00

Another copy: Windward House 1934. The first trade
edition 200.00

Another copy: Dover 1954. Soft cover 10.00

BATES, JOSEPH D., JR.

The Art of the Salmon Fly: Boston 1987. One of 85
lettered copies with salmon fly 900.00

Atlantic Salmon Flies & Fishing: Harrisburg, PA 1970.
One of 24 presentation copies 1,900.00

The Atlantic Salmon Treasury: Montreal 1975. One of
1000 signed and numbered copies with slipcase 275.00

Another copy: As above 165.00

Spinning For Salt Water Game Fish: Boston 1957. First
edition with dust jacket 25.00

Streamer Fly Tying & Fishing: Harrisburg, PA 1966. One
of only 10 presentation copies 2,500.00

Another copy (one of 600 signed
and numbered copies) 275.00

Streamers and Bucktails: New York 1979. One of only 36
deluxe signed and numbered copies . . . .   ˙800.00

Bates was a prolific author and these represent less than half of his titles.

BEACH, WILLIAM N.

In the Shadow of Mount McKinley: Derrydale 1931. One
of 750 numbered copies. Scarce 750.00

BELL, W. D. M.

Bell of Africa: London 1984. Reprint of the scarce 1960
edition. Dust jacket 32.50

Karamojo Safari: London 1949. First British edition with
dust jacket 225.00

As above: First U.S. edition 1949 . . . .   225.00

The Wanderings of An Elephant Hunter: London 1976.
Reprint of the 1923 edition 40.00

As above: Camden, SC 1987 . . . .   40.00

BERGMAN, RAY

Fresh Water Bass: Philadelphia 1942. First edition 85.00

Another: first Borzoi/Knopf edition 1945. Dj 50.00

Just Fishing: Philadelphia 1932. First edition 110.00

Another: First Borzoi/Knopf edition (1943) 35.00

Trout: Philadelphia 1938. One of the deluxe signed and
numbered edition of 149 copies 1,300.00

Another: Philadelphia 1938. First edition 100.00

Another: Borzoi/Knopf 1952 revision 40.00

BORZOI BOOKS FOR SPORTSMEN

Noted bibliophile Isaac Oelgart wrote of these fine volumes as follows: "Book for book, the Borzoi Books for Sportsmen rank among the most important and influential sporting books published in America. This would be true, if for no other reason than the books of Ray Bergman and Jack O'Connor. There are, however, other reasons: Russell Annabel, Bert Claflin, Van Campen Heilner, Ray Holland, John Alden Knight, Clyde Ormond, and illustrators such as Edgar Burke, Arthur Fuller, Lawrence Goadby, Frederick Hilderbrandt and Lynn Bogue Hunt to name a few." Oelgart went on to conclude, "What more could a sportsman ask for?" What, indeed?

With Fly, Plug & Bait: New York 1947. One of the
deluxe signed and numbered edition of 249 copies . . . 225.00

Another: first trade edition (1947) 55.00

BETTEN, E. L.

Upland Game Shooting: Philadelphia 1940. A fine copy of
the first edition 60.00

Another: Borzoi/Knopf edition 1944. Dj 75.00

BIGELOW, HORATIO

Flying Feathers: Richmond 1937. A fine copy of
a scarce book 85.00

Gunnerman's Gold: Huntington 1943. One of 1,000
numbered copies. Fine with dust jacket 140.00

BISHOP, RICHARD

Bishop's Birds: Philadelphia 1936. One of 1,050
numbered copies. Introduction by H. P. Sheldon 300.00

EX LIBRIS

H F Stone

NEW YORK

HARRY WORCESTER SMITH

Three fine and unusual bookplates. *From left to right:* **produced by Richard Bishop for a Philadelphia collector; created by Joel Barber for his friend and fellow decoy collector, H. F. Stone; a multi-sport etching done for Harry Worcester Smith, author of** *A Sporting Family of the Old South***.**

Bishop's Wildfowl: St. Paul 1948. Introduction by Nash
Buckingham 250.00

BLADES, WILLIAM J.

Fishing Flies & Fly Tying: Harrisburg, PA 1951. One of
100 copies. Rebacked 400.00

Another: Harrisburg, PA 1951 first edition. Dj 60.00

BOGARDUS, A. H.

Field, Cover & Trap Shooting: New York 1874. A very
scarce first edition 85.00

BOONE & CROCKET CLUB

American Big Game Hunting: New York 1893. Spine
faded, moderate wear 100.00

Another: As above but in fine condition 200.00

American Big Game in Its Haunts: New York 1904. Spine
faded, moderate wear 100.00

B & C Club's 18th Big Game Awards: Alexandria 1984.
As-new condition with dust jacket 25.00

B & C Club's 19th Big Game Awards: Dumfries 1986. As
new condition with dust jacket 25.00

Hunting & Conservation: New Haven 1925. A very fine
copy of this multi-authored book 250.00

Another: Worn ex-library copy 40.00

Hunting In Many Lands: New York 1895. A very fine
copy with minor head-of-spine wear 300.00

Another: Shelf-worn, inner hinges broken 70.00

Records of North American Big Game: New York 1952. A
very fine copy of a scarce book 325.00

Records of North American Big Game: New York 1958. A
very fine copy in a dust jacket 250.00

Records of North American Big Game: New York 1964. A
very fine copy with a dust jacket 225.00

Records of North American Big Game: Pittsburgh 1971.
Very fine in a fine dust jacket 100.00

BROOKS, JOE

The Complete Book of Fly Fishing: New York 1958. A
fine copy of the first edition. Dj 30.00

Salt Water Game Fishing: New York 1968. A mint copy of
the first edition with dj 30.00

Trout Fishing: New York 1972. A very fine copy of the
first edition with dust jacket 40.00

BUCKINGHAM, NASH

Blood Lines: Derrydale 1938. One of 1,250 copies in very
fine condition 375.00

Another: Putnam 1947. The trade edition 75.00

De Shootinest Gentleman: Derrydale 1934. One of 950
copies in very fine condition 600.00

Another: Nelson 1961. One of 200 signed
and numbered copies 200.00

Another: Putnam 1943. The trade edition 50.00

Game Bag: Putnam 1945. One of 1,250 numbered copies
in very fine condition 150.00

Another: Putnam 1945. The trade edition 50.00

Hallowed Years: Harrisburg 1953. A first edition of
Buckingham's seventh book in fine condition 110.00

Another: as above with wear and no dust jacket 35.00

Mark Right: Derrydale 1936. One of 1,250 copies in
near-mint condition 400.00

Another: As above with dulled spine 300.00

Another: Putnam 1944. The trade edition 75.00

Ole Miss': Derrydale 1937. One of 1,250 copies in near-
mint condition 400.00

Another: Putnam 1946. The trade edition 75.00

Tattered Coat: Putnam 1944. One of 995 numbered
copies in very fine condition with dj 200.00

Another: Putnam 1944. The trade edition 50.00

BURKE, EDGAR

American Dry Flies: Derrydale 1931. One of 500 copies
with flies by Burke on end paper 900.00

Another: As above with slight wear 550.00

CAMP, RAYMOND

Ducks, Boats, Blinds & Decoys: Borzoi/Knopf 1952. A
fine copy of the first edition. Dj 125.00

Fishing the Surf: Boston 1941. A fine copy of the first
edition with a dust jacket 35.00

Game Cookery: New York 1958. A fine copy of a scarce
first edition with "finest" recipes 35.00

CLAFLIN, BERT

Blazed Trails For Anglers: Borzoi/Knopf 1949. A mint
copy of the first edition. Dj 35.00

Muskie Fishing: Borzoi/Knopf 1948. A very fine copy of
the first edition 40.00

CLARK, ROLAND

Gunner's Dawn: Derrydale 1937. One of 950 numbered
copies in fine condition 700.00

Another: As above with library markings 450.00

Pot Luck: Countryman Press 1945. One of 150 signed
and numbered copies with minor cover wear 850.00

Another: One of 460 signed and numbered copies
in worn slipcase 250.00

Another: Countryman Press 1945. The trade edition in
a worn slipcase 50.00

Roland Clark's Etchings: Derrydale 1938. One of 800 in
a repaired box 900.00

Another: As above without box 800.00

Stray Shots: Derrydale 1931. One of 500 copies in
near-mint condition 1,750.00

CLARKE, KIT

The Practical Angler: New York 1895.
Ex-library, internally fine 32.50

Where the Trout Hide: New York 1889. A rare book with
wear and some adhesion in margins 90.00

Another: Front cover missing 47.50

CONNETT, EUGENE V.

American Big Game Fishing: Derrydale 1935. One of 850
copies. Very fine 850.00

American Sporting Dogs. New York 1948. A fine copy
with a fine dust jacket 150.00

Any Luck: New York 1933. A fine copy of the first
edition with a dust jacket 90.00

CONNETT'S DERRYDALE PRESS

Eugene V. Connett established the Derrydale Press in 1927, and until its demise in 1941 published 169 titles, most of which were sporting works. In 1937 Connett wrote: "I believe that the owners of Derrydale Press sporting books can look upon them not only as pleasant and perhaps even valuable things to possess, but also as things produced by a group of real sportsmen with a real idea before them."

Duck Decoys: New York 1953. A fine copy of the first
edition with a good dust jacket 60.00

Duck Shooting Along the Atlantic Tidewater. New York
1947. Very fine copy with worn dj 200.00

Another: later printing 75.00

Feathered Game from A Sporting Journal: Derrydale
1929. One of 550 copies. Very fine 350.00

Fishing a Trout Stream: Derrydale 1934. One of 950
copies in very fine condition 350.00

Random Casts: Derrydale 1939. One of 950 copies
in mint condition 300.00

Upland Game Bird Shooting in America: Derrydale 1930.
One of 850 copies. Very fine copy 350.00

Wildfowling in the Mississippi Flyway: New York 1949. A
fine copy with fine dj. Scarce 250.00

COYKENDALL, RALF

Duck Decoys and How To Rig Them: New York 1955. A
fine copy of the first edition. Dj 65.00

Another: Later printing 20.00

Another: Winchester Press 25.00

COYKENDALL, RALF JR.

You and Your Retriever: Garden City 1963. A fine copy
of the first edition 20.00

Another: As above and signed. Dj 35.00

Wildfowling at a Glance: Harrisburg, PA 1968. Paper
boards. Scarce. Fine 30.00

CROSS, REUBEN

The Complete Fly Tyer: Rockville Center 1971. A
combined edition of the two books below. Very fine . . .   25.00

Fur, Feather & Steel: New York 1940. A fine copy of the
first edition in a dj 120.00

Another: Second printing 50.00

Tying American Trout Lures: New York 1936. A fine copy
of the second printing 50.00

Another: 1937. The third printing. Very good 35.00

CURTIS, PAUL A.

Guns & Gunning: Philadelphia 1934. A fine copy of
the first edition 17.50

Another: Borzoi/Knopf 1943. Dj 25.00

Sportsmen All: Derrydale 1938. One of 950
copies. Very fine 150.00

DALRYMPLE, BYRON W.

Doves and Dove Shooting: New York 1949. One of the
few books on this subject 20.00

Modern Book of Black Bass: New York 1972. A fine first
edition with dust jacket 12.00

DARBEE, HARRY

Catskill Flytier: Philadelphia 1977. One of 125 signed
and numbered copies with Darbee fly and slipcase . . .   550.00

Another: First trade edition. Scarce 75.00

DAVIS, EDMUND W.

Woodcock Shooting: Privately printed 1908. One of only
100 copies printed. Very good 1,200.00

DAVIS, HENRY E.

The American Wild Turkey: Georgetown, SC 1949.
Definitive book on the subject. Fine with dj 250.00

DERRYDALE PRESS

A Decade of American Sporting Books & Prints. One of
950 numbered copies 125.00

Other Derrydale books are listed by author.

DIMOCK, A. W.

The Book of the Tarpon: New York 1911. The scarce
first edition with minor staining 125.00

Another: 1926. Hard to find. Fine 75.00

DUBÉ, JEAN-PAUL

Let's Save Our Salmon: Ottawa 1972. One of 700 copies.
Very fine in slipcase 70.00

Salmon Talk: Clinton 1983. One of 1,000 copies in full
leather with slipcase. Mint 125.00

DUNNE, J. W.

Sunshine and the Dry Fly: London 1924. The scarce first
edition. Very good 50.00

Another: 1950 edition. Very fine. Dj 40.00

EAST, BEN

Danger: New York 1970. A fine copy of the first edition
with dust jacket 15.00

Survival: New York 1967. Fine copy of this first edition
in dust jacket 15.00

EASTMAN, GEORGE

Chronicles of an African Trip: Privately printed
1927. Covers stained 100.00

ECKERT, ALBERT

The Great Auk: Boston 1963. A novel. The first edition
of this "compelling" book. Dj 25.00

The Wading Birds of North America: Garden City 1981.
First edition in fine condition. Dj 50.00

EDMINSTER, FRANK C.

Hunting Whitetails: New York 1954. A very good copy of
the first edition with dj 20.00

EINARSEN, ARTHUR S.

Black Brant: Seattle 1965. A very fine copy of the first
printing with a fine dust jacket 20.00

The Pronghorn Antelope: Washington 1948. A very good
copy of the first printing 30.00

ELLIOT, BOB

All About Brook Trout: Orange 1954. The same book as
below with a different title. Very good with dj 20.00

Eastern Brook Trout: New York 1950. A fine copy of
the first edition 40.00

The Making of an Angler: New York 1975. A mint copy
of the first printing with dust jacket 15.00

ELLIOTT, CHARLES

Fading Trails: New York 1942. A fine copy of
the first printing 15.00

Gone Fishin': New York 1979. A mint copy of the first
printing with dust jacket 27.50

ELMER, ROBERT

Archery: Philadelphia 1926. The scarce first edition in
very fine condition 60.00

Target Archery: Borzoi/Knopf 1945. The first edition in
very good condition. Dj 35.00

Another: first British edition 1952 . . . .   40.00

ESTEY, PAUL C.

The Woodchuck Hunter: Small Arms 1936. The first
printing of a scarce title. Fine 45.00

EVERETT, FRED

Fun with Game Birds: Harrisburg, PA 1954. One of the
limited leather-bound copies 150.00

Another: The trade edition, mint 50.00

Fun with Trout: Harrisburg, PA 1952. One of the limited
leather-bound copies 170.00

Another: The trade edition, mint 50.00

FARRINGTON, S. KIP

Atlantic Game Fishing: New York 1937. A fine copy of
the scarce first edition 250.00

Bill—The Broadbilled Swordfish: New York 1942. Lynn
Bogue Hunt drawings. Juvenile. Very good 175.00

The Ducks Came Back: New York 1945. The Ducks
Unlimited story. A very fine copy 50.00

Pacific Game Fishing: New York 1942. The hard to find
first edition. Very fine 120.00

Fishing the Atlantic: New York 1949. A very fine copy of
the first printing with dj 75.00

Fishing the Pacific: New York 1953. A very fine copy
with a dust jacket. First edition 120.00

Tony—The Tuna: Southampton 1975. A very scarce
juvenile. A. D. "Sandy" Read drawings. Very fine 110.00

FIELD, EUGENE

A Little Book of Tribune Verse: Denver 1901. One of 750
large paper copies. Very good 50.00

The Love Affair of a Bibliomaniac. New York 1896.
Contains "Fender Fishing." Very good 25.00

FISHER, P. (Wm. A. Chatto)

The Angler's Souvenir: London 1835. The first edition in
very fine condition 200.00

Another: As above with spine repairs 160.00

Another: 1877 with loose front hinge 35.00

FLECKENSTEIN, HENRY A.

Shorebird Decoys: Exton 1980. A signed copy of this
important decoy book 35.00

Southern Decoys: Exton 1983. A signed copy of *the* guide
to Virginia and Carolina decoys 35.00

FLICK, ART

Art Flick's Master Fly Tying Guide: New York 1972. A
fine copy in a ragged dust jacket 50.00

Art Flick's New Streamside Guide: New York 1969. A
mint condition copy with a fine dust jacket 30.00

Streamside Guide: New York 1947. Signed copy of the
rare first edition. Very fine 125.00

Another: Later printing 50.00

FORD, COREY

Corey Ford's Guide To Thinking: New York 1961. Heavy
board covers, mint 65.00

Has Anybody Seen Me Lately? New York 1958. Fine in a
fine dust jacket 15.00

Uncle Perk's Jug: New York 1964. The scarce first
edition. Ex-library 75.00

Where The Sea Breaks Its Back: Boston 1966. A very fine
copy with a dust jacket 30.00

You Can Always Tell a Fisherman: New York 1958. A
fine copy of the first edition with dj 75.00

FOSTER, WILLIAM H.

New England Grouse Shooting: New York 1942. The
scarce first edition. 250.00

Another: New York 1947 . . . .   100.00

Another: Oshkosh, WI 1983 . . . .   45.00

FOX, CHARLES K.

Rising Trout: Carlisle 1967. Privately
printed limited edition 110.00

The Wonderful World of Trout: Carlisle 1963. The
privately printed limited edition 90.00

Another: Rockville Center 1971 . . . .   25.00

FRANCIS, FRANCIS

A Book on Angling: London 1867. The first edition with
five hand-colored plates 350.00

FROST, A. B.

Drawings: New York 1904. A book of drawings
introduced by Joel Chandler Harris. Very good 125.00

GARRISON, E. and CARMICHAEL, H.

A Master's Guide To Building A Bamboo Rod: Harrisburg,
PA 1977. First edition. Mint 100.00

GASQUE, JIM

Bass Fishing: Borzoi/Knopf 1945. A very fine copy of the
first edition. Dj 35.00

Hunting & Fishing in the Great Smokies: Borzoi/Knopf
1948. First printing. Mint 50.00

GEE, ERNEST R.

Early American Sporting Books: Derrydale 1928. One of
500 copies. Very fine 250.00

GILL, EMLYN M.

Practical Dry-Fly Fishing: New York 1912. The first
American book on this subject. Fine 80.00

GINGRICH, ARNOLD

The Fishing in Print: New York 1974. Mint condition
with fine dust jacket 25.00

The Joys of Trout: New York 1974. A fine copy with a
fine dust jacket 25.00

The Well-Tempered Angler: New York 1965. A fine copy
of the first edition 40.00

Another: Later printing 25.00

GOODSPEED, CHARLES E.

Angling In America: Boston 1939. One of 795 signed and
numbered copies. Uncut pages. Very fine 240.00

Yankee Bookseller: Boston 1937. One of 310 signed and
numbered copies. Full leather with slipcase 110.00

GORDON, SID

How to Fish from Top to Bottom: Harrisburg, PA 1955.
The first edition in fine condition. Dj 60.00

Another: 1974 edition 25.00

GREENER, W. W.

The Gun and Its Development: London 1881. The scarce
first edition. Fine 200.00

Modern Breech-Loaders: London 1871. The first of
Greener's books. Hinges damaged 110.00

Modern Shot Guns: London 1888. A scarce title in very
good condition 100.00

GREY, ZANE

Tales of An Angler's Eldorado: Grosset. A fine copy in a
fine dust jacket 140.00

Tales of Fishes: Harpers 1919. Not first edition 35.00

Tales of Fishing Virgin Seas: Grosset. Dj 90.00

ZANE GREY FIRST EDITIONS

Recognizing the first editions of Zane Grey's sporting books is not as difficult as you might think, and nowhere as mysterious as the publisher might have intended. The following list should prove useful. All were published by Harper & Brothers.

The Young Lion Hunter	*1911—No code*
Tales of Fishes	*1919—Code "F–T"*
Roping Lions in the Grand Canyon	*1924—Code "B–Y"*
Tales of Southern Rivers	*1924—"First Edition"*
Tales of Fishing Virgin Seas	*1925—"First Edition"*
Tales of An Angler's Eldorado	*1927—"First Edition"*
Tales of Swordfish & Tuna	*1927—"First Edition"*
Tales of Fresh Water Fishing	*1928—"First Edition"*
Tales of Tahitian Waters	*1931—"First Edition"*
Zane Grey's Book of Camps & Trails	*1931—Code "G–F"*
An American Angler in Australia	*1937—"First Edition"*

Another: As above. A fine copy. Dj 100.00

Tales of Fresh Water Fishing: Harpers 1928. A very good copy of the first edition 130.00

Another: As above with dust jacket 250.00

Tales of Southern Rivers: Grosset. Dj 90.00

Another: As above. A fine copy with dj 90.00

Tales of Swordfish & Tuna: Grosset. A fine copy in a fine dust jacket 130.00

GRINNELL, GEORGE BIRD

American Duck Shooting: New York 1901. A fine first edition with Eugene Connett's bookplate 260.00

Another: As above in very good condition 175.00

American Game Bird Shooting: New York 1910. A fine
copy of the first edition 50.00

GROVE, ALVIN R.

The Lure and Lore of Trout Fishing: Harrisburg, PA
1951. The first edition. Very good in a very good dj . . . 65.00

Another: Rockville Center 1971. Fine 20.00

HAGEDORN, HERMANN

Roosevelt in the Badlands: Boston 1921. A very fine copy
in a good dust jacket 60.00

HAIG-BROWN, RODERICK L.

Fisherman's Fall: 1975 reprint. Mint 35.00

Fisherman's Spring: 1975 reprint. Mint 35.00

Fisherman's Summer: 1975 reprint. Mint 35.00

Fisherman's Winter: 1975 reprint. Mint 35.00

A Primer of Fly Fishing: New York 1964. The first
edition. Fine with dust jacket 60.00

Return to the River: 1974 reprint. Fine 20.00

A River Never Sleeps: New York 1946. The scarce
first edition. Fine 70.00

Silver: London 1946. Second edition 30.00

The Western Angler: Derrydale 1939. One of 950 two-
volume sets. Without map. Fine 475.00

Another: New York 1947. The trade edition 45.00

HALL, HENRY M.

A Full Creel: New York 1946. A very good copy of the
first edition with dj 15.00

HALL-MARTIN, ANTHONY

Elephants of Africa: Cape Town 1986. A very fine copy
with dust jacket 50.00

HARDY, CAPTAIN CAMPBELL

Forest Life in Arcadie: London 1869. The first edition
with minor defects 90.00

HEILNER, VAN CAMPEN

A Book on Duck Shooting: Philadelphia 1939. Edition of
99 signed by author and artist L. B. Hunt 1,050.00

Another: Philadelphia 1939. The first edition. Also artist
and author signed 175.00

Another: Borzoi/Knopf 1943. Very fine. Dj 125.00

Another: As above with faded spine 60.00

Salt Water Fishing: Philadelphia 1937. Numbered and
signed edition of 199. Very fine 250.00

Another: 1937. First trade edition. Very fine 100.00

Another: Borzoi/Knopf 1943. Very fine with dj 65.00

Another: Borzoi/Knopf 1952. Hemingway introduction . .   50.00

HENSHALL, JAMES A.

Bass, Pike, Perch & Others: New York 1903. A very good
copy of the first edition 30.00

Another: 1919 edition 20.00

Book of the Black Bass: Cincinnati 1881. First issue of

the first edition. Very good 175.00

Another: Second issue of the first edition 135.00

Another: Facsimile reprint. Mint 15.00

Camping & Cruising in Florida: Cincinnati 1888. A fine
copy of a scarce book 225.00

More About The Black Bass: Cincinnati 1889. The first
edition in fine condition 150.00

Ye Gods & Little Fishes: Cincinnati 1900. A fine copy of
a scarce title 150.00

HIGHTOWER, JOHN

Pheasant Hunting: Borzoi/Knopf 1946. One of a limited
edition, signed and numbered. Fine 150.00

Another: as above. The first trade edition 35.00

HILL, GENE

A Hunter's Fireside Book: New York 1972. The first
edition in mint condition 20.00

Mostly Tailfeathers: New York 1975. One of 475
numbered/slipcased copies 50.00

Another: As above. The trade edition 20.00

HILLS, JOHN WALLER

A Summer on the Test: London 1924. One of 300 signed
and numbered copies with 12 Wilkenson drypoints . . .   700.00

HOLLAND, RAY P.

Now Listen, Warden: West Hartford 1946. One of 475
signed and numbered copies. Very fine 100.00

Another: The trade edition 30.00

Art is often a central factor in determining a collectible book's value. A classic example is found in John Waller Hills's *A Summer on the Test,* which contains twelve original drypoint engravings by Norman Wilkinson. Published in London in 1924 in a limited edition of three hundred, a fine uncut copy sold in 1989 for seven hundred dollars. (Courtesy of Richard Oinonen/Oinonen Book Auctions)

Shotgunning in the Lowlands: West Hartford 1945.
One of 275 signed and numbered copies
with worn slipcase 130.00

Another: The trade edition 75.00

Shotgunning in the Uplands: West Hartford 1944. One of
250 signed and numbered copies with worn slipcase . . 160.00

Another: The trade edition 80.00

HUNT, LYNN BOGUE

An Artist's Game Bag: Derrydale 1936. One of 1,225
numbered copies. Spine wear 350.00

HUNTER, J. A.

Hunter: New York 1952. A fine copy of
this popular book 20.00

Hunter's Tracks: New York 1957. The first edition. Fine
with a good dust jacket 35.00

White Hunter: Long Beach 1986. Reprint of the 1938
edition. One of 1,000 copies 50.00

JANES, EDWARD C.

Hunting Ducks and Geese: Harrisburg, PA 1954. A fine
copy of a hard-to-find title 25.00

Fishing With Lee Wulff: New York 1972. A fine copy
signed by Lee and Joan Wulff 50.00

Fishing With Ray Bergman: New York 1970. Very fine
with a fine dust jacket 15.00

JENNINGS, PRESTON J.

A Book of Trout Flies: Derrydale 1935. One of 850
copies. Green binding. Fine 550.00

Another: Blue binding 600.00

Another: Crown edition with tipped-in fly tied
by the author 425.00

Another: Crown edition, 1971 . . . .   35.00

JOHNSGARD, PAUL A.

The Bird Decoy: Lincoln 1976. A fine copy of this
decoy book. Dj 25.00

North American Game Birds of Upland and Shoreline:
Lincoln 1975. A mint copy 30.00

Waterfowl: Lincoln 1968. A very fine copy of the first edition with a fine dust jacket 47.50

JOHNSON, MARTIN

Camera Trails in Africa: New York 1924. A fine copy . .   35.00

Lion: New York 1929. A very good copy
of the first edition 25.00

Another: Later printing 10.00

Safari: New York 1928. A fine copy with a
sun-faded spine 20.00

JOHNSON, OSA (Mrs. Martin)

Four Years In Paradise: Garden City 1941.
A fine copy 15.00

I Married Adventure: Philadelphia 1940. A fine copy with
a worn dust jacket 17.50

JORGENSEN, POUL

Modern Fly Dressings: New York 1976. A very fine copy
of the first edition 25.00

Modern Trout Flies: Garden City 1979. A fine copy of the
first edition. Dj 30.00

Salmon Flies: Harrisburg, PA 1978. A fine copy with
a dust jacket 20.00

KEENE, JOHN HARRINGTON

Fishing Tackle, Its Materials & Manufacture: London
1886. Avis Marbury's copy. Very good 400.00

Fly Fishing & Fly Making For Trout: New York 1887. Fly-
tying material bound in. A fine copy 260.00

KEITH, ELMER

Big Game Hunting: New York 1948. A very good copy of the first printing 45.00

Hell, I Was There. Peterson 1979. A fine copy of the first edition with a fine dj 35.00

Sixgun Cartridges & Loads: Samworth 1936. The scarce first edition. A fine copy 125.00

Sixguns: Bonanza reprint 25.00

KNIGHT, JOHN ALDEN

Black Bass: New York 1949. One of 150 signed and numbered copies 200.00

Another: The trade edition. Fine with dj 40.00

Field Book of Fresh Water Angling: New York 1944. A very fine copy of the first edition in fine dj 35.00

The Modern Angler: New York 1936. A scarce title in very good condition 25.00

Moon Up—Moon Down: Montoursville 1972. Reprint of the "solunar theory" book 15.00

Ol' Bill & Other Stories: New York 1942. First edition with a good dust jacket 35.00

Ruffed Grouse: Borzoi/Knopf 1947. One of 210 signed and numbered copies in slipcase. Fine 550.00

Another: The trade edition. Fine with dj 100.00

The Theory & Technique of Fresh Water Angling: New York 1940. Fly plates by Burke. Fine 45.00

Woodcock: Borzoi/Knopf 1944. One of 275 signed and numbered copies in slipcase. Fine 400.00

Another: The trade edition. Fine with dj 90.00

KOCH, ED

Fishing The Midge: Rockville Center 1972. The first
edition in very fine condition with dj 40.00

KOLLER, LARRY

Shots At Whitetails: Boston 1948. A fine copy of
the first edition 35.00

Taking Larger Trout: Boston 1950. "Far and away the
author's best book." Very fine with dj 125.00

The Treasury of Angling: New York 1963. Mint
condition first edition 25.00

The Treasury of Hunting: New York 1965. Mint
condition first edition 20.00

KORTRIGHT, F. H.

The Ducks, Geese & Swans of North America. Wash., DC
1942. First edition (trade). Mint 35.00

Another: Fine 25.00

Another: Harrisburg, PA 1960. Full leather 40.00

KREIDER, CLAUDE

Steelhead: New York 1948. A very good copy of
the first edition 30.00

LaBRANCHE, GEORGE M. L.

The Dry Fly & Fast Water: New York 1921. The first
edition of this classic book 20.00

Another: 1926 edition 22.50

*The Dry Fly and Fast Water and The Salmon and The
Dry Fly:* New York 1951. First combined edition 70.00

Another: 1951 first combined edition 75.00

The Salmon and the Dry Fly: Boston 1924. One of 775
numbered copies. Fine 240.00

LAFONTAINE, GARY

Caddisflies: New York 1981. A mint copy with a
fine dust jacket 40.00

Challenge of the Trout: Missoula 1976. A very good copy
in a dust jacket 20.00

LAMB, DANA S.

Bright Salmon and Brown Trout: Barre 1964. One of
350 numbered copies 280.00

Not Far from the River: Barre 1967. One of
1,500 numbered copies 110.00

On Trout Streams and Salmon Rivers: Barre 1963. One
of 1,500 numbered copies 325.00

Some Silent Places Still: Barre 1969. One of
1,500 numbered copies 220.00

Where The Pools Are Bright & Deep: New York 1973.
One of 250 copies 50.00

Wood Smoke and Watercress: Barre 1965. One of
1,500 numbered copies 130.00

LANDIS C. S.

.22 Rifle Shooting: Small Arms 1932. A very good copy of
a scarce book 75.00

LANIER, HENRY W.

A. B. Frost: Derrydale 1933. One of 950
numbered copies. Scarce 450.00

Another: Camden, SC 1985. Fine reprint 110.00

LEFFINGWELL, WILLIAM B.

The Art of Wing Shooting: Chicago 1895. A fair to good
copy of the second printing 40.00

Wild Fowl Shooting: Chicago 1890. A very good copy of
the second printing 65.00

LEISENRING, JAMES E.

The Art of Tying the Wet Fly: New York 1941. A fine
copy of the rare first printing with dj 275.00

Another: As above but ex-library 100.00

Another: New York 1971 . . . .   30.00

LEOPOLD, ALDO

Game Management: New York 1933. A very good copy of
a scarce first edition 45.00

Round River: New York 1953. A fine copy of
the first edition 50.00

A Sand County Almanac: New York 1966. A mint copy
with chipped dust jacket 75.00

Another: Madison 1977. Mint with fine dj 75.00

Another: As above. Fine 40.00

LINCOLN, ROBERT PAGE

Black Bass Fishing: Harrisburg, PA 1952. A fine copy of
the first printing in a dust jacket 30.00

The Pike Family: Harrisburg, PA 1953. A fine copy of the
first edition with a dust jacket 26.00

LONG, JOSEPH W.

American Wild Fowl Shooting: New York 1879. A good
copy of the second edition 75.00

LYMAN, HENRY

Bluefishing: Boston 1950. The limited edition bound in
blue leather. Very fine 40.00

Another: New York 1955 . . . .   15.00

LYONS, NICK

Fisherman's Bounty: New York 1970. A very fine copy of
the first edition 40.00

Fishing Widows: New York 1974. A very fine copy in a
fine dust jacket 20.00

The Seasonable Angler: New York 1970. A mint copy in a
fine dust jacket 22.50

McCLANE, A. J.

The American Angler: New York 1954. A very fine copy
with a torn dust jacket 20.00

McClane's Standard Fishing Encyclopedia: New York
1965. The first edition. Very fine. Dj 50.00

Another: Later printing 35.00

The Practical Fly Fisherman: New York 1953. The first
edition in very fine condition. Dj 130.00

Another: As above. Fine 110.00

Spinning for Fresh and Salt Water Fish: New York 1953.
Fine with a worn dust jacket 20.00

Wise Fisherman's Encyclopedia: New York 1951. The first
edition in fine condition 35.00

McDANIEL, JOHN M.

The Turkey Hunter's Book: Clinton 1980. One of 1,000
signed and numbered slipcased copies. As new 200.00

Another: The trade edition 25.00

McDONALD, JOHN

The Complete Fly Fisherman: New York 1970. One of 50
copies. As new 1,000.00

As above: One of 950 copies 250.00

Another: New York, 1989 . . . .   30.00

The Origins of Angling: Garden City 1963. Translation of
Dame Berners. Mint 75.00

Quill Gordon: New York 1972. A fine copy
with cover-soiling 35.00

MacDOUGAL, ARTHUR R.

Doc Blakesley Angler: Portland 1949. One of 500 copies.
Fine in original glassine wrapper 150.00

Another: The first trade edition 40.00

Dud Dean and His Country: New York 1946. One of 450
signed and numbered copies. Very fine with dj 100.00

Another: The first trade edition 40.00

The Sun Stood Still: Bingham 1939. A signed and
numbered copy of the limited edition. Fine 110.00

Trout Fisherman's Bedside Book: New York 1963. A copy
in mint condition 15.00

Under a Willow Tree: New York 1946. A very fine copy.
Milton Weiler illustrations 40.00

Where Flows the Kennebec: New York 1947. A very good
copy of the first edition 45.00

MACKEY, WILLIAM J. JR.

American Bird Decoys: New York 1965. A fine copy of an
important decoy book 65.00

Another: Reprint edition 20.00

MARBURY, MARY ORVIS

Favorite Flies and Their Histories: Boston/New York
1892. A good copy of the second printing 210.00

Another: Fourth printing 250.00

MARINARO, VINCENT

In the Ring of the Rise: New York 1976. A mint copy
with dj of the first edition 50.00

A Modern Dry-Fly Code: New York 1950. A very fine copy
of the first edition 100.00

Another: 1970 edition 30.00

MELLAND, FRANK

Elephants in Africa: London 1938. A fine copy of the
first printing. Illustrated 75.00

MERKT, DIXON

Shang—A Biography of Charles E. Wheeler: 1985. One of
500 signed and numbered copies. Slipcase. Mint 75.00

Another: The trade edition 40.00

MERRILL, SAMUEL

The Moose Book: New York 1916. The first edition
in "fabulous" condition 90.00

MERSHON, WILLIAM B.

The Passenger Pigeon: New York 1907. A very fine copy
with a chipped dust jacket 150.00

Another: As above. Signed by author 150.00

MORDEN, HAROLD L.

Across Asia's Snows and Deserts: New York 1928. A fine
copy of a scarce book 100.00

MORSE, IRA H. and JULIE B.

Yankee in Africa: Boston 1936. A very good copy of the
first edition. Dust jacket 50.00

Another: As above. No dj 45.00

MURPHY, JOHN M.

American Game Bird Shooting: New York 1882. A very
good copy of the first edition 85.00

Another: 1892 edition 65.00

NEMES, SYLVESTER

The Soft-Hackled Fly: Bozeman, MT 1988. One of 180
signed and numbered copies. Slipcase. New 125.00

The Soft-Hackled Fly Addict: Bozeman, MT, 1988. One of
276 signed and numbered copies. Slipcase. New 125.00

NETBOY, ANTHONY

The Atlantic Salmon: Boston 1968. A very fine copy of
the first edition 35.00

The Salmon: Boston 1974. A very fine copy of
the first printing 30.00

Salmon: Tulsa 1980. A very fine copy of
the first edition 18.00

NORMAN, GEOFFREY

The Orvis Book of Upland Bird Shooting: New York
1985. Mint in mint wrapper 16.00

NORMAN, J. R.

History of Fishes: New York 1948. A very fine copy of the
first U.S. edition 25.00

O'CONNOR, JACK

The Art of Hunting Big Game in America: New York
1967. Fine first edition. Dj 25.00

The Best of Jack O'Connor: Clinton 1977. One of 1,000
signed and numbered copies. As new in slipcase 275.00

The Big Game Rifle: Borzoi/Knopf 1952. A fine copy of a
scarce book with a dust jacket 150.00

The Complete Book of Rifles and Shotguns: New York
1961. A fine first edition 20.00

The Complete Book of Shooting: New York 1965. A fine
copy with a chipped dust jacket 20.00

Game in the Desert: Derrydale 1939. One of
950 numbered copies 600.00

Another: Ex-library 500.00

Game in the Desert Revisited: Clinton 1977. One of 1,000
signed and numbered copies. As new in slipcase 275.00

Hunting in the Rockies: Borzoi/Knopf 1947. A very
scarce first edition 185.00

Hunting in the Southwest: Borzoi/Knopf 1945. A fine
copy with minor spine wear 100.00

Hunting on Three Continents with Jack O'Connor: Long
Beach 1987. One of 500 copies. New 45.00

The Hunting Rifle: New York 1970. A mint copy with a
fine dust jacket 25.00

The Rifle Book: Borzoi/Knopf 1949. A fine copy of the
third printing with dj 25.00

The Shotgun Book: New York 1965. A fine copy of the
first edition with dust jacket 45.00

ORDEMAN, JOHN T.

Frank Benson: Master of the Sporting Print: Privately
printed 1983. One of 50 signed and numbered copies . .   450.00

Another: One of 950 signed and numbered copies 150.00

Another: Second printing 40.00

*To Keep A Tryst With The Dawn: An Appreciation of
Roland Clark:* Privately printed 1989. One of 100 signed
and numbered copies 150.00

Another: One of 1,000 signed and numbered copies . . .   40.00

William J. Schaldach: Artist, Author, Sportsman: Privately
printed 1987. One of 150 signed and numbered copies   250.00

Another: One of 1,000 signed and numbered copies . . .   42.00

ORVIS, C. F. and CHENEY, A. N.

Fishing With The Fly: Boston 1886. A very good copy
with shelf wear 100.00

Another: Rutland, VT 1968 . . . .   30.00

OVINGTON, RAY

Tactics on Bass: New York 1983. A mint copy in
a fine dust jacket 20.00

Tactics on Trout: New York 1969. A very fine copy of the
first edition with dust jacket 15.00

PAGE, WARREN

One Man's Wilderness: New York 1973. A fine copy with
a fine dust jacket 45.00

PFEIFFER, C. BOYD

Shad Fishing: New York 1975. A very fine copy in a
good dust jacket 15.00

PHAIR, CHARLES

Atlantic Salmon Fishing: Derrydale 1937. One of 950
copies. Minor damp staining 675.00

PHILLIPS, JOHN C.

George Washington—Sportsman: Privately printed 1928.
One of 100 copies. Very fine 275.00

John Rowe: Privately printed 1929. One of 150
copies. Scarce. Mint 200.00

A Natural History of the Ducks: Boston/New York 1922–
26. 4 volumes. Rare. Fine 3,750.00

Another: 1986 2-volume reprint 100.00

The Sands of Muskeget: Privately printed 1931. One of
250 copies. Spine chipped 125.00

A Sportsman's Scrapbook: Boston 1928. A very fine copy
in a fine dust jacket 75.00

Another: Very good 45.00

A Sportsman's Second Scrapbook: Boston 1933. A fine
copy in a fine dust jacket 75.00

Another: Very good 35.00

PHILLIPS, JOHN C. and LINCOLN, FREDERICK C.

American Waterfowl: Boston 1930. A very good copy of
the first edition with a very good dj 70.00

PHILLIPS, JOHN C. and HILL, LEWIS W.

Classics of the American Shooting Field: Boston 1930. A
good copy of the first edition 45.00

PICKERING, H. C.

Angling of the Test: Derrydale 1936. One of 197 copies.
Very fine in worn two-part box 600.00

Dog Days on Trout Waters: Derrydale 1933. One of 199
copies. Spine and covers show wear 950.00

Merry Xmas, Mr. Williams: Derrydale 1940. One of 267
copies. Mint 600.00

Neighbors Have My Ducks: Derrydale 1937. One of 227
copies. Very scarce. Mint 650.00

POPOWSKI, BERT

Calling All Game: Harrisburg, PA 1952. A very fine copy
with a fine dust jacket 25.00

Calling All Varmints: Harrisburg, PA 1952. A fine copy
of a scarce book with dj 30.00

Crow Shooting: New York 1946. A very fine copy of
the first edition 15.00

Olt's Hunting Handbook: Omaha 1948. A fine copy of
a scarce title 25.00

PRYCE-TANNATT, T. E.

How to Dress Salmon Flies: London 1914. A fine copy of
the first edition 280.00

Another: 1986 reprint 27.50

QUEENY, EDGAR M.

Prairie Wings: Philadelphia 1947. A fine copy of
this "classic book" 270.00

Another: As above 275.00

QUICK, JIM

Fishing the Nymph: New York 1960. A very fine copy
with a fine dj 20.00

Trout Fishing and Trout Flies: New York 1957. A very
fine copy with a fine dj 18.00

REIGER, GEORGE

Fishing with McClane: Englewood Cliffs, NJ 1975. A fine
copy of the first edition with dj 20.00

Floaters and Stick-Ups: Boston 1986. A fine copy in a
fine dust jacket 45.00

Profiles in Salt Water Angling: Englewood Cliffs, NJ
1973. A fine copy of the first edition with dj 30.00

The Undiscovered Zane Grey Fishing Stories: New York
1984. First edition. Mint 17.50

Wanderer on My Native Shore: New York 1983. A fine
copy with a fine dust jacket 15.00

The Wings of Dawn: New York 1980. A fine copy in a
fine dust jacket 30.00

Zane Grey: Outdoorsman: Englewood Cliffs, NJ 1972.
Third printing. Fine with dj 30.00

RHEAD, LOUIS

American Trout Stream Insects: New York 1916. A fine
copy of the first edition 135.00

The Speckled Brook Trout: New York 1902. One of 350
large paper copies. Signed and numbered 400.00

Another: The 1902 trade edition. Very fine (dj) 195.00

RIKHOFF, JIM

Hunting the Big Cats: Clinton 1981. One of 1,000 signed
and numbered two-volume sets. Very fine 250.00

RILING, RAY

The Powder Flask Book: New York 1953. A reprint in
fine condition with dust jacket 50.00

Rifles and Shotguns: New York 1951. One of 1,500
copies. Very good with repaired dust jacket 110.00

Another: 1982. One of 500 copies 60.00

RITZ, CHARLES

A Flyfisher's Life: New York 1972. New edition of this
popular book. Mint with dj 75.00

Another: Lacking dust jacket 70.00

ROBINSON, JIMMY

Forty Years of Hunting: Minneapolis 1947. A very good
copy signed by the author 30.00

Hits and Misses (Trap & Skeet): Minneapolis 1942. A
very good copy of a scarce book 50.00

Hunting Adventures with Jimmy Robinson: Minneapolis
1958. A very good presentation copy 40.00

RONALDS, ALFRED

The Fly Fisher's Entomology: Liverpool 1913. One of 250
two-volume sets with actual trout flies. Fine 1,800.00

Another: Secaucus, NJ 1990. Reprint of the above 15.00

ROOSEVELT, KERMIT

The Happy Hunting Grounds: New York 1920. The
scarce first edition 50.00

Another: 1921 edition 25.00

The Long Trail: New York 1921. The first edition in a
repaired box 35.00

Another: 25.00

ROOSEVELT, THEODORE

African Game Trails: Scribners 1910. A very good copy of
the first edition 75.00

Another: Syndicate 1910. A very good copy
of this edition 50.00

A Book-Lover's Holiday in the Open: New York 1916. Ex-
library first edition. Fine 65.00

Hunting Trips of a Ranchman: New York 1886. A fine
copy with head of spine torn 75.00

Another: Presidential edition 40.00

Outdoor Pastimes of an American Hunter: New York
1905. A fine copy of the first edition 35.00

Another: Later printing 25.00

Ranch Life and the Hunting Trail: New York 1906.
The Elkhorn edition 100.00

The Wilderness Hunter: New York 1893. A very good copy
of the first edition 95.00

ROOSEVELT, THEODORE and ROOSEVELT, KERMIT

East of the Sun and West of the Moon: Blue Ribbon
edition. Very fine with a dust jacket 40.00

Trailing the Giant Panda: New York 1929. A fine copy
with the fold-out map 60.00

ROOSEVELT, THEODORE with ELLIOT, STONE, and VAN DYKE

The Deer Family: New York 1902. A very good copy of
the first edition 60.00

Another: The Grosset reprint 15.00

ROOSEVELT, THEODORE and HELLER, EDMUND

Life Histories of African Game Animals: New York 1914.
A two-volume set. Good ex-library 175.00

ROSENE, WALTER

The Bobwhite Quail: Rutgers Press 1969. One of 250
signed and numbered copies in slipcase. As new 200.00

RUARK, ROBERT

Horn of the Hunter: New York 1953. A very fine copy of
the first printing with a fine dj 150.00

Another: Lacking dust jacket 125.00

Another: 1987 printing 50.00

The Old Man and the Boy: New York 1957. A very fine
copy of the first edition with chipped dj 75.00

The Old Man's Boy Grows Older: New York 1961. A very
fine copy of the first edition with dj 80.00

Use Enough Gun: New York 1966. A very good copy of
the first edition with a fine dj 45.00

RUSSELL, JACK

Jill and I and the Salmon: Boston 1950. A signed copy
of the first edition. Fine 45.00

RUSSELL, KEITH

The Duck Huntingest Gentleman: Privately printed 1974.
One of 1,000 signed and numbered copies. Very fine . .   65.00

Another: Tulsa 1980. First trade edition 20.00

RUTLEDGE, ARCHIBALD

From the Hills to the Sea: Indianapolis 1958. A fine copy
of the first edition 55.00

Home by the River: Indianapolis 1955. A signed copy of
the large paper edition 35.00

Another: the 1941 first edition. Very good 20.00

Old Plantation Days: New York 1921. A very good copy
of the first edition 85.00

RUTTERFORD, KEN

Collecting Shotgun Cartridges: Vermont 1987. A mint
copy in a fine dust jacket 45.00

SAGE, DEAN

The Restigouche and Its Salmon Fishing: Goshen, CT
1973. One of 250 slipcased copies. Mint 1,050.00

SAGE, DEAN and OTHERS

Salmon and Trout: New York 1902. A very good copy of
the first edition 45.00

Another: 1904 edition 30.00

SANDS, LEDYARD

The Bird, the Gun and the Dog: New York 1939. A very
good copy of the first edition with dj 75.00

SAWYER, FRANK

Keeper of the Stream: London 1952. A fine copy of the
first edition with a fine dust jacket 75.00

SCHALDACH, WILLIAM J.

Carl Rungius—Big Game Painter: New York 1945. One
of 1,250 copies. Very fine 750.00

Another: As above 750.00

Coverts and Casts: New York 1943. One of 160 signed
and numbered copies 300.00

Another: The trade edition 40.00

Coverts and Casts/Currents and Eddies: Rockville Center
1970. The Freshet reprint. Mint 50.00

Currents and Eddies: New York 1944. One of 250 signed,
numbered, and slipcased copies 275.00

Another: The trade edition 40.00

Fish: Philadelphia 1937. One of 1,560 copies in the
original box. A "gorgeous" copy 350.00

Another: A fine copy 200.00

The Path to Enchantment: New York 1963. A very fine
copy of the first printing with fine dj 35.00

Upland Gunning: New York 1946. A very fine copy of the
first edition in a fine dust jacket 75.00

Another: As above 100.00

The Wind on Your Cheek: Rockville Center 1972. One of
200 numbered, slipcased copies 195.00

Another: The trade edition 25.00

SCHUEREN, ARNOLD C.

Foxy's Lion Tales: Privately printed 1943. One of 990
copies. Map endpapers. Very good 75.00

Another: As above 55.00

SCHWIEBERT, ERNEST

Death of a Riverkeeper: New York 1980. A fine copy of
the first edition in a fine dj 30.00

Matching the Hatch: New York 1955. A fine copy of the
scarce first edition 150.00

Nymphs: New York 1973. An inscribed copy of the first
printing. Fine with a fine dust jacket 75.00

Another: 1977 edition 40.00

Remembrances of Rivers Past: New York 1972. A mint
copy of the first edition with fine dj 25.00

A River for Christmas: Lexington 1988. A mint copy with
a fine dust jacket 20.00

Salmon of the World: New York 1970. One of 750 signed
and numbered copies. Slipcase. Very fine 1,500.00

Trout: New York 1978. Fine edition of the two-volume
first printing. Slipcase 200.00

Another: Very good in very good slipcase 100.00

Another: 1984 revision 75.00

SHARP, HENRY

Modern Sporting Gunnery: London 1906. A good copy of
the scarce first printing 125.00

SHAW, HELEN

Flies for Fish and Fishermen: Harrisburg, PA 1989. A
mint signed first edition 40.00

Fly Tying: New York 1963. A very good copy of a
scarce first edition 45.00

SHELDON, CHARLES

The Wilderness of Denali: New York 1930. A very fine
copy of the first edition . . . .　300.00

The Wilderness of the N. Pacific Coast Islands: New York
1912. Fine copy of a scarce book . . . .　200.00

The Wilderness of the Upper Yukon: New York 1913. The
second printing. Very scarce. Very fine . . . .　300.00

SHELDON, COL. H. P.

Tranquillity: Derrydale 1936. One of 950 numbered
copies. Very fine . . . .　225.00

Tranquillity Revisited: Derrydale 1940. One of 485
numbered copies. Very fine . . . .　475.00

The Tranquillity Stories: New York 1974. One-volume
edition of the three Tranquillity books . . . .　50.00

*Tranquillity—Tranquillity Revisited—Tranquillity
Regained:* New York 1945. One of 475 sets. Fine　. . . .　500.00

Another: The trade edition of the above. Fine　. . . . . .　85.00

Another: Willow Creek edition . . . .　45.00

SHELDON, WILLIAM G.

The Book of the American Woodcock: Amherst 1971. The
corrected second printing. Mint with dj . . . .　25.00

SKUES, G. E. M.

Minor Tactics of the Chalk Stream: London 1910. A very
good copy with cover wear . . . .　130.00

The Way of a Man with a Trout: London 1977. One of
150 two-volume sets with trout flies　. . . . .　750.00

SMEDLEY, HAROLD H.

Fly Patterns and Their Origins: Muskegon 1943. A fine
first edition, signed with a repaired dj 200.00

Another: Fourth edition 85.00

More Fly Patterns: Muskegon 1944. A rarely seen
supplement to the above. Very good 100.00

SMITH, EDMUND WARE

The Further Adventures of the One-Eyed Poacher: Crown
1947. One of 750 signed and numbered copies. Fine . .   185.00

The One-Eyed Poacher and the Maine Woods: New York
1955. A very fine first edition with dj 60.00

The One-Eyed Poacher of Privilege: Derrydale 1941. One
of 750 numbered copies. Very fine 200.00

Tall Tales and Short: Derrydale 1938. One of 950
numbered copies. Very fine 220.00

A Tomato Can Chronicle: Derrydale 1937. One of 950
copies. Very fine 220.00

A Treasury of the Maine Woods: New York 1958. A
scarce title in very fine condition with dj 50.00

SMITH, HARRY WORCESTER

A Sporting Family of the Old South: Albany 1936. A very
fine copy with a fine dust jacket 150.00

Another: As above in good condition 75.00

SOWLS, LYLE K.

Prairie Ducks: Harrisburg, PA 1955. A fine copy with a
fine dust jacket 65.00

Another: As above. Very good 35.00

SPILLER, BURTON L.

Firelight: Derrydale 1937. One of 950 numbered
copies. Very fine 400.00

Fishing Around: New York 1974. A very fine copy in a
fine dust jacket 20.00

Grouse Feathers: Derrydale 1935. One of 950 numbered
copies. Very fine 300.00

Another: 1947 trade edition 35.00

Another: 1972 edition 25.00

Grouse Feathers/More Grouse Feathers: Crown 1972. One
of 750 signed and numbered sets. Very fine 300.00

Another: Set. Very good 250.00

More Grouse Feathers: Derrydale 1938. One of 950
numbered copies. Very fine 300.00

Another: 1947 trade edition 35.00

Another: 1972 edition 25.00

Thoroughbred: Derrydale 1936. One of 950 numbered
copies. Very fine and bright 250.00

STOUT, GARDNER D.

The Shorebirds of North America: New York 1967. A very
fine copy of the first edition with dj 175.00

Another: Second printing 120.00

SWISHER, DOUG and RICHARDS, CARL

Fly-Fishing Strategy: New York 1975. A signed copy
(Richards) of the first edition. Fine with dj 40.00

Selective Trout: New York 1972. A very fine copy of the
first printing with dust jacket 60.00

TAPPLY, H. G. "TAP"

The Fly Tyer's Handbook: New York 1949. A scarce title
in fine condition with a dust jacket 35.00

The Sportsman's Notebook & Tap's Tips: New York 1964.
A mint copy with dust jacket 20.00

Tackle Tinkering: New York 1946. A very fine copy of
a first printing 15.00

TAVERNER, ERIC

Salmon Fishing: London 1948. A very good copy of this
hard-to-find book 75.00

Trout Fishing from All Angles: London 1948. A very fine
copy with a dust jacket 45.00

TAVERNER, ERIC and OTHERS

Salmon Fishing: London 1931. One of 275 deluxe copies
with salmon flies 1,400.00

TAYLOR, JOHN

African Rifles and Cartridges: Samworth 1952. A very
fine copy of a scarce book 90.00

THOMSON, WILLIAM

Great Cats I Have Met: Boston 1896. A very good copy of
a very scarce book 40.00

TRAVER, ROBERT (John Voelker)

Anatomy of a Fisherman: New York 1964. A very fine
signed copy of the first edition with dj 150.00

Another: As above but no signature 120.00

Trout Madness: New York 1960. A mint copy of
this popular book 30.00

Trout Magic: New York 1974. A mint copy of
another popular book 75.00

TRUEBLOOD, TED

The Angler's Handbook: New York 1949. A good copy of
the first edition 35.00

The Ted Trueblood Hunting Treasury: New York 1978. A
mint copy with dj 20.00

UNDERWOOD, LAMAR

Bass Almanac: Garden City 1979. A mint copy in a
fine dust jacket 20.00

The Deer Book: Clinton 1982. One of 1,000 signed and
numbered copies in slipcase. As new 200.00

Hunting the North Country: Clinton 1982. One of 1,000
signed and numbered slipcased copies. As new 220.00

VAN DE WATER, FRED F.

In Defense of Worms: New York 1949. A fine copy of the
first edition with dust jacket 25.00

VAN DYKE, THEODORE S.

The Still Hunter: New York 1943. A very fine copy in a
fine dust jacket 45.00

Another: 1922. First printing. Ex-library 27.50

WALDEN, HOWARD T. 2d

Big Stony: Derrydale 1940. One of 550 copies. A
fine signed copy 225.00

Another: New York 1940 . . . .   35.00

Familiar Fresh Water Fishes: New York 1964. A mint
copy in a fine dust jacket 15.00

The Last Pool: New York 1972. The above two books as
one volume. Very fine with dj 25.00

Upstream and Down: Derrydale 1938. One of 950 copies.
Gold leaf rubbed, otherwise fine 250.00

Another: The trade edition 35.00

IZAAK WALTON, THE COMPLEAT ANGLER

Collecting the hundreds of editions of Izaak Walton's The Compleat
Angler *is an art unto itself. The serious collector knows this, and the
amateur should become serious. The few editions that follow here are
introductory.*

WALTON, IZAAK

The Compleat Angler: 1784. The Fourth Hawkins edition
with light edge wear 100.00

Another: 1822. The Ninth Hawkins edition. Very good . .   75.00

Another: 1825. The First Pickering edition. Fine 150.00

Another: 1893. The First McClurg edition. Very good . .   100.00

Another: 1897. The First La Gallienne edition. Fine . . .   125.00

WARD, ROLAND

Roland Ward's Records of Big Game: London 1903.
Fourth edition. Very good 250.00

Roland Ward's Records of Big Game: London 1964.
Eleventh edition. Africa addendum. Ex-library 15.00

Roland Ward's Records of Big Game: London 1969.
Thirteenth edition. Very good 65.00

WATSON, FREDERICK

Hunting Pie: Derrydale 1931. One of 750 copies in
very fine condition 125.00

Another: London 1931. The trade edition 50.00

WETZEL, CHARLES M.

American Fishing Books: Privately printed 1950. One of
200 signed and numbered copies. Very fine 1,650.00

Another: Stone Harbor 1990. One of 500 copies 45.00

Practical Fly Fishing: Harrisburg, PA 1955. One of a
limited edition in full leather binding 625.00

Another: The first trade edition 120.00

Another: The 1979 facsimile reprint 25.00

WHELAN, TOWNSEND

Hunting Big Game: Harrisburg, PA 1947. A very fine
two-volume set with djs 150.00

The Hunting Rifle: Harrisburg, PA 1940. A very good
copy of a scarce first edition 40.00

WHITE, FREDERICK

The Spicklefisherman and Others: Derrydale 1928. One
of 740 copies. Very fine 150.00

WHITE, STEWART EDWARD

African Camp Fires: Garden City 1913. A very good copy
of the first printing 50.00

The Forest: New York 1903. A fine copy of the hard-to-
find first edition 17.50

The Land of Footprints: Toronto 1914. A fair copy of the
first Canadian edition 22.50

Lions in the Path: Garden City 1926. A very good copy of
the first printing 50.00

The Mountains: New York 1904. A very fine copy of the
scarce first edition 32.50

The Pass: New York 1906. A fine copy of the
scarce first edition 25.00

The Rediscovered Country: Garden City 1915. A very
good copy of the first printing 40.00

WILLIAMS, BEN AMES

The Happy End: Derrydale 1939. One of 1,250
numbered copies. Fine 175.00

WITTER, DEAN

Meanderings of a Fisherman: San Francisco (no date). A
very fine copy 35.00

Solo Safari: San Francisco (no date). A very fine copy
about a Kenyan safari 35.00

WRIGHT, BRUCE S.

Black Duck Spring: New York 1966. A fine copy of the
first edition with a fine dj 30.00

High Tide and an East Wind: Harrisburg, PA. The hard-
to-find first edition. Fine with fine dj 65.00

WULFF, LEE

The Atlantic Salmon: New York 1958. One of 200 signed
and numbered copies. Very fine in very good slipcase . . 400.00

Another: The trade edition. Third printing 30.00

Leaping Silver: New York 1940. One of 540 signed and
numbered copies. Fine in very good slipcase 450.00

Lee Wulff on Flies: Harrisburg, PA 1980. A very fine
signed copy with fine dj 35.00

The Sportsman's Companion: New York 1968. A very
good copy with good dust jacket 15.00

Trout on a Fly: New York 1986. One of 500 signed and
numbered copies. As new in a very fine slipcase 150.00

Another: The trade edition 35.00

YOUNG, PAUL H.

Making and Using the Dry Fly: Birmingham 1934. A very
rare book by the rodmaker. Very fine 300.00

Making and Using the Fly and Leader: Privately printed
by the rodmaker. Third edition 100.00

Another: Second edition 130.00

ZERN, ED

A Fine Kettle of Fish Stories: New York 1971. Fine copy
in dust jacket 20.00

How to Catch Fishermen: New York 1951. A fine copy in
a good dust jacket 35.00

How to Tell Fish from Fishermen: New York 1947. A
very fine copy 30.00

Hunting and Fishing from A to Zern: New York 1985. A
very fine signed copy 25.00

To Hell with Fishing: New York 1945. A fine copy of the
first printing with fine dj 30.00

To Hell with Hunting: New York 1946. A fine copy in a
fine dust jacket 25.00

with the best wishes of Ed Zern

Ed Zern's humor and zany drawings have brought joy to sportsmen for many years. A front endpaper sketch such as this one increases the enjoyment and value of his books. This is from a copy of *To Hell with Hunting* that I bought for my son—the godson, I'm proud to say, of Ed and his late wife Evelyn.

SPORTING CATALOGS

They may be catalogs to some, but to me these printed offerings of sporting goods for sale are, and always will be, *look books.* They fueled the fires of my youth, provided a warm comfort on winter nights, and were the stuff dreams are made from. I don't remember getting anything from any of the many catalogs I kept and cherished; mostly I think I just looked, and, I am happy to recall, that was enough.

Times change, and catalogs, like all things "sporting," have become costly. Some now truly are "look books" because only a very few people can afford them. These old-time compendiums of everything under the sun make an interesting and potentially valuable collection. There is only one thing to keep in mind: Many of the "old" catalogs you see in today's marketplace are recent reprints. The illustration for this chapter of a signed Joel Barber catalog is from a reprint. Look books should be looked at carefully.

ABBIE & IMBRIE

Fine Fishing Tackle: 1889 wholesale catalog with price list laid in. Fine 500.00

Another: 1893. Good with cover staining 110.00

ABERCROMBIE & FITCH

Shooting: 1965. The fall catalog of guns. A fine copy . . 65.00

CATALOGUE

AFG
EXHIBITION
WILDFOWL DECOYS
1931

SEPTEMBER 26-28-29-30
1931

Joel Barber

Used Guns: 1942	25.00
Another: 1952	25.00
Another: 1964	25.00
Used & Antique Guns: 1966	95.00
Another: 1971	95.00

ABERCROMBIE, DAVID T.

Abercrombie's Camp Outfits: 1927. A very fine copy	40.00

ALLCOCK, S. & CO.

Allcock's Angler's Guide: 1938–39. Profusely illustrated. Very good	30.00
Another: As above. Fine	20.00
Another: 1968	20.00

ANGLERS & SHOOTERS BOOKSHELF

Anglers & Shooters Bookshelf Catalogs. A complete run of
20 from 1977 through 1985 . . . .   150.00

BATE, THOMAS H. & CO.

Thomas H. Bate & Co: Circa 1853 catalog. Store copy.
Handcolored plates. "Fabulous" 1,500.00

BRISTOL ROD CO.

Fishing Rods, Reels, and Lines: Catalog #39. A very good
copy of an early catalog 140.00

J. T. BUEL CO.

J. T. Buel & Co. catalog: Circa 1932. A mint catalog in
original envelope 45.00

BURBERRYS

Hints On Alpine Sports: A circa 1911 catalog in
very fine condition 50.00

CROSS ROD COMPANY

Cross Custombuilt Rods: 1931 catalog. A very good copy
with woodgrain cover 325.00

CROSSROADS OF SPORT

Crossroads of Sport catalog: 1970–71. A fine copy
with Pleissner cover 15.00

Another: 1977–78 . . . .   10.00

Another: 1978–79 . . . .   10.00

DARBEE, E. B. & H. A.

E. B. & H. A. Darbee catalog: With inked-in 1951
prices and date 200.00

DICKERSON, LYLE

Dickerson Rods catalog: In its
original mailing envelope 375.00

HARDY BROS.

Anglers Guide & Catalog: 1925. A very good copy of the
forty-seventh edition 90.00

Another: 1929 . . . .   75.00

Another: 1934 . . . .   50.00

Another: 1963 . . . .   30.00

HERTER'S

Herter's catalog: 1969 . . . .   8.00
Another: 1978 . . . .   8.00

HILL BROS. FUR CO.

Trapper's Friend: 1935–36 catalog complete with
shipping tags, etc. 12.00

ITHACA GUN CO.

Ithaca Guns: 1940 catalog illustrated in color and black
and white. Very good 15.00

IVER JOHNSON SPORTING GOODS

Fishing—Camping: Circa 1922 catalog. Heddon lures in
color. Very good 40.00

MASON DECOYS

Mason Decoys: 1910–12 catalog in good condition 350.00

MEISSELBACH, A. F. & BROS.

Fishing Reels & Landing Nets: Circa 1906 catalog with
two fliers tipped in 75.00

MILLS, WILLIAM & SON

William Mills & Son: 1909 catalog with pencil marking
on cover 140.00

Another: 1912 . . . .   200.00

Another: 1941 . . . .   35.00

ORVIS, CHARLES F. CO.

Finest Rods, Reels, Flies, & Fishing Tackle: Circa 1902
catalog. Very good condition 185.00

Another: Catalog #30 (1930) 165.00

PARKER BROTHERS

Parker Guns: Circa 1920s. Fine condition 137.00

PAYNE, E. F. CO.

E. F. Payne Rod Co: Catalog circa 1951 with taped-in
inscription to Harry Darbee 180.00

PFLUEGER

Fishing Tackle: 1926 catalog with Zane Grey ad on back
cover. Very good 55.00

Another: 1938. A fine copy with
hundreds of photographs 40.00

SMITH, ALBERT

Fishing Tackle: 1939. Catalog #19 of "tackle that is
worth fishing with" 30.00

THOMAS, F. E.

F. E. Thomas—Bangor, Maine: Catalog for 1935 with
writing on back cover 250.00

VOM HOFE, EDWARD

Edward Vom Hofe catalog: 1937. "70th Anniversary Fine
Fishing Tackle Catalog" 130.00

VOM HOFE, JULIUS

Julius Vom Hofe: Catalog for 1915 with "1916"
date overstamped. Excellent 150.00

WILKENSON, JOHN & CO.

Angler's & Sportsman's Guide: Circa 1890. Very good
with some pencil marking 120.00

Tackle & Camp Equipment: 1896. Advertises the Kosmic
rods, reels, and lines 150.00

WINCHESTER

Retail Price List: Revised to December 30, 1955. Thirty-
six pages. Fine 8.00

Another: Revised to December 15, 1956 . . . .   8.00

DUCK STAMPS AND DUCK-STAMP PRINTS

Duck stamps—properly termed Federal Migratory Bird Hunting and Conservation Stamps, and duck-stamp prints have attracted collectors and controversy since their inception in 1940. When California became the first state to require a state duck stamp in 1971 and another "limited edition duck-stamp print" became available, the race was on for the waterfowler's and the print collector's dollars. There are now forty-six states with duck stamps and "first of state duck-stamp prints," and when you add this to the fifty-seven federal duck stamps and "limited edition prints," it seems logical to ask not where it all began, but where it will end—and what the various values will be when it does. There are now only four states left without duck stamps, and thus the ability to offer "first of state prints," so the end is indeed in sight. Only the question of value remains, and to explore this it is necessary to go back to the beginning—where today's so-called limited editions have their roots, and when the stamps themselves were what it was all about.

Severe drought conditions persisted in the United States from 1915 into the 1930s, threatening the already-depleted waterfowl population. In 1934 two important things happened: Jay N. "Ding" Darling was appointed to head the Bureau of Biological Survey, and one of his sketches became the art for the very first "duck stamp." Duck-stamp dollars and emergency funds fought for by Darling and authorized by President Franklin Roosevelt were used for the restoration of breeding grounds. The emergency funds ran out in 1939, but by that time the drought had ended and the duck stamp had proven its potential.

In order to appeal to a wider audience than that of the waterfowl gunners who were required to buy the stamp, the duck stamp was designed to appeal also to conservationists and wildlife art lovers as well as stamp collectors. To that end, the Bureau of Biological Survey invited well-known wildlife artists to design each of the early black-and-white stamps, and the work of Frank Benson, Richard Bishop, Joseph Knapp, Roland Clark, Lynn Bogue Hunt, and others was used. The chief of the Bureau's public relations division, Colonel H. P. Sheldon, in 1936 voiced the Bureau's philosophy: "Each issue of the stamp should have a value beyond that of the privileges which its possession conveys. If you never kill a duck, you will still have acquired something that gives any sportsman a thrill whenever he looks at it."

By the late 1940s, the invited-artist policy came apart as many other artists submitted their designs for duck stamps, and in 1950 a contest was held to determine who would illustrate the upcoming stamp. Eighty-eight designs were submitted by sixty-five artists: a far cry from the original one-artist-one-stamp plan, and an even farther cry from the two-thousand-plus entries that were to become commonplace as artists winning the duck stamp competition became instant millionaires through the sale of duck-stamp prints.

Duck-stamp prints were not offered for sale until 1940, when Ed Thomas and Ralph Terrill of Abercrombie & Fitch's art department convinced Richard Bishop to make an etching of his 1936–37 duck stamp. In 1942, Thomas was able to get Frank Benson to follow suit, and by the time Jay N. Darling turned out an estimated three hundred prints of his duck-stamp design in 1944, duck-stamp artists were routinely making limited-edition prints of their designs. Darling turned out the aforementioned three hundred prints and Frank Benson only one hundred, but Dick Bishop, who did not believe in limiting his prints, turned out not one but two unlimited editions of his stamp art— and today's values reflect that long-ago decision. J. D. Knapp produced 260 prints, Lynn Bogue Hunt came up with two editions of 100 each, and Francis Lee Jaques turned out three editions with a total of 260 prints.

This pattern of truly limited editions continued through the 1960s, with print editions climbing slowly to an average of six hundred or so each. This changed with the 1970–71 duck-stamp print when artist Ed Bierly turned out one thousand prints of his winning watercolor stamp design at sixty dollars each. The print sold out quickly, and the handwriting was on the wall: Color had come to the duck stamp, and collectors craved color.

In 1971–72 and 1972–73, duck-stamp prints in color editions of 950 each sold out almost immediately, as did Lee LeBlanc's winning design of Steller's eiders in 1973–74 in an edition of 1,000 prints. Grabbing the bull by the horns, David Maass then offered his winning wood-duck stamp design to all who ordered it before a given deadline. Twenty-seven hundred prints were sold, and the meaning of "limited-edition print" changed forever.

From then on, duck-stamp prints were turned out in ever-increasing numbers, and in 1980–81 Richard Plasschaert's design sold 12,950 print copies. Two years later, David Maass's winning design sold a record-setting 22,250 copies, to be bested in 1983–84 when 31,900 copies of the year's duck-stamp print were sold in all editions. Duck-stamp print sales might well have spiraled to unheard-of numbers had not some well-meaning official closed the barn door and limited the number of prints produced to twenty thousand, beginning with the 1987–88 print. But it was too late. The horse was gone and the truly limited edition duck-stamp print was lost forever.

STATE DUCK-STAMP PRINTS

California is known for setting trends that later sweep the nation, and so it did with state duck-stamp prints. In 1971 the Golden State became the first to require a state duck-stamp, and the artist, Paul Johnson, was the first to offer a state duck-stamp print to the public. Iowa joined the parade in 1972 and Maryland and Massachusetts tagged along in 1974. By 1980, eighteen states had jumped on the bandwagon and today only four states are without state duck stamps and duck-stamp prints: Connecticut, Hawaii, Nebraska, and New Mexico. Of these, only one is considering a state duck stamp at this time, but there are still a total of forty-six individual "first of state" duck stamps and duck-stamp prints available to collectors. Sad to say, all too many of these are in the unlimited "limited edition" category that has diminished the value of the federal duck-stamp prints. The Colorado duck-stamp print issued in 1989 was offered in five editions with a total of 17,750 prints.

No one can tell you what to collect—those choices are up to you. But the following lists of duck stamps, federal duck-stamp prints, selected state duck stamps, and "first of state" duck-stamp prints can help. The prices are retail and the prints unframed, and anyone wishing to sell should expect to realize not more than one-half of these prices, although more than half can be expected from the more scarce early stamps and prints. On the other hand, less than one-half to nothing may be offered for the later prints because many dealers are overstocked. The final listing shows prices realized at the July 1990 decoy auction of Richard A. Bourne at Hyannis, Massachusetts, for a group of framed federal duck-stamp prints that included the appropriate stamp in the framing.

Federal Duck Stamps

	Used*	Unused*	Mint*
1934–35	$ 95.00	$125.00	$425.00
1935–36	100.00	180.00	400.00
1936–37	50.00	85.00	225.00
1937–38	30.00	60.00	195.00
1938–39	30.00	60.00	195.00
1939–40	20.00	40.00	125.00
1940–41	20.00	40.00	125.00
1941–42	20.00	40.00	125.00
1942–43	20.00	40.00	125.00
1943–44	20.00	30.00	50.00
1944–45	18.00	25.00	45.00
1945–46	13.00	18.00	30.00

*Prices in all three categories are for stamps in fine to very fine condition. Lesser quality stamps are worth less, and fine and extra fine quality stamps are worth considerably more, as are such things as plate blocks, errors, and artist-signed stamps. More information may be obtained from the National Wildlife Galleries, P.O. Box 061397, Fort Myers, Florida 33906, to whom I am deeply indebted.

The 1947–48 federal duck stamp and duck-stamp print by Jack Murray, depicting snow geese. (Courtesy Richard A. Bourne Co., Inc.)

1946–47	10.00	18.00	30.00
1947–48	10.00	20.00	30.00
1948–49	10.00	20.00	40.00
1949–50	8.00	22.00	40.00
1950–51	8.00	22.00	45.00
1951–52	7.00	22.00	45.00
1952–53	7.00	22.00	45.00
1953–54	7.00	22.00	45.00
1954–55	6.00	24.00	55.00
1955–56	6.00	24.00	50.00
1956–57	6.00	22.00	55.00
1957–58	5.00	25.00	55.00
1958–59	5.00	25.00	50.00
1959–60	5.00	35.00	65.00
1960–61	7.00	35.00	65.00
1961–62	7.00	35.00	65.00
1962–63	7.00	45.00	75.00
1963–64	7.00	55.00	70.00
1964–65	7.00	50.00	70.00

1965–66	. . . . .	7.00	. . . . .	55.00	. . . . . .	70.00
1966–67	. . . . .	7.00	. . . . .	55.00	. . . . .	70.00
1967–68	. . . . .	6.00	. . . . .	50.00	. . . . .	70.00
1968–69	. . . . .	5.50	. . . . .	35.00	. . . . .	50.00
1969–70	. . . . .	5.00	. . . . .	30.00	. . . . .	45.00
1970–71	. . . . .	4.50	. . . . .	30.00	. . . . .	45.00
1971–72	. . . . .	4.50		18.00	. . . . .	25.00
1972–73	. . . . .	4.50		12.00	. . . . .	18.00
1973–74	. . . . .	4.50	. . . . .	12.00	. . . . .	14.00

Average pricing:
1974–75 through
1990–91 . . . . .   5.00   . . . . .   10.00   . . . . .   15.00

Federal Duck-Stamp Prints

Prices are for unframed prints without stamps.

Year and Artist		Quantity		Value
1934–35: Darling		300*		4,400.00
1935–36: Benson		100		8,000.00
1936–37: Bishop		unlimited		850.00
1937–38: Knap		260		3,000.00
1938–39: Clark		300		3,800.00
1939–40: Hunt	(1st ed.)	100		7,500.00
. . . . . .	(2nd ed.)	100		7,000.00
1940–41: Jaques	(1st ed.)	30		10,000.00
. . . . . .	(2nd ed.)	30		7,500.00
. . . . . .	(3rd ed.)	200		3,500.00
1941–42: Kalmbach	(flopped)	100*		4,500.00
. . . .	(2nd ed.)	unknown		1,300.00
1942–43: Ripley		unlimited		1,200.00

*Number of prints unconfirmed, but believed correct

The 1949–50 federal duck stamp and duck-stamp print by Roger Preuss, depicting common goldeneyes. (Courtesy Richard A. Bourne Co., Inc.)

1943–44: Bohl	(1st ed.)	290	1,500.00
	(2nd ed.)	unknown	500.00
1944–45: Weber	(flopped)	100	4,700.00
	(2nd ed.)	200	2,700.00
	(3rd ed.)	90	700.00
1945–46: Gromme		250	6,500.00
1946–47: Hines	(1st ed.)	300*	1,600.00
	(2nd ed.)	380	200.00
1947–48: Murray		300	2,700.00
1948–49: Reece	(1st ed.)	200	1,500.00
	(2nd ed.)	150	1,000.00
	(3rd ed.)	400	600.00
	(4th ed.)	300	500.00
1949–50: Preuss	(1st ed.)	250	3,000.00
	(2nd ed.)	395	200.00
1950–51: Weber	(1st ed.)	250*	1,500.00
	(2nd ed.)	300	250.00

*Number of prints unconfirmed, but believed correct

The 1951–52 federal duck stamp and duck-stamp print by Maynard Reese, depicting gadwalls. (Courtesy Richard A. Bourne Co., Inc.)

1951–52: Reece	(1st ed.)	250	1,200.00
	(2nd ed.)	400	600.00
1952–53: Dick	(1st ed.)	250*	2,100.00
	(2nd ed.)	300	150.00
1953–54: Seagers	(1st ed.)	250*	2,000.00
	(2nd ed.)	1,500	150.00
1954–55: Sandstrom	(1st ed.)	275	1,600.00
	(2nd ed.)	400	150.00
1955–56: Stearns	(1st ed. 1st prt.)	250	1,200.00
	(1st ed. 2nd prt.)	53	1,100.00
	(2nd ed.)	100	600.00
1956–57: Bierly	(1st ed. 1st prt.)	325	1,000.00
	(1st ed. 2nd prt.)	125	800.00
1957–58: Abbott	(1st ed.)	253	1,000.00
	(2nd ed.)	500	300.00
	(3rd ed.)	1,500	150.00
1958–59: Kouba	(1st ed.)	250	1,300.00

*Number of prints unconfirmed, but believed correct

. . . . . . (2nd ed.)	250	. . . . .	1,000.00
. . . . . . (3rd ed.)	300	. . . . .	300.00
1959–60: Reece . . . . . . (1st ed.)	400	. . . . .	4,000.00
. . . . . . (2nd ed.)	300	. . . . .	2,000.00
. . . . . . (3rd ed.)	400	. . . . .	1,500.00
1960–61: Ruthven . . . . (1st ed.)	400	. . . . .	1,000.00
. . . . . (2nd ed.)	300	. . . . .	600.00
. . . . . (3rd ed.)	400	. . . . .	500.00
1961–62: Morris	275	. . . . .	1,500.00
1962–63: Morris	275	. . . . .	1,500.00
1963–64: Bierly . . (1st ed. 1st prt.)	550	. . . . .	1,000.00
. . (1st ed. 2nd prt.)	125	. . . . .	800.00
1964–65: Stearns . . . . . (1st ed.)	665	. . . . .	1,100.00
. . . . . (2nd ed.)	100	. . . . .	650.00
1965–66: Jenkins . . . . . (1st ed.)	700	. . . . .	850.00
. . . . . (2nd ed.)	100	. . . . .	600.00
. . . . . (3rd ed.)	250	. . . . .	250.00
1966–67: Stearns . . . . . (1st ed.)	300	. . . . .	1,100.00
. . . . . (2nd ed.)	300	. . . . .	400.00
1967–68: Kouba	275	. . . . .	900.00
1968–69: Pritchard	750	. . . . .	1,200.00
1969–70: Reece	750	. . . . .	1,000.00
1970–71: Bierly . . . . . . (1st ed.)	1,000	. . . . .	2,500.00**
. . . . . . (2nd ed.)	2,150	. . . . .	200.00
1971–72: Reece	950	. . . . .	5,200.00
1972–73: Cook . . . . . . (1st ed.)	950	. . . . .	2,700.00**
. . . . . . (2nd ed.)	900	. . . . .	150.00**
1973–74: LeBlanc . . . . . . (1st ed.)	1,000	. . . . .	2,000.00**
. . . . . (2nd ed.)	900	. . . . .	150.00**
1974–75: Maass	2,700*	. . . . .	1,100.00
1975–76: Fisher	3,150	. . . . .	1,000.00**
1976–77: Magee . . . . . (reg. ed.)	3,600	. . . . .	800.00
. . . (medallion ed.)	1,000	. . . . .	1,300.00

*Number of prints unconfirmed, but believed correct
**Indicates remarqued prints available and worth more

1977–78: Murk	5,800	450.00**
1978–79: Gilbert	7,150	450.00**
1979–80: Michaelson . . . . (reg. ed.)	7,000	350.00
(medallion ed.)	1,500	500.00
1980–81: Plasschaert	12,950	600.00
1981–82: Wilson	16,000	350.00
1982–83: Maass	22,250	350.00
1983–84: Scholer . . . . . . (reg. ed.)	17,400	500.00
. . (medallion ed.)	6,700	1,000.00
1984–85: Morris . . . . . . (reg. ed.)	20,400	175.00
. . . (medallion ed.)	11,500	350.00**
1985–86: Mobley . . . . . . (reg. ed.)	18,200	135.00
. . . (medallion ed.)	6,650	250.00
1986–87: Moore . . . . . . (reg. ed.)	16,310	135.00
. . . (medallion ed.)	4,670	250.00
1987–88: Anderson, A. . . . (reg. ed.)	20,000	135.00
(medallion ed.)	5,000	250.00
1988–89: Smith . . . . . . (reg. ed.)	22,000	200.00
. . . (medallion ed.)	6,500	350.00
1989–90: Anderson, N. . . (reg. ed.)	20,000	145.00
(medallion ed.)	7,000	325.00
1990–91: Hautman . . . . . (reg. ed.)	14,500	145.00
. . (medallion ed.)	5,500	325.00

**Indicates remarqued prints available and worth more

STATE DUCK STAMPS OF EXTRAORDINARY INTEREST

California

1971—Pintails	scarce*
1972—Canvasbacks	scarce*
1978—Hooded Mergansers	150.00

*Very rare, often unobtainable

Delaware

1980—Black Ducks	100.00
1981—Snow Geese	90.00
1982—Canada Geese	95.00

Florida

1979—Green-wing Teal	195.00

Illinois

1975—Mallard	scarce*
1976—Wood Duck	scarce*
1977—Canada Goose	250.00
1978—Canvasback	115.00
1979—Pintail	115.00
1980—Green-wing Teal	115.00
1981—American Widgeon	115.00
—American Widgeon misprint	795.00

Iowa

1972—Mallards	175.00

Michigan

1977—Canvasbacks	325.00

Missouri

1979—Canada Geese	795.00
1980—Wood Ducks	185.00

New Hampshire

1983—Wood Ducks	175.00
1984—Mallards	150.00
1985—Blue-wing Teal	125.00

North Carolina

1983—Mallards	110.00

*Very rare, often unobtainable

North Dakota

      1982—Canada Geese 135.00

South Carolina

      1981—Wood Ducks 100.00

      1982—Mallards 100.00

      1983—Pintails 125.00

Tennessee

      1979—Mallards. *Resident* 225.00

      —Mallards. *Nonresident* . . . . scarce*

      1980—Canvasbacks. *Resident* 50.00

      —Canvasbacks. *Nonresident* . . . . scarce*

Texas

      1983—American Widgeon 225.00

Wisconsin

      1978—Wood Ducks 150.00

*Very rare, often unobtainable

FIRST OF STATE DUCK-STAMP PRINTS

Some collectors seek out "first of state prints" and buy them for a variety of reasons. Early first of state prints in very limited numbers have appreciated greatly in value; many others, issued in unlimited "limited" editions, have not. The following state-by-state listing is in order of year of issue, and values are for unframed prints at top retail prices.

    California—1971 . . . . 1,500.00

    Iowa—1972 . . . . 10,000.00

Maryland—1974	5,000.00
Massachusetts—1974	1,500.00*
Illinois—1975	3,500.00
South Dakota—1976	2,000.00
Michigan—1976	3,500.00
Mississippi—1976	2,500.00
Indiana—1976	2,000.00
Minnesota—1977	1,500.00
Wisconsin—1978	500.00
Nevada—1979	1,500.00
Florida—1979	750.00
Alabama—1979	750.00
Missouri—1979	1,500.00
Tennessee—1979	750.00
Delaware—1980	750.00
Oklahoma—1980	750.00
Arkansas—1981	900.00
Texas—1981	900.00
South Carolina—1981	1,500.00
Ohio—1982	350.00
North Dakota—1982	450.00
New Hampshire—1983	500.00
North Carolina—1983	750.00
Pennsylvania—1983	750.00
Oregon—1984	350.00
New Jersey—1984	700.00
Maine—1984	350.00
Alaska—1985	650.00
New York—1985	300.00

*The 1974 Massachusetts duck stamp was taken from a print by Milton Weiler for the "Classic Decoy" series published by Winchester Press. The Winchester print was signed, but Weiler died before he could sign the Massachusetts print. There are those who consider the 1975 Massachusetts print by Tom Hennessey the "true" first of state print. The 1975 print is worth much less than the 1974 print.

Kentucky—1985 . . . .   250.00
Wyoming—1985 . . . .   250.00
Georgia—1985 . . . .   250.00
Washington—1986 . . . .   250.00
Montana—1986 . . . .   250.00
Vermont—1986 . . . .   250.00
Utah—1986 . . . .   200.00
Arizona—1987 . . . .   200.00
Idaho—1987 . . . .   200.00
Kansas—1987 . . . .   200.00
West Virginia—1987 . . . .   200.00
Virginia—1988 . . . .   200.00
Louisiana—1989 . . . .   149.50
Rhode Island—1989 . . . .   200.00
Colorado—1990 . . . .   169.00

DUCK-STAMP PRINTS AT AUCTION

The following federal duck-stamp prints were offered at auction on July 25, 1990, by the Richard A. Bourne galleries of Hyannis, Massachusetts. Each was framed with matching stamp in a simple mat and plain black frame. Five of the twenty-three prints were "passed," and the remaining eighteen sold at a fraction of their estimated values in what can only be called a buyer's market. It should be noted that this particular collection of prints had been cut, trimmed, and taped. The condition was far from pristine, a fact that was noted in the auction catalog, which illustrates that serious collectors demand the very best.

I am indebted to the Bourne galleries for their cooperation and for the photographs included in this chapter.

1936–37: Richard Bishop (evenly faded and toned) . .   375.00
1937–38: J. D. Knap (evenly faded and toned) 575.00
1946–47: Bob Hines (evenly toned)   . . . .   Passed

1947–48: Jack Murray (slight foxing) 500.00
1948–49: Maynard Reese (slight foxing) 350.00
1949–50: Roger Preuss (evenly toned, broken frame) 675.00
1950–51: Walter Weber (excellent) 300.00
1951–52: Maynard Reese (excellent) 325.00
1952–53: John Dick (excellent) . . . . Passed
1953–54: Clayt Seagers (excellent) . . . . Passed
1954–55: H. Sandstrom (slight foxing) 225.00
1955–56: Stanley Stearns (evenly faded and toned) . . Passed
1956–57: Edward Bierly (excellent) 150.00
1957–58: Jackson Abbott (excellent) . . . . Passed
1958–59: Les Kouba (evenly faded) 175.00
1959–60: Maynard Reese (evenly toned) 800.00
1960–61: John Ruthven (uneven fading) 100.00
1961–62: Edward Morris (evenly toned) 175.00
1962–63: Edward Morris (evenly toned) 200.00
1963–64: Edward Bierly (slight fading) 175.00
1964–65: Stanley Stearns (evenly faded & toned) . . . 225.00
1966–67: Stearns #204 of 300 (evenly faded) 225.00
1967–68: Les Kouba (excellent) 175.00

Several books have been written about duck stamps and duck-stamp prints: David McBride's *The Federal Duck Stamp,* and *Duck Stamp Prints* by Russell Fink and Jean Stearns are invaluable resources for the serious collector.

ANTIQUE AND CLASSIC SPLIT-CANE RODS

I n the 1840s, Sam Philippi made the first all-bamboo rod, gluing four split strips together. In 1869 Hiram Lewis Leonard went Philippi two better and created the six-side split-cane rod as we know it today in his Bangor, Maine, rod shop. By the early 1880s, his fame assured, Leonard moved his shop to central valley New York to be closer to his customers. Happily, before he left Maine, Leonard trained a few good men—men like Eustis Edwards and Edward Payne—who in turn trained their sons in the art of fine rod-making. It is one thing to buy a fine old split-cane rod and another to remember the men who sought perfection and passed the dream along. It is their product that makes today's prices possible.

Few, if any, areas of interest in the field of sporting antiques and collectibles offer the beginner more hazards than does the purchase of split-cane rods. One need not be a craftsman to realize that a rod has been reworked badly, but when the remaking is done with great care it can be very difficult to find any faults. It is not wise to make summary judgments, but in most cases you are better off with a rod that needs work than with one that has been reworked, because *you* can then select the craftsman. Split-cane rods are big business and should be approached as you would any other business venture—with care.

Collecting fine split-cane rods cannot be approached haphazardly; I strongly urge that you learn as much as you can about these delicate tools before you collect them. There are books on the subject, private and museum collections to be seen, and tackle sales and auctions to attend. The knowledgeable collector has the advantage.

Condition is the watchword when collecting fine rods, and its importance cannot be overstated. The monetary difference between an almost-new unfished rod by a given maker and the same rod in good average condition can be shocking. Rods in the almost-new category are rare indeed, and it is not uncommon to discover differences in value ranging in the hundreds of dollars. This varies of course, depending upon the longevity and productivity of a given maker, but it can be an important factor in a sale.

Rods that do not fall into the "almost-new" or "as-new" categories can fall into just about as many categories as you can imagine, and it is here that the beginning collector gets lost. It is not uncommon for a fine old split-cane rod to have been used and to show the resultant wear and tear. Broken tips, missing parts, and similar disfiguring defects are obvious demerits and can be serious enough to render a fine rod worthless. Minor defects are not as serious, and there is no reason to fault a fine rod that has been refinished by an expert who has preserved the original integrity of the maker. This is a tricky area in collecting bamboo rods, and if you have any doubts about a refinished rod, seek expert advice or pass up the offering. If you take the time to familiarize yourself with the varied styles of the collectable-rod makers, you will save time and money somewhere down the stream.

Today's collectable rods fall into two distinct categories: classic handmade rods, and the less-desirable production rods produced by Shakespeare, Montague, and others. Both categories are found in the price guide to come, but I will concern myself with the classic makers here.

Any listing of classic rod-makers must begin with Hiram Lewis Leonard, for he laid the foundation for all that followed both within the Leonard organization and outside it, as well. Leonard perfected the fly rod as we know it and trained those makers who followed him. Reuben Leonard contributed to the Leonard Company's success, as did George Reynolds, who was active there until 1965. A complete list of Leonard rods would fill pages, but the mention of models such as the Catskill Fairy or Hunt Pattern are enough to set collector's mouths in determined grins. Happily enough, fine early Leonard rods are available to keep this particular market active.

Edward Payne apprenticed in the Leonard shop in Bangor, Maine, and

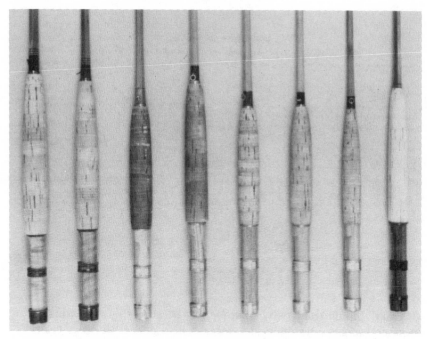

Various Leonard trout rods. (Courtesy of Oliver's Auction Galleries)

many believe his rods and those by his son James are the finest ever built. From the beginning, Payne rods have been in great demand, and it is interesting to note that when Jim Payne passed away in 1970, the cost of a Payne at Abercrombie and Fitch in New York City jumped from two to four hundred dollars almost overnight. Payne rods are still in demand and prices are still going up.

Another Hiram Leonard apprentice whose work is in demand was Fred Thomas, who stayed on in Maine and made rods that are considered by many to be the equal of Leonard's. His Brownstone and Special models bring big bucks on today's market.

Howard "Pinky" Gillum began his career with Payne, and his work shows the influence of Payne, as well as of Eustis Edward and Edward Hewitt, but what sets Gillum's rods apart is the exclusivity that carried over into his work. Couple this with all the characteristics of a perfectionist and you come

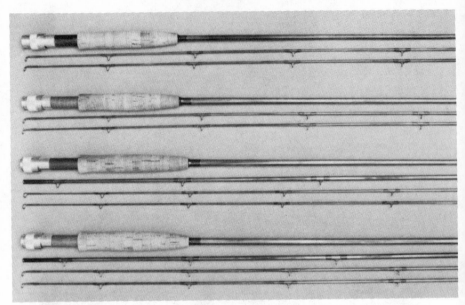

"Pinky" Gillum trout rods. *From top to bottom:* a six-foot six-inch $2\frac{5}{8}$ ounce two-piece two-tip rod; a seven-foot $3\frac{7}{8}$ ounce two-piece two-tip rod; a seven-foot eight-inch $4\frac{3}{4}$ ounce three-piece two-tip rod; and an eight-foot $5\frac{1}{4}$ ounce three-piece two-tip rod. (Courtesy of Oliver's Auction Galleries)

up with a very limited number of truly classic and collectable split-cane rods that cost dearly.

I have mentioned Eustis Edwards and Edward Hewett, and their names belong on this brief list, as do those of Lyle Dickerson, Edwin Powell, Gary Howells, and Paul Young. George Halstead belongs here, as do Everett Garrison and Goodwin Granger. A nod goes also to Bill Phillipson and Sam Anson, who led the production at Wright and McGill and James Heddon & Sons, respectively. No list of this sort could end before the names of Douglas Merrick, guiding light at the R. L. Winston Rod Company, and Wes Jordon of Cross and, later, Orvis fame are included. Remember these names well: These are the individuals who made what you collect collectable.

There is little point in paying out good money for something unless you are prepared to care for it properly, and fine split-cane rods require special care. Insurance is a serious consideration; you should take care to see that your collection is protected as it grows. A separate rider is a good choice, and professional appraisal should be considered. Beyond financial protection, fine rods also require a bit of TLC. A light coating of fine furniture wax will protect rods from drying out, and should be applied periodically. This is true no matter whether you display your rods or keep them in cases. If displayed, they must be dusted and checked more frequently and rewaxed if they show signs of drying. If there is one rule that always applies to all rods under all circumstances, it is to store them in the vertical position. Assembled or unassembled, cased or uncased, rods can develop a set if they are allowed to lie around, so keep them on their toes and make them stand up straight.

If a quick look at the prices for fine split-cane rods that follows fails to scare you off, study the entries carefully. If shouldn't take you long to discover that short rods bring more money than do long ones. There are two reasons for this: The shorter rods are scarcer and, of course, easier to use; but the primary reason for the price is that collectors like to display their treasures, and rods over eight feet do not fit in the average home.

L. L. BEAN CO.

$7\frac{1}{2}'$ *"L. L. Bean" trout rod:* Made for Bean by Heddon. A 2/2* in excellent condition 375.00

C. W. CARLSON

6' Carlson "Four" #803462: A four-sided 2/2 in original bag and tube 4,000.00

$7\frac{1}{2}'$ *Riverton:* A six-sided 2/2 rod in near-mint condition 2,250.00

7'9" Streamer Special: A four-sided 2/2 rod with elongated tips. Near-mint with letter 3,250.00

9' Light salmon rod. A four-sided 3/2 with agate stripper guide and butt. Near-mint 1,600.00

CONSTABLE

Set of two rods: With identical tips and two butt sections
making a 6' and 6½' rod, or one with an extra tip. As-
new with bag and tube . . . .　425.00

6'9" R. H. Woods Classic trout rod: A 2/2 rod with agate
stripper guide, bag, and tube . . . .　325.00

CROSS

10' SDF: a 3/2 rod with a 6½" extension butt in original
bag and tube. Midsection repair . . . .　220.00

DICKERSON

7½' Model 7615: Owned and marked by Art Flick. A 2/2
in near-excellent condition . . . .　4,500.00

8' Dickerson 801611–D: A 3/2 for #6 line with repair
to one tip . . . .　2,200.00

8½' Custom trout rod: Made in 1941. This 3/2 4½ oz. rod
has owner's name. Near-mint . . . .　3,100.00

9' Dickerson #901812–C trout rod: 3/2
and shows wear . . . .　650.00

EDWARDS

6' Quadrate: A 2/2 with agate stripper guide in original
bag and tube. Overvarnished wraps . . . .　2,700.00

8' A & F Triton: A 3/2, 3⅞ oz. for #5–6 line. This rod
has varnish meltdown . . . .　480.00

8' Quadrate #50: A 3/2 with overvarnish on wraps and a
slight butt bruise. Bag and tube . . . .　625.00

8½' Quadrate #54: A 3/2 with agate
stripper guide. Excellent condition . . . .　450.00

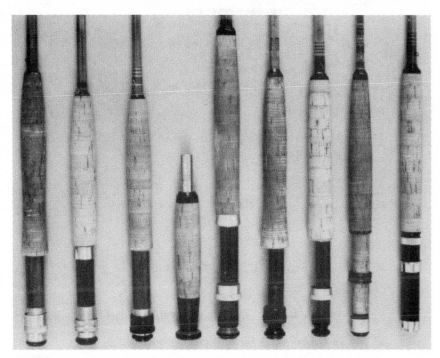
Various Edwards trout and salmon rods.

7' Quadrate spinning rod: A 2/1 in original bag and
tube. Light soiling 200.00

GARRISON

7' Garrison #198 I–7–4: A 2/2 light-line rod refinished
to new condition with bag and tube 6,000.00

7'9" Garrison #206 C–7 9–6: An early 2/2 trout rod with
minor problems. Original bag and tube 4,000.00

8' Garrison #212 J–80–1: A 3/2 rod with agate stripper
guide. Excellent condition 7,000.00

GILLUM

$6\frac{1}{2}'$ #1963 trout rod: A 2/2, $2\frac{5}{8}$ oz. rod for HFH line.
Slight tip set. Near-mint 10,000.00

7' #1901 trout rod: A 2/2, $3\frac{7}{8}$ oz. rod in original bag
and labeled tube 6,000.00

$7\frac{1}{2}'$ #1950 trout rod: A 2/2, 4 oz. rod. Near-mint with
original bag and tube 4,500.00

7'8" #1978 trout rod: A 3/2, $4\frac{3}{4}$ oz. rod in near-mint
condition with bag and tube 9,500.00

8' #1972 trout rod: A 3/2, $5\frac{1}{4}$ oz. rod in near-mint
condition. Original bag and tube 5,250.00

GRANGER

8' Registered model: A 3/2 with plastic still on the grip
of this mint 1950 rod 850.00

9' Aristocrat: A 3/2 for #7/8 line with varnish marks . .   250.00

9' Victory model: A 3/2 for #8 line in nearly new
condition with bag and tube 280.00

$9\frac{1}{2}'$ Stream & Lake trout rod: Made for Wright & McGill.
Mint in original bag and tube 160.00

HARDY

$6\frac{1}{2}'$ C. C. DeFrance: A 2/1, $2\frac{3}{8}$ oz. rod in
rare, sparkling condition 340.00

$7\frac{1}{2}'$ Marvel. A 3/2 with second tip short. Shows
very careful use 480.00

$8\frac{1}{2}'$ Salmon Deluxe: A 3/2 with shortened midsection.
6 oz. for #8 line 250.00

8'9" Hardy LRH: A 3/2 for #6 line. Ferrule plugs, bag,
and tube. As-new 510.00

9' McDonough: A 3/1, $4\frac{1}{2}$ oz. rod for #6 line
in excellent condition 210.00

9½' Salmon rod: A 3/2, 6¾ oz. rod with 4″ extension butt
in unused condition 320.00

HEDDON

7½' Featherweight Model 14: A 2/2, 3½ oz. rod for #4/5
line with original bag and tube 460.00

8' Expert #125: A 3/2 for HDH or F line, this rod has
original bag and tube. Near-mint 300.00

8½' Black Beauty #17: A 3/2 with original handle-
covering in labeled bag and tube 350.00

8½' Thoroughbred #14: A 3/2, 4¾ oz. rod in mint
condition with bag and tube 225.00

9' Rod-of-Rods #1000: A 3/2 with both midsection and
one tip 1″ short 300.00

KOSMIC

7½' Kosmic: A 3/2/2 (2 midsections, 2 tips). This rod is
marked "H. A. Whittemore—Boston" and
in excellent condition 1,750.00

10' Kosmic serial #2422: A 3/2 with Edwards and Hawes
ferrules and U.S. Net & Twine Co. markings.
Very minor restoration 2,400.00

LEONARD

6' Model 37 ACM #289: A 2/3 (one tip shortened) in
near-mint condition with bag and tube 1,300.00

7' Model 38H #3654: A 2/2 for #4/5 line in original
buckskin leather case 1,400.00

7' Catskill Special 48–4 #8457: A mint 3/2 for #4 line.
Unused condition with bag and tube 2,900.00

7' Catskill 38–4: A 2/2 made without handle checks.
Mint with bag and tube 2,600.00

7½' Custom #4481: A 2/2 in mint condition with original
handle-covering, bag, and tube 2,000.00

7½' Model 38½ Fairy Catskill: A pre-fire rod. 3/2 with
minor reel-seat marking. Bag and tube 3,750.00

8' Model 40 #2294: A 2/2, 4⅜ oz. rod for #6 line.
Reportedly used once 530.00

8' Model 50 Tournament: A 3/2, 3⅝ oz. rod for #4
line. Professionally restored 1,200.00

8' Deluxe Duracane: A 2/2 for #6/7 line. Rod was
reportedly never used. Labeled tube 540.00

8' "Mills and Son Maker" marking: A 3/2 rod in near-
mint condition with bag, tag, and tube 900.00

8½' Catskill Model 42: A 3/2, 3½ oz. for #4 line. This
1920s rod has only minor repair 1,550.00

12' Model 91: Low-water salmon rod. A 3/2, 12⅛ oz.
medium-action. Needs rewraps 575.00

Model 15 bait casting rod: A 2/2, 5½ oz., 5'3" rod with
rough varnish in labeled bag and tube 400.00

Black Bass rod: 7½', 3/2 rod has been refinished 250.00

ORVIS

4'4" Banty trout rod #33304: 2/1 as-made with
bag and tube 600.00

5'9" Ultra-Light #65–9XX. 2/1 as-made with
original bag and tube 520.00

6½' Battenkill Flea rod #80–9XX: 2/2, 2 oz.
for #4 line 460.00

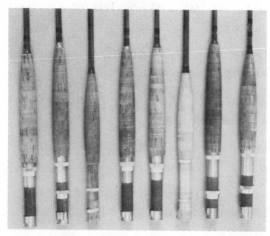

Orvis trout rods. *From left to right:* Battenkill, Battenkill, Deluxe, Special, Special, Superfine, Battenkill, and Madison. (Courtesy of Oliver's Auction Galleries)

$6\frac{1}{2}'$ Battenkill rod #49715: 2/2, $2\frac{5}{8}$ oz. for #6 line in original bag and tube 315.00

7' Madison Grade #74–3XX. 2/1 as-sold in original bag and tube 280.00

7' Battenkill #81–3XX: 2/2, $2\frac{3}{8}$ oz. with two-band cork seat. Circa 1977 . . . . 475.00

$7\frac{1}{2}'$ Model 99 trout rod #31538: 2/2 for #7 line. Slight wear 325.00

8' Varnished Battenkill #3942: From the 1940s. A 3/2 rod for #6 line in excellent condition 775.00

8' Battenkill #85–6XX. 2/2, $4\frac{1}{8}$ oz. for #6 line. As-new 580.00

8' Battenkill #52348: 2/2, $5\frac{1}{8}$ oz. for #9 line in original bag and tube 200.00

8' Wes Jordon: A 2/2 for #8 line. This rod is somewhat
dulled. Circa 1971 . . . .   850.00

8½' Limestone Special #71–5XX. 2/2, 4½ oz. for #6 line.
As-new in original bag and tube 480.00

8'9" Orvis SSS #72–5XX: A 2/2 for #10 line with 2½"
pull-out butt. Never fished 450.00

9½' Battenkill #11402. 3/2, 6¾ oz. for #9 line in original
bag and tube 200.00

9½' Salmon rod #21603: A 3/2, 7¾ oz. rod with
removable extension butt. Near-mint 230.00

Rocky Mountain two-rod set: From 1956. A 6½' 3/2 fly
rod and a 6½' 3/1 spinning rod in a presentation case
with original lock, key, and sales papers 1,400.00

6' Universal spinning rod: A heavy-duty one-piece rod
in original case 80.00

6½' Battenkill spinning rod #27843: A 2/1, 5⅛ oz. rod
in mint condition 225.00

7' Battenkill spinning rod #17–XXX: A 2/1 lightweight
model in unused condition 270.00

7½' Battenkill heavy duty spinning rod #32109: A 2/1, 8¼
oz. rod in mint condition 110.00

8' Battenkill heavy-duty spinning rod #30923: A 2/1, 8½
oz. rod in mint condition 190.00

PAYNE

6' Model 96: A 2/1 for #2/3 line. Very good original
condition in A & F/Payne tube 1,950.00

6½' Model 96: A 2/1 marked "made for Abercrombie and
Fitch" in near-mint condition 2,500.00

$7\frac{1}{2}'$ *Jim Payne:* A 2/2, $3\frac{7}{8}$ oz. for #5 line. This rod
has been refinished 2,100.00

8' *Model 102–H:* A 2/2, $4\frac{1}{2}$ oz. "Sold by A & F" rod in
original bag and tube 1,950.00

8' *Model 102:* A 2/2, $3\frac{7}{8}$ oz. rod with "A & F" marking in
excellent used condition 1,300.00

8' *Model 102:* With "E. F. Payne" marking. A 2/2, $3\frac{3}{4}$ oz.
with agate stripper guide. Repaired 700.00

8' *trout rod:* With "A & F" marking. A 3/2 with agate
stripper guide and one tip broken 1,400.00

8' *Model 202:* A 3/2, $4\frac{1}{4}$ oz. rod with "A & F" marking.
Agate stripper guide and ferrule plugs 1,200.00

8' *Model 200:* A 3/2, $3\frac{7}{8}$ oz. rod with "A & F" marking
and ferrule plugs 1,100.00

$8\frac{1}{2}'$ *Canadian Canoe rod:* A 3/2, $3\frac{7}{8}$ oz. rod made without
extension butt. Ferrule plugs 4,500.00

$8\frac{1}{2}'$ *Model 205:* A 3/2, 5 oz. rod with "A & F" marking
and minor repair 950.00

9' *Light salmon rod:* A 2/2, $5\frac{3}{4}$ oz. rod for #9 line, this
is reported to be the last rod Jim Payne finished before
his death. 2,100.00

9' *Light salmon rod:* A 2/2 with "A & F" marking
in excellent condition 1,100.00

9'3" *Model 310 salmon rod:* A 3/2, $6\frac{5}{8}$ oz. rod for #9 line
with "A & F" marking, bag, and tube 1,250.00

9'8" *Special fly rod:* A 3/2, 8 oz. rod with 2" extension
butt, ferrule plugs, bag, and tube 1,750.00

10' *Salmon rod:* A 3/2, $9\frac{1}{2}$ oz. rod for #10 line.
Refinished by Payne in 1966 .... 1,000.00

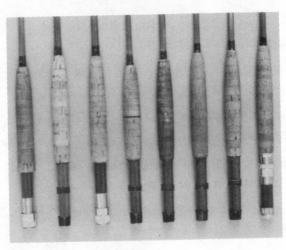

Various Payne trout rods.

7' Spinning rod: A 2/1 rod for regular-weight lures in
tagged bag and tube. As-new 950.00

PHILLIPSON

6'3" Peerless midge rod: Detachable handle and two tips.
Add additional butt for a 8'6". As-new 430.00

7½' Peerless 5: A 2/2, 3¾ oz. rod for #5 line in original
bag and labeled tube 335.00

8' Peerless 5: A 3/2, 4¼ oz. rod for #5 line. Light soiling,
original bag and tube 315.00

F. E. THOMAS

7'9" Dirigo trout rod: A 3/2 in very good condition in
original bag and tube 550.00

8½' Brownstone streamer fly rod: A 3/2, 5¼ oz. with
extended butt in labeled bag and tube 900.00

8½' Dirigo trout rod: A 3/2 with some varnish mars in
velvet-covered wood form 425.00

8½' Dirigo trout rod: A 3/2 (one short tip) with varnish mars, wood form 150.00

9' Brownstone Special trout rod: A 3/2 in excellent condition in original bag and tube 525.00

9' Special fly rod: A 3/2, 5¼ oz. rod for #7/8 line. Very good with original bag and tube 325.00

9' Bangor Rod trout rod: A 3/2 in excellent-plus condition with bag and labeled tube 375.00

9½' Special trout rod: A 3/2 in excellent condition with original bag and tube 300.00

VOM HOFE, EDWARD

9½': A 5-piece rod (2 midsections, 3 tips) with metal tarnish and varnish crazing. Excellent 500.00

PAUL YOUNG

6'3" Midge #XX: A 2/2 for #4/5 line in excellent condition with original bag and tube 1,800.00

6'3" Midge made for Arnold Gingrich: A 2/2, 1¾ oz. rod. Near-mint with provenance 3,000.00

7'2" Driggs with flamed finish: A 2/2, 3 oz. for #3/4/5 line. Used once or twice 1,950.00

7½' Made for Martha Marie: A 2/2, 3⅝ oz. rod made for Mrs. Paul Young. Near-mint 2,250.00

8' Para–15 #4942: With wet- and dry-fly tips, this rod is reportedly new and unused 1,700.00

There are many worthwhile books about split-cane rods and rod-making, but a single volume will get you started and probably prove to be the only one you'll need or want. I unhesitatingly recommend it: *Classic Rods and Rod Makers,* by Martin J. Keane.

FISHING REELS

Fishing reels, in one form or another, have been in use since the 1600s, but it remained for a small group of early watchmakers in Kentucky to put them on the map in the years after the American Revolution. George Snyder was the first of these reel-makers to be recognized for his work, but it was the brothers Meek who made Kentucky reels a commercial success. Needless to say, these early Kentucky reels are rare and expensive and often hard to authenticate because it was not until about 1875 that reels were stamped with the maker's or manufacturer's name. Deal only with people who guarantee what they sell, and do so in writing.

After the Civil War, and in part because of it, reel-making hit its stride in America as machines slowly replaced hand-work, and nickel and German silver replaced brass and silver construction. This was the so-called Golden Age of American reel-making, and makers such as Leonard, Milam, Meiselbach, Orvis, and Talbot left a legacy collectors clamor for today. Collecting these golden age reels is not as costly or as chancey as collecting Kentucky reels, but condition is, and should be, of the utmost importance. If you take a look at the prices that follow, you will note several instances where condition is a definite consideration.

If you are just starting to collect old fishing reels, I suggest you learn a good deal more than this simple guide can begin to tell you. Go to fishing-tackle shows and sales, visit individual and museum collections, and read and reread anything and everything you can get your hands on. One of the finest tools you can get is one or more of the Oliver Galleries fishing-tackle auction catalogs that are available by mail for about twenty-five dollars each.

Another suggestion for the beginning reel collector is to specialize in one or two of the many possible areas of interest: bait and casting reels, fly reels for trout and/or salmon, or the larger saltwater reels. Very few spinning reels have any real collector value, but a very interesting collection can nevertheless be put together for very little money. If you are after appreciation over the long term you will probably do better if you stick with early casting reels or the earliest and smallest trout reels by a variety of makers at a variety of costs. In recent years these have appreciated more rapidly than have other reels. Again, let me caution you to the importance of condition. One reel in fine condition is far more valuable than are two or three of the same item in poor shape. Know what you are collecting and deal only with reputable individuals. Nothing can nip the collecting bug faster than can being reeled in by a fishy deal.

Another no-no, and one that anyone with an ounce of sense can avoid, is the temptation to "clean" or otherwise improve upon the condition of a fine old reel. More fine collectibles have been ruined by fumble-fingered fools than one can begin to imagine. There are a good many more "don'ts" than "do's" on this short list, but if you follow these simple rules you will save yourself later anguish and embarrassment:

- Don't use steel wool or any other abrasive.
- Don't try to straighten bent brass or German silver.
- Do use soap and water and common sense.
- Don't try to take any reel apart unless you have jeweler's tools.
- Don't polish a reel that has a fine old patina.
- Do seek expert advice.

When working with fine old collectable fishing reels, you will do well to remember that many of the earliest reels were made by jewelers and watchmakers with exacting precision. Don't be the one to undo what made a given reel collectable in the first place.

REEL STORIES

For more than twenty years I have had my hand in the edge of the sporting antiques and collectibles pie, and I am continually amazed when something of value turns up in a strange or unexpected place. The following experience happened only last summer and should give you all the reason you need to be out and about at every opportunity.

On the dubious theory that early birds collect the most worms, I am almost always out early on Saturday mornings in pursuit of yard sales, flea markets, and whatever comes my way, but on this particular Saturday I got off to a late start. I arrived at the first of my scheduled stops well after nine, thinking about all the bargains I had missed at the heavily trafficked flea market. I was greeted almost immediately by a sign in rather large letters at a dealer's set-up offering a "Vom Hofe reel 4-sale" at a price that seemed to good to be true. As it turned out, I purchased a fine little two-inch Julius Vom Hofe rubber and German-silver trout reel for forty-five dollars. The dealer happily took his sign down, and I went on my way wondering how many people had seen and ignored the offering.

I traveled well over one hundred miles that morning and early afternoon without finding another thing and, knowing I was three hours from home, I nearly passed up an estate sale in one of Vermont's better-known villages. Everything at the sale was overpriced, but the owners were charming and I stopped to chat with them before leaving and it was only then that I spotted the rod, reel, and creel in the garage. Remembering the other prices, I was almost afraid to ask if they were for sale, but I did and the owners showed me that there was indeed a tag on the rod and reel. The tag said "$8.00" and I said "sold," only to be handed the fine old center-hole creel that I was told was part of the deal. I bid the charming couple a good day and headed home with the second Julius Vom Hofe of the day: a slightly dirty $2\frac{1}{8}$-inch trout reel of rubber and German silver and more than a little value, and the miles seemed to melt away.

If there is a moral to this story it is simply to get out and look. I traveled well over two hundred miles on that particular Saturday and stopped at forty or fifty flea markets and sales. All in all, it was a so-so day, which is to say that I have enjoyed better ones. The finds are there if you will only take the time to seek them out.

The twentieth century brought changes to the fishing tackle industry as America discovered the sport and reels were turned out by the thousands to meet the ever-growing demand. Fine reels were still made by dedicated makers and a new group of hand-made reels has surfaced. These fine reels, together with examples by Heddon and Winchester, are or are not antiques, but they are collectable and therefore included here. The prices that follow represent prices realized or asked during 1990. Future editions of this guide will carry additional makers, manufacturers, and costs.

ABBEY & IMBREY

Multiplying reel made by Julius Vom Hofe: Early size
2/00 reel dating from the 1860s 200.00

Early Latch-Stop trout reel: With the A & I logo, this
nickel-plated reel is excellent 375.00

Bait casting reel: With circle A & I logo. An early
transitional reel. Good-plus 45.00

ABERCROMBIE & FITCH

Multiplying salmon reel made by Bogdan: Marked
"AF–200–M" on foot. Light wear, uncleaned 750.00

Multiplying salmon reel made by Bogdan: Marked as
above and with owner's name. Very good 800.00

Another: New, in A & F green box 1,800.00

BATE, T. H. & CO.

T. H. Bate & Co: Marking on tiny #5 circa 1850 brass
ball-handle reel 350.00

T. H. Bate & Co: Marked brass ball-handled $2\frac{1}{8}''$
multiplying reel. Circa 1840 . . . .   450.00

BOGDAN

Handmade steelhead reel: Set for left-hand wind. $3\frac{1}{8} \times 1''$ finished in silver and black. Unfished 1,450.00

Handmade single-action click reel: $3\frac{3}{8} \times \frac{7}{8}''$ finished in silver and black. New in pouch 1,250.00

Early single-action salmon reel: A large $4\frac{1}{4} \times 1\frac{1}{2}''$ reel with wear and minor scratches 1,750.00

Multiplying salmon reel in "150" size: Shows wear at top of rims 1,300.00

Multiplying salmon reel: $3\frac{5}{8} \times 1\frac{1}{8}''$ spool in gold and black. Scratches 1,300.00

Narrow-spool Baby Trout reel: All black. $2\frac{3}{4} \times \frac{1}{2}''$ spool. New, unfished 2,000.00

Narrow-spool Baby Trout reel: Silver with black plates and a $2\frac{3}{4} \times \frac{1}{2}''$ spool 2,000.00

Wide-spool Baby trout reel: $2\frac{3}{4} \times \frac{3}{4}''$ spool. New unfished condition 1,350.00

Wide-spool standard trout reel: For left-hand use. New in leather pouch 2,000.00

BLUE GRASS (*See* Horton and Meek)

BLUE GRASS REEL WORKS (Meek)

Blue Grass Reel Works: Louisville, KY. No. 3 is marked on this German-silver reel 675.00

BRADFORD'S

Bradford's Boston: Name is the only marking on this unpolished brass trout reel 425.00

Bradford's Boston: Name marked on handle of circa 1850 $2\frac{1}{2}'' \times 1''$ German-silver trout reel 2,200.00

CAMPBELL, J. W.

J. W. Campbell—Bowling Green, KY: Name engraved on this $2 \times 1\frac{3}{8}''$ German-silver reel 4,250.00

CARLTON MFG. CO.

Carlton Mfg., Co. Rochester NY Bait Caster: Patent Oct 27 –03″ is marked on this old reel 250.00

CONROY, THOMAS J.

Thos. J. Conroy, Maker, NY: Name is marked on this $2\frac{1}{8}''$ German-silver bait-casting reel. Uncleaned 225.00

FOSS, AL

Al. Foss, Cleveland, O—Easy Control #3–25: Ivory handles and in mint condition 575.00

HARDY

Size 3″ Bougle trout reel: Once owned by Eugene V. Connett III. Very good 1,700.00

Early 3″ brass-faced Perfect trout reel: With obvious wear but in very good condition 1,450.00

Ancient $3\frac{1}{8}''$ Hardy Perfect: With old-style copper strap over drag knob. With original box 520.00

St. George Junior. $2\frac{9}{16}''$ reel in very good condition with original box 525.00

The 1930s Cascapedia multiplying salmon reel is one of the scarcest of all the Hardy reels. (Courtesy Oliver's Auction Galleries)

Another: As above. With considerable wear and
dressed foot ends 425.00

Flyweight: A silent-check 2½″ reel in very good
used condition. Rare 95.00

LEONARD

Rare Leonard-Mills: Made for the 1 oz. Leonard Model
36L rod. Aluminum frame. Excellent 1,500.00

H. L. Leonard, Maker marking: With orange and black
marbleized hard rubber. 2⅜″ reel is near-mint 8,500.00

Leonard-Mills Model 44: With special foot for Fairy
Catskill rods. Near-mint 1,450.00

Early H. L. Leonard Pat. #101813 (Philbrook's): Of
German silver and bronze. Click rough 1,000.00

A marbleized hard-rubber and German-silver trout reel marked "H. L. Leonard Maker," circa 1877–80. (Courtesy Oliver's Auction Galleries)

Mills (Leonard) "Fairy" trout reel: Made for the Leonard "Baby" Catskill rod. Near-mint 950.00

Larger size "Fairy"-type: Click reel with protective front rim. Excellent 375.00

Leonard-Mills Model 44B trout reel: Reel has back-sliding click switch. Excellent 1,350.00

Leonard-Mills Model 50B trout reel: A $3\frac{1}{8}''$ with $1\frac{1}{8}''$ pillars in excellent condition 950.00

Leonard-Mills Model 51 trout reel: A rare narrow spool in excellent condition 950.00

H. L. Leonard Pat #191813 (Philbrook's): A 3" reel with $\frac{7}{8}''$ pillars. Excellent 1,050.00

Leonard Model 50 wide-spool trout reel: With maker marking "Julius Vom Hofe" 850.00

Scarce U.S.A. Model 3⅛" Unique: With silent drag. Shows
wear, very good 1,250.00

Old Unique 4" salmon reel: With duplicated
stamping. Shows wear 350.00

HEDDON

Model 3–15 bait-casting reel: A German-silver reel.
Unpolished, but excellent 210.00

Early Model 3–24, serial #1028: With ivory knobs and
covered oil port 225.00

HORTON MFG. CO.

Blue Grass #5 bait-casting reel: German silver
with several faults 325.00

Meek (Horton) #3 Tournament casting reel: With
owner's name. Excellent 150.00

Blue Grass #34 Simplex: Free-spool
tournament casting reel 275.00

Blue Grass #3 casting reel: German silver, missing
rear bearing cap 110.00

Blue Grass #34 Simplex: Free-spool bait-casting reel in
original (fair) box 200.00

Meek (Horton) #3 bait-casting reel: Serial #6118
in excellent condition 300.00

MEEK, B. F. & SONS

Blue Grass Reel: Made by B. F. Meek & Sons Louisville,
KY. #3 marked. Near-mint 500.00

As above: In very good condition 145.00

#25 Blue Grass: Carter's Pat. July 5, 04, Nov. 28, 05.
Bait-casting reel 375.00

Blue Grass Reel: With front marking "Pat. Jul. 5,
04—Patent Pending" 180.00

#33 Blue Grass: Name marked on front and Carter's
Patent data on back. Very good 200.00

MEEK & MILAM

Meek & Milam, Frankfort, KY. #3: Marked brass bait-
casting reel. Engraved. Excellent 3,400.00

Meek & Milam, Frankfort, KY. #1: Marked brass bait-
casting reel with numbered screws 5,000.00

**A German-silver casting reel in excellent condition, marked "Meek and
Milam Frankfort, KY NO 2." (Courtesy Oliver's Auction Galleries)**

MILAM, B. C.

The Frankfort Kentucky Reel #2: Marked bait-casting
reel. #8328 on foot 1,200.00

M AND M AND M AND . . .

Brothers Meek and Meek set up shop in Kentucky in about 1835. Milam was their apprentice and, later, partner. In 1851 he opened a shop of his own.

B. C. Milam & Son: "Kentucky" bait-casting reel. A 4″ German-silver reel #11712 . . . .   1,200.00

Rustic 3″ B. F. Milam & Son: Marked bait-casting reel. Excellent 625.00

As above: With slightly different yoke support and considerable wear 125.00

MEISELLBACH

Rainbow Model 621: A 1 × 3¼″ trout reel with considerable brass showing 25.00

Tri-Part Model 581: A free-spool with 80-yd. capacity. Model patents '04, '07, and '09 . . . .   55.00

Tri-Part Model 580: 80-yd. capacity in very good, clean condition 40.00

OCEAN CITY

Ocean City trout reel: A 3″ reel with center drag ring. Circa 1950 . . . .   25.00

3″ Viceroy trout reel: With perforated all-aluminum reel. Click broken 15.00

ORVIS

1874 Patent Trout Reel: Reel foot narrowed and original box with missing latch 900.00

As above: With dressed foot ends and in very good
original wooden box 1,000.00

As above: With unaltered foot, but with
a homemade handle 350.00

As above: But without box and showing years
of careful use 250.00

Orvis SSS 9/10: Antireverse left-hand reel in
padded case. Excellent 220.00

Battenkill trout reel: $1 \times 3\frac{1}{4}''$ with adjustable drag in
padded zip case. Excellent 40.00

PETTINGILL

Pettingill Mohawk #4: Side-mounted trout reel with
brake-drag lever. Very good 525.00

PFLUEGER

Pflueger Sal-Trout Model 100: Ferris-wheel
design. Machined brass 35.00

Medalist 1495: Showing light wear. A circa 1965 reel
in excellent condition 40.00

As above: With considerable wear 25.00

Pflueger Taxi: In natural metal finish and
with bulldog logo 35.00

Early Pflueger Supreme: Casting reel with original bag,
box, booklet, etc. Excellent 100.00

SHAKESPEARE

Shakespeare Marhoff casting reel: With "S" handle.
Very good condition 25.00

Miller Autocrat 6/0 size ocean reel: With lined case and
felt bag. Mint condition 225.00

GEORGE W. SNYDER

A jeweler and watchmaker by trade, Snyder was president of the Bourbon County (Kentucky) Angler's Association, and America's first documented precision reel-maker.

SNYDER, GEORGE W.

Rare circa 1810 George Snyder casting reel: "G. S." in raised relief on click switch 18,500.00

Rare George Snyder bait-casting reel: Brass $1\frac{7}{8}''$ diameter reel with 2″ pillars 14,000.00

TALBOT, Wм. H.

Early Wm. H. Talbot Reel Co., Nevada, Mo.: ELI marked bait-casting reel. Mint condition 550.00

A circa 1905 Ben Hur trout reel made by William H. Talbot for Abercrombie and Fitch. (Courtesy Oliver's Auction Galleries)

Wm. H. Talbot Reel Co., Nevada Mo.: Meteor casting reel #4880. Very good 325.00

Talbot Reel & Mfg. Co.: German-silver casting reel, serial #13274 . . . .   150.00

Scarce Talbot Ben Hur trout reel: With early Nevada, Mo. and A & F markings. Near-mint 9,500.00

VOM HOFE, EDWARD

Rare Edward Vom Hofe #722 Big Game Reel: In 12/0 size. Excellent uncleaned condition 1,350.00

Edward Vom Hofe #732 Big Game Reel: In 14/0 size. $7\frac{1}{4}''$ diameter with $5\frac{3}{8}''$ pillars 1,800.00

Edward Vom Hofe—Patentee marked: #5 trout reel. German silver and hard rubber. Poor 1,100.00

Edward Vom Hofe Ocean Reel #811— 4/0: 1896 and '02 patent markings. Excellent 325.00

Edward Vom Hofe Handmade Model 550: A size 3 Ocean Reel with a V.L.& A. case. Excellent 400.00

Edward Vom Hofe Model 621–4/0: Ocean reel with a 6-point star drag. Very good 150.00

THE VOM HOFES

Frederick Vom Hofe was the father of both Edward and Julius, and he trained them well.

VOM HOFE, FREDERICK & SON

F. Vom Hofe & Son, Maker marked: "250" brass ball-handle reel. Excellent unpolished condition 350.00

VOM HOFE, JULIUS

Very rare Julius Vom Hofe trout reel: Nickeled finish and
Oct. 8, 1889 patent date. Mint 1,350.00

Rare 4″ Julius Vom Hofe 6/0 salmon reel: With
adjustable drag. Excellent with case 650.00

Tiny Julius Vom Hofe trout reel: Size 3 of hard rubber
and German silver. Excellent 650.00

Julius Vom Hofe trout reel: With 1889 patent date.
German silver and aluminum. Excellent 500.00

As above: In poor condition 205.00

Julius Vom Hofe "4$\frac{1}{4}$" salmon reel: Without maker name
strip in very good condition 275.00

WALKER, ARTHUR

3/0 Salmon Reel Model 100: Circa 1950s reel has been
professionally restored 800.00

TR–1 Trout Reel with left-hand wind: One pillar screw
missing. Very good 1,125.00

TR–2 Trout Reel: With adjustable drag and left-hand
wind. Near-mint with original bag 1,550.00

TR–2 Trout Reel: With fixed drag-click. Screw slots
show use, otherwise mint 1,025.00

TR–3 Trout Reel: With fixed drag-click in
near-mint condition 1,150.00

WINCHESTER

Winchester—1312 trout reel: A 2″ diameter reel in
near-excellent shape 180.00

Winchester—4350 "Takapart": A 100-yd. capacity casting
reel. Very good 80.00

ZWARG, OTTO

Otto Zwarg Model 300 2/0 salmon reel: With a front click
and rear click-stop drag 1,400.00

Model 400 3/0 salmon reel: With the early Brooklyn, NY
marking (1946–47) 1,200.00

A Rare 2/0 Otto Zwarg: With the 1946–7
Brooklyn marking. Excellent 1,475.00

Very rare 1/0 Model 300 salmon reel:
In "spectacular" condition 1,750.00

HAND-TIED FLIES

If you think two or three hundred dollars is too much to pay for a little bit of fluff and feather tied on a two-bit hook, collecting flies is not for you. If, on the other hand, you see these smallest of all sporting collectibles as the art form they are, the time to buy is now. Prices for flies tied by well-known fly tiers like Art Flick, Elsie and Harry Darbee, and Carrie G. Stevens are high and going higher. In fact, I'll stick my neck out and say that authenticated examples of these flies will be the most sought-afteor sporting collectibles of this century's last decade, and will rise in price to double and triple the costs listed here.

There are four basic groups of flies: trout, salmon, bass, and saltwater, but each of these can be broken down into many individual categories, and beginning collectors will do well to identify each before beginning a collection. Books with good color illustrations can help, as can a close look at a collection. Fine collections are on display at many museums, such as the American Museum of Fly Fishing in Manchester, Vermont. A beginner should take the time and trouble to inspect fine flies firsthand before spending any money.

Once you know something about flies, you are then faced with the question what to collect, and this presents myriad choices. Too many beginning fly collectors start out by picking up just about anything and everything, and end up with next to nothing. Avoid this approach by planning ahead. If you are determined to put together a good collection that will increase in interest and value, you must be selective. Decide what you are going to collect and then collect identified and authenticated flies that fit the mold of your intended goal. The only time to alter this systematic approach is when you are offered fine flies at a reasonable price that you can trade for whatever it is you collect. You will discover that trading is a common practice among collectors of flies, and quite often is the only way you can get what you want.

We have all seen fly books and boxes containing relics that once were fine flies. Flies are delicate and require special handling and care if they are going to last. Hooks rust, fur and feathers are subject to the ravages of insects, and sunlight will cause flies to fade. The best and most attractive way to preserve fine flies is to frame them with or without accompanying artwork. Mounting and framing a collection of flies is best done by an expert. The framed flies should be hung where sunlight does not touch them. Unframed flies are best stored in a wooden fly box, such as those preferred by serious fishermen. These are expensive, but are well worth the expense when you consider the cost of collectible flies. Moisture can be controlled with silica gel packets, which must be changed frequently. A few flakes of camphor or paradichlorobenzene (moth flakes) will help control insects. All flies, framed or unframed, should be checked periodically for moisture and insect infestation.

There are those who feel that steaming old flies helps bring them back to life and those who swear the steam will cause irreparable damage. I have found that a high-speed hair dryer works wonders. If the fly has been steamed the dryer will get rid of potentially damaging moisture, and if it hasn't the dryer will help fluff dried-out materials. A light coat of very fine machine oil will prevent rust on the exposed metal of the hook, but great care must be taken to be certain the oil doesn't touch the other materials, or it will discolor them. Silicone will also work to protect the metal. Severely dried-out feathers may be treated with feather dressing purchased from fly-tying suppliers. A good rule of thumb for treating old flies is to handle them as little as possible and take steps to preserve them from further deterioration.

Once you have learned a little about flies and how to care for them, the matter of actually collecting them can be faced. Putting together a collection of valuable flies requires that you obtain only fine flies by known tiers that *can be authenticated.* This is no easy matter. Like most sporting collectibles, flies can turn up just about anywhere, from attics to antique shops, and the tricky part is finding those tied by the "collectable" tiers.

COLLECTIBLE FLY TIERS

Collectible fly tiers fall into several categories: authors whose flies are detailed in their books; tiers who have originated a given pattern or patterns; and commercial tiers who are famous for given patterns. The following list of collectible tiers is far from complete, but it is a beginning.

Arsenault, Clovis:	tier/innovator
Atherton, John:	author/artist
Bates, Joe	author/innovator
Bergman, Ray:	author/innovator
Blades, William:	author/innovator
Borders, Larry:	tier/innovator
Boyd, Megan:	tier/innovator
Burke, Edgar:	author/artist/tier
Cross, Rube:	author/innovator
Darbee, Elsie:	tier/innovator
Darbee, Harry	tier/innovator
DeFeo, Charles:	tier/innovator/artist
Deren, Jim:	tier/seller/innovator
Dette, Walter:	tier/innovator
Drury, Esmond:	tier/innovator
Fabbeni, Brian:	tier/innovator
Flick, Art:	author/tier/innovator
Fulsher, Keith:	author/tier/innovator

Gillum, "Pinky":	innovator/tier
Glasso, Syd:	tier/innovator
Gordon, Theodore:	tier/innovator
Grant, George:	tier/innovator
Greig, Elizabeth:	tier/innovator
Haas, Edward:	tier/innovator
Hewitt, Edward:	author/tier/innovator
Howard, Herb:	tier/innovator
Jennings, Preston:	author/artist/tier
Jorgensen, Poul:	author/innovator
Kreh, Lefty:	author/tier/innovator
LaBranche, George:	author/tier/innovator
Leisenring, James:	author/innovator/tier
Leonard, Edson:	author/tier
Marbury, Mary Orvis:	author/tier
Marinaro, Vincent:	author/tier
Martinez, Belarmino:	tier/innovator
Messinger, Joe:	tier/innovator
Oatman, Lew:	tier/innovator
Pryce-Tannatt, T. E.:	author/tier/innovator
Rhead, Louis:	author/tier/innovator
Rhodes, Homer:	tier/innovator
Rogan, Alex:	tier/innovator
Rosborough, Polly:	author/tier/innovator
Schwab, Peter:	tier/innovator
Shaw, Helen:	author/tier/innovator
Schwiebert, Ernest:	author/tier/innovator
Stearns, Frances:	tier/innovator
Stevens, Carrie:	tier/innovator
Trueblood, Ted:	author/tier/innovator
Vinciguerra, Matthew:	photographer/tier/innovator
Wetzel, Charles:	author/tier/innovator
Whitlock, Dave:	author/artist/tier
Wulff, Lee:	author/tier/innovator

The following flies and prices are from 1990 sales, auctions, and catalogs.

ARSENAULT, J. CLOVIS

Green Highlander: Hairwing salmon flies in sizes 8, 4, and 2. Set of three 70.00

Low-water salmon flies: On wire hooks in Rat family patterns together with a low-water nymph.
Set of three 70.00

Low wing: Double salmon fly 100.00

BATES, JOSEPH D., JR.

Four salmon flies: Crossfield, Black Dose, Orange Blossom and Bates Turkey. Set of four 375.00

BERGMAN, RAY

Hendrickson 500.00
Feist Special 250.00

BOYD, MEGAN

Blue Charm: Salmon fly on treble hook 185.00
Blue Charm: Salmon fly on double hook 115.00
Irish Hairy Mary: Salmon fly on double hook 75.00
Garry Dog: Salmon fly on double hook 215.00
March Brown: Salmon fly on double hook 65.00

BORDERS, LARRY

Double-White-Wing Akroyd: Salmon fly 90.00

BURKE, DR. EDGAR

Cahill style: Dry fly 300.00

COHEN, ALBERT J.

Black and Gold: Salmon fly in display dome 200.00

CROSS, RUBE

Six dry flies: In frame with authentication 500.00
Cream hackle: gold-ribbed body 250.00

DARBEE, ELSIE and HARRY

March Brown: #10 . . . .   100.00
Hendrickson: #12 . . . .   120.00
Red Quill: #12 . . . .   120.00
Light Cahill: #14 . . . .   100.00
Grey Fox: #18 . . . .   100.00
Blue-Wing Olive: #16 . . . .   110.00
Quill Gordon: #14 . . . .   110.00
Dun Variant: #12 . . . .   125.00
Black-Nosed Dace: streamer #4 . . . .   130.00
Dun Super Spyder 185.00

DE FEO, CHARLES

Muskers Fancy: Salmon fly 75.00
Salmon nymph 110.00
Three salmon flies 235.00

DRURY, ESMOND

General Practitioner: Salmon fly on double hook 235.00
General Practitioner: Variation 70.00

FABBENI, BRIAN

The Columbia: Originated by Joe Bates to commemorate
the first space shuttle flight of Columbia. Framed 100.00

The Bishop of Parsons: Salmon fly 160.00

Goldon Parson: Salmon fly 240.00

Avon Eagle: Salmon fly 80.00

FLICK, ART

Black-Nosed Dace	125.00
Dun Variant	125.00
Hendrickson	125.00
Full set of ten dry flies: From Flick's book, *A Streamside Guide to Naturals and Their Imitations*	1,800.00

GILLUM, H. S. "PINKY"

Winged eastern dry flies	75.00

GLASSO, SYDNEY

Gold Riach: Salmon fly on card	475.00
Abinger: Salmon fly with gut eye on card	500.00
Jockie Double: Salmon fly	850.00

GORDON, THEODORE

Wood-duck wing dry fly: With provenance	4,000.00

GRANT, GEORGE

Four flies: Trude, Murder Orange, Integration, and Badger Royal in original box together with a copy of Grant's *Montana Trout Flies*	110.00
Six nymphs: In original box together with a copy of Grant's *The Art of Weaving Hair Hackles for Trout Flies*	160.00
Nine flies: Together with a sample of Grant's patented woven hackle	150.00

HAAS, EDWARD

Polar Shrimp	50.00
Four steelhead flies	70.00

HEWITT, EDWARD

Yellow Nymph #14 . . . .   650.00

HOWARD, HERB

Irresistible 110.00
Spinner 85.00

LaBRANCHE, GEORGE

Whirling Dun 600.00
Queen of the Waters 600.00

LEISENRING, JAMES E.

Framed set of "Favorite Flies": Once hung in the tap
room at the Hotel Rapids on the Brodheads Creek
in Analomink, Pennsylvania 6,000.00

MARTINEZ, BELARMINO

Martinez Special: Salmon fly 195.00
Sweep: Salmon fly 60.00
Black Doctor and Silver Doctor: Two salmon flies 260.00
Blue Rat: Salmon fly with card 125.00
Pas River: 4/0 salmon fly on card 125.00
Green Highlander: 4/0 salmon fly with card 125.00
Durham Ranger: 3/0 salmon fly with card 125.00
Rio Deva: 2/0 salmon fly 150.00
Rio Cares: 2/0 salmon fly 150.00
Martinez Plateada: 2/0 salmon fly 150.00

ORVIS, CHARLES F. CO

Ten cards with about forty trout flies: Dated from
1902 to 1912 . . . .   400.00

Thirteen cards with about forty trout flies: Dated
from 1901–1912 . . . .   300.00

PRYCE-TANNATT, DR. T. E.

Blue Doctor: Gut-eye salmon fly in glass dome 1,200.00

Bonne Bouche: Variation salmon fly 500.00

RHODES, HOMER

White bucktail 200.00

Pink bonefish fly 300.00

SCHWAB, PETER

Queen Bee 150.00

SHAW, HELEN

Authenticated fly: Mounted and under a glass dome . . . 120.00

SHIELDS & CO.

Eight gut-eye salmon flies: Circa 1875
on labeled cards 175.00

Salesman's sample board with 30 bass flies: In a
25″ × 21″ frame 500.00

STEARNS, FRANCES

Twenty-three full-dressed salmon flies: On dark green
velvet in a 13″ × 19″ frame 1,300.00

Thirty-two streamer flies: For salmon, trout and bass.
Labeled, signed, and framed 650.00

STEVENS, CARRIE

Judge: Streamer fly 240.00

Jitterbug: Streamer fly 200.00

America: Streamer fly 220.00

Casablanca: Streamer fly 240.00

Golden Witch: Streamer fly 210.00

Rapid River: Streamer fly 210.00
Kelly's Killer: Streamer fly 220.00
Queen of the Waters: Streamer fly 225.00
Royal Coachman: Streamer fly 260.00

Collection: Of seventy-eight different patterns of which
forty-one are mounted on Stevens's cards and
identified in her hand 20,000.00

WHITLOCK, DAVE

Sculpin 150.00

WULFF, LEE

Threadless black streamer 50.00
Royal Wulff 150.00

MISCELLANEOUS

Drop-front oak fly chest: With twenty-one slide-out trays
containing approximately 600 salmon flies 3,600.00

Malloch's metal fly box: With seven lift-out trays
containing about eighty-five old salmon flies 875.00

Brass fly box: With fifty circa 1910
gut-eye salmon flies 250.00

Pigskin trout-fly case: Circa 1870–90 . . . .   110.00

Hardy "Neroda" fly box 145.00

Twenty-four-drawer fly chest 850.00

Twenty-eight-drawer fly chest 450.00

Metal fly chest: With five lift-out trays and
about 550 flies 1,050.00

SELECTED BIBLIOGRAPHY

There are nearly as many books about flies and fly fishing as there are fly patterns, but the beginning collector will be well served by the following informative volumes:

Bates, Joseph D.
> *The Art of the Atlantic Salmon Fly*
> *Atlantic Salmon Flies and Fishing*
> *Streamer Fly Tying and Fishing*

Blades, William F.
> *Fishing Flies and Fly Tying*

Flick, Art
> *Master Fly-Tying Guide*

Leonard, J. Edson
> *Flies*

Smedley, Harold H.
> *Fly Patterns and Their Origins*

Wetzel, Charles
> *Practical Fly Fishing*

Fishing Lures, Plugs, and Spoons

Fifteen years ago an acknowledged expert stated that he did not believe there were more than five hundred lure collectors in the entire world. That was then and this is now, and although no one has counted them lately, there are at least fifty thousand eager collectors, antique dealers, and entrepreneurs seeking the scarce lures that were like pebbles on a beach only a few short years ago. If you plan to compete for the lures that are left, there are some things you should know before you begin your quest.

Fishing lures in one form or another have been around as long as human civilization. Primitive peoples made barbed hooks and spears and simple "spoons" and spinners from bone and stone. Civilized peoples followed suit, and a metal lure that resembled a minnow was in use in Europe before Columbus discovered the New World. This early history of lures is of passing interest to today's collectors because, for them, collectable lures fall into one of two categories: metal spoons and spinners from the 1800s; and wooden lures or plugs (often called "baits") made in the late 1800s and preplastic 1900s. Early rubber frogs are eagerly sought after and command premium prices, as do rare examples of metal and wooden frogs. The would-be collector should learn all he or she can about lures, and the best way to do this is at one or more of the many shows held each year in all parts of the country. Information about these shows may be obtained from the National Fishing Lure Collectors Club (see the address at the end of this chapter). Membership in the NFLCC is a must for the lure collector. You will save the modest

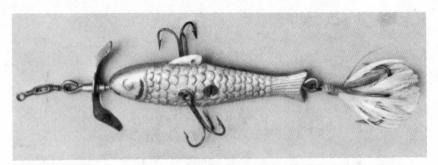

A circa 1907 Van deCar Bonafide Minnow. (Courtesy Oliver's Auction Galleries)

membership cost hundreds of times over when you set out to compete in the marketplace as a better-prepared collector.

There is no single answer to the question of where to find old fishing tackle, because it can turn up anywhere. Auctions such as the exciting ones held by the Richard W. Oliver Galleries of Kennebunk, Maine, are a source, as are the many specialized shows where dealers display and sell their wares. Many dealers, such as John Shoffner of Fife Lake, Minnesota, publish periodic price lists of lures and other tackle, and these too are a resource for collectors.

An early Jersey Expert, by the Adams Manufacturing Company. (Courtesy Oliver's Auction Galleries)

Antique shops can be an excellent source of rare lures. Most of these dealers know little about lures and have a smattering for sale only because the lures are collectable. Usually these are overpriced common lures, but now and then you will find a gem among the also-swams.

Flea markets and yard sales are potential lure sources, and although most of what turns up is of little or no interest, don't be discouraged. Only last year I turned up, for fifteen dollars, a mint-condition "Neverfail" rigged Pflueger minnow in a 1911 Four Brothers mint-condition box, complete with papers authenticating the package. (1911 was the year Pflueger patented the Neverfail name, and "Four Brothers" was one of their product trade names.) The very same day I bought two tackle boxes jammed with lures for $175. I removed one lure and sold the rest for what I had invested. The lure I kept (temporarily) was a Creek Chub model #5000 Clothes Pin with a book value of four hundred dollars. Days like this may be few and far between, but they are what keep collectors collecting.

THE TERRIBLE TACKLE BOX

There's an old timer in a town near here who has three boxes full of lures that haven't been touched in thirty years and that a collector would kill for. Not much farther away is a weekly auction house that routinely sells beat-up old tackle boxes filled with worthless discards for from twenty to fifty dollars to unsuspecting, unknowledgeable collectors. Know what you are buying and don't let a dream become a costly nightmare.

If you put your thinking cap on you will discover that there are many more ways to find old collectable lures. The attics and cellars of friends and relatives are good possibilities, as are those of strangers you can bring into the act with "wanted" ads in local papers and with posters placed where such notices are permitted. I know of two individuals who built up fine collections this way. When you come right down to it, you are limited only by your purse strings and by the time and energy you are prepared to spend. There are hundreds of fine old lures out there just waiting to be discovered.

ABBEY & IMBREY

Abbey & Imbrey Glowbody Minnow: This circa 1920s glass-body bait is excellent 80.00

ARBOGAST

Rare Arbogast Walleye Metal Bait: A $2\frac{1}{2}''$ lure with superficial wear on back 750.00

Arbogast Northern Pike Metal Bait: A $2\frac{3}{4}''$ lure in excellent condition 275.00

Small-size Sunfish Metal Bait: A $1\frac{3}{4}''$ lure in excellent condition 150.00

ARNTZ

Arntz Michigan Life-Like Minnow: A $2\frac{3}{4}''$ green and white lure with paint chipping 205.00

BING'S

Bing's Weedless Namahbin Minnow: A $3\frac{1}{2}''$ glass-eye minnow with some chipping 325.00

BONAFIDE MANUFACTURING CO.

Rare Van DeCar Bonafide Aluminum Minnow: A 1907 patent shows lure/decoy uses. Rare and excellent 3,750.00

BUEL, J. T.

#6 Kidney Casting Spoon: 3″ overall. Metal and yellow paint. Single fixed hook. Mint 12.00

#3 Arrowhead Trolling Spoon: Silver and copper with plain treble hook. "T" name and address 25.00

> ### CHRISTMAS "T"
>
> *Collecting early spoons and spinners is an increasingly popular pursuit, and J. T. Buel is a popular manufacturer. Buel lures with the manufacturer's name and address in the form of a "T" or "Christmas tree" are the earliest Buels, and the most valuable.*

CHAPMAN & SON

Chapman & Son "Allure" in large (3⅜") body
size: Mint condition 275.00

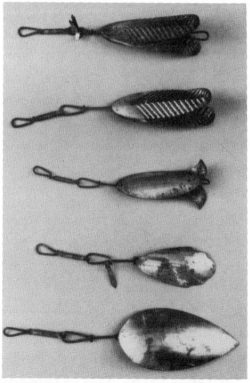

Chapman & Son baits from the 1870s. (Courtesy Oliver's Auction Galleries)

Allure Pat. Imp. 1883: 1/0 marked bait
in excellent condition 225.00

W. D. Chapman—Theressa, N.Y.–3": Name and address
marked on this "The Boss" bait 675.00

Chapman & Son—Minnow Propeller: Name and model
marked on this $3\frac{3}{8}''$ bait in excellent condition 245.00

CHARMER

Charmer Wooden Minnow: A $3\frac{1}{2}''$ in bronze and red in
near-mint condition 300.00

CREEK CHUB

Creek Chub Sarasota Minnow: A $4\frac{1}{2}''$ perch scale lure.
One tiny hook mark 110.00

Creek Chub Fin Tail Shiner: A 4" bait with red fiber fins
and tail. Very good condition 130.00

Underwater Minnow (5-hook): A very rare lure with
minor hook rust 475.00

The Musky Wigglefish: Golden Shiner finish with
minor hook scrapes 135.00

Another: Shad finish. Single tie. Minor hook scrapes on
bottom. Very good 160.00

The Musky Wigglefish: Silver flash. Single-tie. A scarce
lure in excellent condition 225.00

Gar Minnow (#2900): A good to very good lure with
rusty hooks. Scarce 110.00

Polly Wiggle: Pollywog finish. Missing weed guard,
otherwise very good 115.00

Lucky Mouse (#3600): All black with missing ears 45.00

Baby Jigger: Green frog finish with only minor
chips. In box 115.00

Jigger (#4100): Red head and white body with
body scrapes. Good 25.00

Husky Dinger (#5700): In golden shiner finish with the
big tail. Excellent 180.00

Another: All black finish. Near-mint 180.00

Dinger (#5500): In silver flash finish with red and white
tail. Very good 30.00

Midget Dinger (#6100): In golden shiner finish with big
tail. Near-mint 55.00

Surface Dingbat (#5400): In all black finish
in near-mint condition 35.00

Another: In perch finish. Excellent 22.00

Dingbat (#5100): Frog finish in near-mint condition . .   35.00

Surfster (#7300): In blue flash finish
in excellent condition 58.00

Another: In mullet finish. Minor scrapes 48.00

DECKER

Decker Surface Water Bass Bait: Circa 1913 in original
box. Near-mint 250.00

Decker Plug Bait: $3\frac{1}{2}''$ all yellow with three single
hooks. Excellent. Scarce 75.00

DETROIT

Detroit Glass Minnow Tube: In tired original box.
Lure needs cleaning 300.00

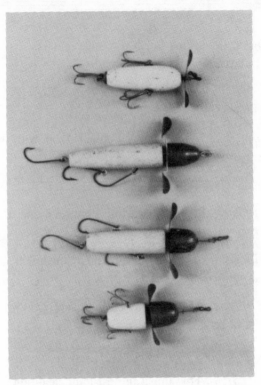

Decker surface baits, circa 1910–18. (Courtesy Oliver's Auction Galleries)

DONALY

Donaly Redfin Floater: A $2\frac{7}{8}''$ lure with several chips . . .   80.00

Donaly WOW: 3". Black with gold markings and red mouth. Minor chipping 90.00

DUNK'S

Dunk's Swim-A-Lure: A $4\frac{1}{4}''$ long lure in new condition in an excellent box 225.00

EUREKA BAIT COMPANY

Eureka Little Giant Wiggler: A $3\frac{1}{4}''$ lure. White with red hole decoration. Very good 115.00

Eureka Wiggler: A strawberry-spotted lure 4″ in length.
Rate. Very good 175.00

EXPERT

The Expert: Marked lure. A 3⅝″ bait with aluminum and
green body. Missing one hook 200.00

EXPERT MINNOWS

The Expert minnow was designed by Franklin Woods and Company, but a relative of Woods, Charles Shaffer, sought and obtained the patent in 1903. Experts marked "Holzwarth" were made by Woods. Five years later, J. L. Clark began marketing "Expert" minnows, as did Fred Keeling after 1914 when he obtained the rights.

Five-Hook Expert Minnow marked "Holzworth": In
aluminum and green. Very good condition 525.00

The Expert: Marked minnow. A 3⅝″ lure in green and
aluminum. Very good 100.00

Keeling Expert Minnow: A tiny 2″ lure in the original
box. Very good condition 240.00

Keeling's Expert Minnow: Marked 5-hook, 3½″ lure in
original box. Very good 225.00

The Expert: Marked 3⅜″ early lure. Paint off weights,
otherwise excellent 175.00

HEDDON

Wooden Frog: Carved by James Heddon in 1898 before
the company was founded 3,000.00

Heddon #7001 8″ Minnow: One of only three known to
exist. Replaced hooks. Good 1,000.00

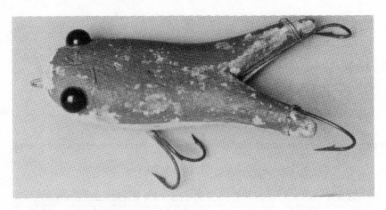

A wooden frog carved by James Heddon, circa 1898. (Courtesy Oliver's Auction Galleries)

Heddon Baby Coast Minnow: $2\frac{3}{8}''$ crackle-back body with hand-painted gills. One chip 400.00

Uncataloged #900-Type Lure: With unpainted gills in very good condition 325.00

#900 Swimming Minnow: A $4\frac{1}{2}''$ long lure in yellow with green and black spots 225.00

#800 Swimming Minnow: $3\frac{1}{8}''$ lure in very good shiny condition 275.00

As above: In white and green. Very good 195.00

Heddon L-Rigged Dummy Double: A $3\frac{1}{4}''$ white with red and green spots and original box 370.00

#10 Series Variation: White with red and green spots in shiny mint condition 300.00

#10 Series Variation: Yellow, red, and green with hand-painted gills 375.00

#10 Series Variation: White body with red head and one tiny chip 150.00

Heddon Musky Vamp: 8″ lure with green-scale body in very good condition 175.00

Heddon Red and White Luny Frog: A scarce lure in mint condition 300.00

Giant River Runt (#7510): Toilet-seat rig. Only made for one year. Near-mint 550.00

Another: "Teddy Bear" (white body with red tail and red around eyes) finish. Excellent 550.00

Dowagiac Minnow (#100): Cup rig. Slate back and hand-painted gill marks. Very good 42.00

Another: Early perch finish. Very good 75.00

Another: "L" rig. Fat-bodied rainbow finished 55.00

Another: As above in red and white finish 75.00

Another: As above in all-red finish. Scarce 85.00

Zaragossa (#6500): In red head with frog-scale finish in near-mint condition 165.00

Another: As above in green-scale finish. Good 55.00

Musky Three-Hook Minnow: Cup rig in rainbow finish. Tiny nicks, otherwise mint. Rare 485.00

River Runt (#110): 2-piece rig in dace-scale finish. Near-mint 58.00

Surface Bait (#200): "L" rig in frog finish and 3-pin collar. Very good 35.00

Surface Bait (#210): As above in red and white with tail cap. Age lines 25.00

Another: Blue and white. Slight soiling 28.00

Punkinseed (#730): "S" rig in bluegill finish. Near-mint 45.00

Another: As above but scuffs 28.00

Another: 2-piece rig. Crappie finish 30.00

Heddon Basser (#8500): H.D.L. rig. Shiner-scale
finish. Near-mint 25.00

Another: As above. Strawberry-spotted finish 25.00

Another: As above. Perch-scale. Two-hooker 15.00

King Basser (#8500–5): Blue-herring-scale in very good
condition 45.00

Little Luny Frog (#3400): Green frog finish with
toilet-seat rig 70.00

Luny Frog (#3500): Green frog finish. Toilet-seat rig.
Minor scuffs 45.00

Another: As above in tan frog finish 40.00

Baby Crab Wiggler (#1900): "L" rig. Natural crab finish.
Very good 22.00

Another: As above in perch-scale finish 20.00

Another: As above. Strawberry-spotted 40.00

Crab Wiggler (#1800): In natural crab. Inch-worm tie
and "U" collar. Flaking 18.00

S.O.S. Wounded Minnow (#160): "L" rig in luminous
finish. Soiled. Good 15.00

Another: Dace-scale finish. Very good 20.00

Another: In "Silver flitter" finish. Excellent 35.00

Meadow Mouse (#9800): In black-mouse finish with
"L" rigged hooks 15.00

Another: White-mouse with double hooks 42.00

Another: White with black back stripe. Early 35.00

Lucky 13 (#2500): 2-piece rig. Red head with white
body. Rusty hooks 24.00

Another: As above in red-head frog-scale finish 20.00

Musky Lucky 13: A $5\frac{1}{2}''$ lure with red head and
green-scale finish and white eyes. In a 2-piece
wood box. Rare 135.00

JAMISON, W. J. CO.

Jamison #1 Winged Mascot: An all-white 4" lure with
minor age lines. Excellent 150.00

Jamison Struggling Mouse: In frog finish. Only minor
wear. Very good 135.00

Jamsion #3 Weedless Coaxer: White with red ears and
feathers. Very good 20.00

JERSEY EXPERT

Jersey Expert: Patent Pending, Adams Mfg. Co.,
Morristown, NJ marked on this very rare lure's box . . . 1,900.00

KEELING (See also Expert)

Keeling Tom Thumb: In-surface model. A $3\frac{1}{2}''$ lure in
original box in excellent condition 140.00

LOCKHART, E. J.

Lockhart Pollywag: $2\frac{5}{8}''$ white with red holes in
very good condition 95.00

Lockhart Wiggler: $3\frac{7}{8}''$ all-white lure with red
holes. Very good 70.00

Lockhart Baby Wiggler: $2\frac{7}{8}''$ lure. All red with
yellow holes. Excellent 95.00

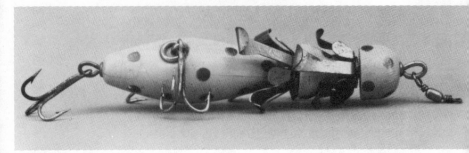

A Miller Reversible Minnow, circa 1916. (Courtesy Oliver's Auction Galleries)

MILLER

Circa 1916 Miller's Reversible Minnow: Rare $4\frac{1}{2}''$ lure
in near-excellent condition 3,400.00

As above: Hook marks and age lines 1,500.00

MOONLIGHT

Moonlight Pikaroon: Red head, white body, black eye
circles. Very good condition 30.00

Another: White, green, black eye circles 30.00

Moonlight Jointed Pikaroon: All black with green eye
circles. Very good 45.00

PAW PAW BAIT COMPANY

Paw Paw Baby Wottafrog: $3\frac{1}{4}''$ with green-splatter finish
and plain trebles. Very good 35.00

Paw Paw Wottafrog: $3\frac{3}{4}''$ with yellow-splatter finish
and plain trebles 28.00

Jointed Musky Minnow: Perch finish with
rusty metal parts 38.00

Paw Paw Natural Hair Mouse: Grey head with natural-
hair body. Excellent 48.00

Paw Paw Trout Caster: $3\frac{1}{2}''$ in dark green with red ribs and gold scales. Very good 28.00

Another: Dark grey with silver scales and red belly stripes. Excellent condition 45.00

Another: $4\frac{1}{2}''$ size in pike finish. Good 35.00

Another: 5″ size in perch finish. Tail chipped 38.00

Another: As above. In brown with gold. Excellent 65.00

Paw Paw Pike Caster: $5\frac{1}{4}''$ in chain-pickerel finish. Very good condition 68.00

Another: In black with silver scales. Excellent 68.00

PEPPER, JOSEPH E.

Pepper Red Devil Spinner: Nickel with red beads and two single hooks 18.00

Another: As above with white-feathered treble 14.00

Baby Red Devil Spinner: Nickel with red beads. In mint condition 18.00

PFLUEGER

Early Indian Bead Spoon: 2″ long nickeled blade with original silk trace 35.00

Fine Pflueger Competitor Minnow: $2\frac{1}{2}''$ lure with hand-painted gills 250.00

Surprise Minnow: With early washered screw-eye rig in silver. Minor chipping 75.00

Neverfail Minnow: Early see-through wire rig with three hooks. Green crackle-back. Very good 95.00

Neverfail Minnow: 3-hook. Green crackle-back finish with Neverfail hardware. Very good 85.00

THE AMERICAN FISH HOOK COMPANY

The company that we know today as Pflueger Fishing Tackle began in 1864 when E. F. Pflueger founded the American Fish Hook Company in Akron, Ohio. This became the Akron Fishing Tackle Works and then the Enterprise Manufacturing Company before the Pflueger name was used. The company has been making and marketing tackle for 127 years— longer than any other.

Another: Red head with white body. Excellent 50.00

Another: Perch finish. Two hooks missing 30.00

Neverfail Minnow: 5-hook. Rainbow finish with minor chipping. Otherwise excellent 60.00

Pflueger Monarch Minnow: In box with 1911 patent date. Excellent condition 325.00

Globe: $3\frac{5}{8}''$ see-through wire. Luminous. Early and scarce. Very good 68.00

Globe: $5\frac{1}{4}''$ red head and pike scale. Not spring loaded. Very good 18.00

Another: As above. Yellow-gold spots. Mint 22.00

RHODES, JAY (See Shakespeare)

RUSH, J. K.

Rush Tango Minnow: 5″ white with green and yellow mottled back. Minor chipping. Very good 28.00

Rush Tango Junior: $4\frac{1}{4}''$ yellow with red and green mottled back. Very good 28.00

Rush Troutango: $1\frac{3}{4}''$ red head with a white body in mint condition 35.00

SHAKESPEARE

Rhodes Wood Minnow: In Shakespeare box with 1904 patent date. Near-mint 525.00

Evolution Rubber Bait: With "Pat. Appl'd For" prop marking. Near-mint 200.00

As above: But with 1901 patent date and minor defects   150.00

Scarce Baby Revolution: With the very early "Pat. Appl'd For" marking. A 3" lure 250.00

REVOLUTION/EVOLUTION

Shakespeare's "Revolution" bait was patented in 1900 and the name indicates that the lure revolves. The "Evolution" appeared in 1902 and the term advertises the "evolution" the company hoped for from live minnows to this rubber bait.

Shakespeare Five-Hook Minnow: In wooden box. Lure is excellent, box is age-soiled 400.00

Shakespeare #709 Hydroplane Bait: A $4\frac{1}{2}$" lure in a tired old box 65.00

Waukazoo Surface Spinner: In frog finish with hook hanger missing 65.00

SOUTH BEND

South Bend Vacuum Bait: A $2\frac{3}{8}$" lure in yellow with red and green spots 145.00

Peach Oreno (#502): A metal lure with red head and white body. Lacking leader butt 25.00

Another: In nickel finish. Very good 25.00

THE EYES HAVE IT ?

The earliest South Bend lures had no eyes. Glass eyes were introduced in about 1913 and tack eyes in the 1930s as a cost-saving measure in those hard times.

Swanberg Peach Oreno (#503): A 4½" metal lure in frog-spot finish. Excellent 100.00

Swanberg Peach Oreno (#504): A 5" metal lure in frog finish with minor flaking 75.00

Three-Hook Panatella Minnow: In green-scale finish with considerable wear 30.00

Another: In yellow with strawberry spots. Good 38.00

Five-Hook Panatella Minnow: Red head and white body with tail cap. Very good in worn box 65.00

Another: In brown and yellow. Missing two hooks 14.00

Five-Hook Underwater Minnow: Yellow with strawberry spots. Minor flaking 38.00

Another: White with black stripe and some flaking . . . 35.00

Another: Yellow with red back. Very good 48.00

Fish Oreno: Yellow with strawberry spots. Mint in fine original box 35.00

Another: In pike-scale finish. Very good 12.00

WAKEMAN, ARCHER

Circa 1886 Skeleton Bait: A 4" Cape Vincent, NY lure. Excellent 1,000.00

As above: But in medium (3⅜") size 300.00

WILSON, R. T.

Wilson's Bassmerizer: A white-on-white lure with minor chipping. Very good 165.00

Wilson Six-in-One Wobbler: Yellow with red on head and chin. Chip on head. Very good 115.00

WINCHESTER

Winchester #9212: 5-hook minnow in blended brown finish. Excellent 525.00

Winchester #9200 Multi-Wobbler: A 3½″ lure with minor chips 180.00

Winchester #9538 Crusader Fluted Spinner: A 7″ nickel and red with treble hook 45.00

Winchester #9539 Crusader Kidney Spinner: 7″ nickel and red with feathered treble 60.00

WINCHESTER VS. WINCHESTER

There are two Winchesters that made collectable lures: the Winchester Repeating Arms Company of New Haven, Connecticut, and the Winchester Bait and Manufacturing Company of Winchester, Indiana. The lures from New Haven have the well-known Winchester trademark.

WRIGHT AND McGILL

Flapper Crab: 2½″ natural crab finish. Near-mint in a shelfworn box 95.00

Baby Flapper Crab: 1¾″ natural crab finish. Missing feelers. Very good 45.00

Another: 2″ grey, black, yellow. Missing feelers 65.00

EMPTY BOXES

Lures in their original boxes are similar to books in their original dust jackets, and their value is increased from ten to as much as fifty percent more when in the box. Early wooden lure boxes sell for upwards of a hundred dollars in good condition.

Bass Nabber: 3½″ rainbow finish in
near-mint condition. Scarce 150.00

Wiggling Shrimp: Silver with green finish. Missing legs,
otherwise very good 250.00

Bass-O-Gram: 4″ red and white finish with a small slice
out of belly. Otherwise near-mint 425.00

Whirlwind Spinner: Nickel with red beads in
original box. Mint 65.00

The lures listed and priced here are only the tip of an enormous iceberg. The National Fishing Lure Collectors Club can help you see the whole picture. Contact them in care of Rich Treml, P.O. Box 1791, Dearborn, MI 48121.

Two well-illustrated books about lures, plugs, and spoons are: *Luckey's Identification and Value Guide to Old Fishing Lures and Tackle,* and the highly recommended *Streeter's Reference Guide to Old Fishing Lures.*

FISHING ACCESSORIES

Accessories is a wonderful word, for it enables the eclectic collector to sort out just what it is he or she is interested in. Fishing accessories—creels, nets, fly books, and such—are hot collectibles.

Line dryers, gut cutters, and, particularly, split-shot containers with gun company names on them are scarce and very collectable. Creels are collected by fishing enthusiasts as well as basket freaks, and they are eagerly sought in a marketplace that has less and less to offer the discriminating buyer. Nothing should be overlooked: Even the 1950s and 1960s signs that say things like "Old fishermen never die—they just smell that way" are collected by someone somewhere. If you see something that says "fish" at an affordable price, you probably should buy it to sell or trade.

The following list of various fishing accessories is short, but a more comprehensive tally could easily fill this entire guide.

Bronze of a hooked trout: Signed G. Marchegay. Made to
display with a fly. 11" long 2,600.00

Embossed match safe: With fly fisherman in
relief. Excellent condition 130.00

1900s mug with fishing scene and a fly: With
Staffordshire markings. Minor crazing 80.00

Signed Limoges 9" plate: With a grayling and
decorative border. Excellent 155.00

Ten Limoges dinner plates and platter: All with fish
scenes. Very good condition 525.00

Walnut angler's kit: Marked "Killanney." Has grove for
leaders and center for flies 65.00

1895 marked "Edward Vom Hofe" portable line dryer:
With carry case and in excellent condition 170.00

Pegley-Davies angler's knife: Name marked on this
German silver knife. Some blade rusting 175.00

Abercrombie & Fitch: Name marked on this wood tackle
box with brass hardware. Very good condition 450.00

As above: But with canvas cover and 45 wood and plastic
fishing lures. Box is excellent 550.00

Circa 1930s Olson gut cutter: A tweezer-style cutter in
very good condition 600.00

Scarce #3 Hardy Anglers Knife: With virtually all working
parts. Very good condition 380.00

Classic 1960s Case fly fishing knife: In the original
display box. New condition 325.00

Ash splint creel: In a pot-bellied design with center hole.
Circa 1880s. Fine condition 210.00

Split-ash creel: With a wooden "spring" woven in front
to secure lid. Used clean condition 170.00

Early splint creel: Made "necked down" rather than with
a lid to retain fish 450.00

Early willow creel: With woven rim design and with
original latch, strap, and hinges 300.00

Ladies toleware creel: With matching worm box. Both
painted green with stenciled roses 800.00

CREELS AND CREELS AND CREELS

Good creels are hot, and poor creels and most "antique" creels are probably not. Be careful to learn the differences between old finely crafted creels and those you can buy today brand new for around twenty dollars.

Tiny whole willow creel: With overlapping center hole lid. Replaced hinge and latch 110.00

16' Adirondack guide scull: A circa 1880s cedar boat with copper stapping. Revarnished 2,750.00

Restored Old Town Yankee model canoe: A 1930 canoe that has been completely restored 3,000.00

Canoe Paddle with painted brown trout: Classy trout on classic paddle. Very good 350.00

Russell lock-back knife: With bone handle. 4" serrated back blade. Very good 235.00

Hardy collapsible wood net: With triangular "ring" and 3' to 6' handle 300.00

Long-handled wooden net: With brass and bronze fittings. Very good condition 325.00

Edward Vom Hofe-marked gaff: With brass and German-silver fittings. Excellent 425.00

Unmarked Marble's spring gaff: A $26\frac{1}{2}$" gaff with wood handle and aged metal parts 180.00

English combination priest and telescopic gaff: In excellent condition 190.00

A. Carter & Co.-marked telescopic gaff: With brass extending handle 225.00

T. J. Conroy's Floating Bait Bucket: Name marked on
this very good bucket 500.00

St. Lawrence Bucket: Name marked on stenciled bait
bucket. Very good 110.00

Two-compartment cricket cage: With sliding end
lids. Very good 115.00

Shakespeare Honor Built tackle box: With 2 lift-out
trays and contents 170.00

Winchester marked tackle box: With 2 lift-out trays in
very good condition 160.00

"Live Bait For Sale" sign: With painting of a pickerel.
15" x 22" 275.00

19" carved brook trout: With old crazed paint on an
oval oak plaque 900.00

WILDFOWL DECOYS

For all intents and purposes, decoy collecting began in 1919 when a New York City architect "discovered" his first decoy and termed it "floating sculpture." The architect was Joel Barber, who, posthumously, would be called "The Father of the Decoy." His fascination with decoys became the foundation upon which all that followed was built. Barber's innovative book *Wild Fowl Decoys* was published in 1934 and found few buyers. He died in 1952 before gaining the fame he enjoys today, and his entire collection of hundreds of decoys was sold for about the price of one really decent decoy on today's market.

Decoy collecting continued in relative obscurity for a decade after Barber's death. There was a handful of farsighted individuals who put together fine collections in those quiet times, but for the most part the writing on the wall was ignored or went unnoticed, even though it meant the end of an era that had endured for a century and more. The writing on the wall said "plastic" and signaled the change that created a marketplace for old wooden decoys—the "floating sculpture" Barber had appreciated. Decoys were Americana, and Americana was in, but only a handful of buyers knew anything about the decoys they were buying.

In 1963 Hal Sorenson of Burlington, Iowa, started a small publication, *The Decoy Collector's Guide,* to, as he stated, provide a "meeting place" for collectors from the various areas of the country and to provide "a bridge" for knowledge to be shared. It is interesting to note that in the final regular issue in 1965, readers found advertisements for both William Mackey's and Adele Earnest's new decoy books—the first such books in thirty-one years. What Barber had begun and Sorenson kept alive, Mackey and Earnest guaranteed a place in history for. Decoys were here to stay and collectors were learning the ropes.

In the summer of 1968 the decoy market changed forever when the Richard A. Bourne Galleries of Hyannis, Massachusetts, held the first all-decoy auction. For the first time collectors had comparison and competition, and prices reacted accordingly as good decoys brought good prices. A fine turned-head black-duck decoy by Elmer Crowell was the highlight of the sale at $900. It was a far cry from today's prices, but $900 was considered high in 1968.

If 1968 was the beginning for decoy sales and prices, then the eight-part auction by the Bourne Galleries of William Mackey's extensive collection in 1973 and 1974 was, and in many ways still is, the living end. Prices had more or less doubled since 1968, but Mackey's better birds brought better prices,

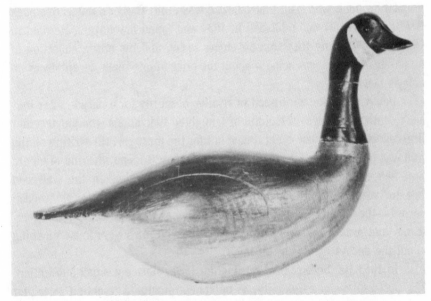

A Canada goose stick-up made by John Tax of Osakis, Minnesota, in 1917. (Photograph by David Beane for James Julia—Gary Guyette)

and the highlight of the two-year event was the sale of a William Bowman curlew decoy for $10,500—twice what Barber's heirs received for his entire collection twenty years earlier. The stage had been set, and it was only a matter of time until a decoy brought six figures. This happened in 1968 when a wood duck by Joe Lincoln was sold by the Bourne Galleries for over $200,000, and a fine Canada goose by Elmer Crowell was auctioned by the Richard Oliver Galleries of Kennebunk, Maine, for more than $300,000.

It goes without saying that a few sentences and a handful of prices cannot, in themselves, be considered either a history or a price guide, but they most certainly are indicative of the seventy-year trend that has brought us from Barber to today's wildfowl decoy marketplace. There is more to know; learn all you can about decoys *before* you ever make a purchase. Get and read the Barber, Mackey, and Earnest books, which are all available as reprints. Go to museums and decoy shows and talk to other collectors. Get a feel for the regional styles. You may feel you are wasting precious time in the learning period, but the time you "waste" will be repaid in the marketplace where fine decoys are still available at all price ranges for those who know what to look for.

For those who like to categorize things, wildfowl decoys can be separated into six reasonably distinct groups: ducks, geese, shorebirds, crows and owls, doves, and miscellaneous species such as seagulls, terns, blackbirds, and such. Each of these six groups can be further divided into hand-carved and factory-made groupings and divided yet again into species and/or materials used in manufacture. Without getting involved in algebraic formulations, it should suffice to say that someone, somewhere, collects every possible combination—from the finest hand-carved ducks and geese to the lowliest papier-maché crows and owls that have yet to curry favor with many serious collectors. I have no intention of telling you what or what not to collect. I will, however, offer some friendly advice that you can take with as many grains of salt as you see fit.

The first caution is to avoid decoys that have been repainted, have undergone major repair, or otherwise differ greatly from what they originally were. A fine Mason decoy with the original untouched paint can be worth thousands of dollars, but the very same decoy repainted may be worth next to nothing. There is a very thin line between "touch-up" and "repaint," and the difference can prove worth more than you want to waste. A great many decoys come on the market with "professional restoration" and only the astute collector is in a position to evaluate these repairs. If you have questions, ask them, and if they are not answered to your satisfaction, pass on the sale.

Another area of confusion for beginning collectors is the remark "attributed to." If you have not learned to recognize the styles and peculiarities of given makers from given parts of the country, don't let "attributed to" talk you into anything. When in doubt, pass.

One last word of caution, and the word is "fakery." Don't be blinded by an attractive duck or goose of questionable origin. Deal only with reputable organizations and individuals who stand behind what they sell and won't dissemble when you question the pedigree of a given decoy.

The following listing of decoys by their makers covers a little of everything, from collectables to investment-quality carvings that may be the six-figure birds of the future. The list is a compilation from major decoy auctions held in 1990, and I am deeply indebted to the Richard A. Bourne Galleries of Hyannis, Massachusetts; Gary Guyette and Jim Julia of Fairfield, Maine; and the Richard W. Oliver galleries of Kennebunk, Maine, for their cooperation. Each of these organizations has auction catalogs detailing recent sales and prices, and I can think of no better guides to today's decoy market than these profusely illustrated volumes. Detailed information on obtaining these catalogs is found at the end of this chapter.

ALGARD, WALLY: CHESTERTOWN, MARYLAND

Canvasback hen: In original paint with minor wear . . . 1,750.00

Another: In excellent original paint. Some age cracks . . 800.00

Canvasback drake: In original paint with
touch-up to white 2,200.00

ANGER, KEN: DUNNVILLE, ONTARIO

Canada goose: In original paint with some aging 5,000.00

Another: In original paint with some
checking at seams 3,500.00

Wood-duck drake: In excellent original condition 4,750.00

Bluebill pair: In original paint with minor
wear and dents 1,450.00

Canvasback drake: In original paint with some wear   . .   1,850.00

Canvasback pair: In near-mint condition 4,250.00

ANIMAL TRAP DECOYS: PASCAQOULA, MISSISSIPPI

Mallards (4): In worn original paint 210.00
Mallard drake: In good worn original paint 25.00

BACH, FERDINAND: DETROIT, MICHIGAN

Redhead drake: In outstanding original
paint. Near-mint 15,500.00

BALDWIN, WILLARD: STRATFORD, CONNECTICUT

Bluebill drake "sleeper": In near-mint condition 1,200.00
Black duck: Hollow. In original touched-up paint 525.00

BARNES, SAM: HAVRE DE GRACE, MARYLAND

Canvasback drake: In old working repaint 350.00

Redhead drake: In fine original paint
with minor aging 450.00

BIRCH, CHARLES: WILLIS WHARF, VIRGINIA

Canada goose: In a solid body with
worn original paint 900.00

Pintail drake: In fine worn original paint 2,750.00

Brant: Hollow. In touched-up
original paint. Excellent 3,700.00

Canada goose: Hollow. In exceptional original paint . . .   17,000.00

Bluebill drake: In worn old working repaint 650.00

BLAIR, JOHN SR.: PHILADELPHIA, PENNSYLVANIA

Canada goose: Circa 1860
with professional restoration 17,500.00

Blue-wing teal drake: Attributed to Blair 3,200.00

BLISS, ROSWELL: STRATFORD, CONNECTICUT

Black duck: Hollow. In touched-up original paint 375.00
Another: In original paint with minor wear 350.00
Bluebill drake: In old working repaint 425.00
White-wing scoter: In mint condition 625.00

BOWMAN, WILLIAM: LAWRENCE, NEW YORK

Long-billed dowitcher: In spring
plummage. Near-mint 30,000.00

Golden plover: In original paint. Bill restoration 15,000.00

BOYD, GEORGE: SEABROOK, NEW HAMPSHIRE

Canada goose: Canvas-covered in original paint 3,750.00
Another: As above. Excellent 5,750.00
Yellowlegs: In outstanding original condition 3,400.00
Another: As above. Original paint shows wear 1,500.00

BRADY, WALTER: OYSTER, VIRGINIA

Canada goose: In fine repaint by Ira Hudson 34,000.00
Another: In worn original paint 50,000.00
Brant: In worn repaint (from the Mackey collection) . . 4,500.00

CHADWICK, KEYES: MARTHA'S VINEYARD, MASSACHUSETTS

Common merganser pair: In near-mint condition 4,500.00

CHAMBERS, THOMAS: TORONTO, ONTARIO

Redhead drake: In worn original paint 900.00
Another: Repainted 500.00
Canada goose: In restored original paint 3,500.00

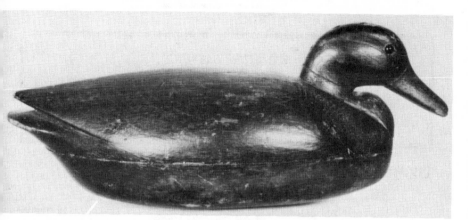

A black-duck decoy by James Cobb of Cobb's Island, Virginia. (Courtesy James Julia—Gary Guyette)

COBB, NATHAN: COBB'S ISLAND, VIRGINIA

Canada goose: In exceptional old paint 30,000.00

Another: "Shot over by Jefferson Davis" 21,000.00

Brant: With fine old working repaint 6,500.00

Black duck: In excellent condition 10,000.00

Bluebill hen: Hollow. In original touched-up paint 9,000.00

Bluebill drake: Hollow. In old working repaint 4,500.00

Another: With restored original paint 10,000.00

Bufflehead: In worn original paint (from
the Mackey collection) 30,000.00

Curlew: In running mode. Original worn paint 4,000.00

COOMBS, FRANK: ALEXANDRIA BAY, NEW YORK

Bluebill pair: In fine original paint 1,600.00
Bluebill drake: In original paint with minor wear 500.00
Another: As above 400.00
Goldeneye drake: In fine original paint 1,400.00

MINIATURE CARVINGS

Elmer Crowell, George Boyd, Joe Lincoln, and dozens of other decoy makers also turned out fine miniature and decorative carvings, and these will be a feature of the next edition of this guide.

CROWELL, ELMER: EAST HARWICH, MASSACHUSETTS

Black duck: In swimming mode with
fine original paint 10,500.00

Another: In standard position with touch-up 2,200.00

Another: As above. Fine original paint 4,250.00

Canvasback drake: In outstanding near-mint condition   20,000.00

Redhead drake: In original paint with slight wear 7,500.00

Another: In worn original paint 5,500.00

Black-breasted plover shorebird decoy by Elmer Crowell of East Harwich, Massachusetts. (Courtesy James Julia—Gary Guyette)

Canada goose: In touched-up original paint 8,700.00

Merganser drake: In near-mint condition 15,500.00

Green-wing teal drake: Made as a
doorstop. Light wear 4,000.00

Black-breasted plover: In outstanding condition 10,000.00

Yellowlegs: In excellent condition (from
the Starr collection) 11,500.00

Yellowlegs: In running mode.
In near-mint condition 8,500.00

DENNY, SAM: CLAYTON, NEW YORK

Redhead drake: In original paint with slight chipping . . 350.00
Bluebill drake: With touched-up paint 225.00

DILLEY, JOHN: QUOGUE, NEW YORK

Knot: In original paint with minor wear 3,700.00

Dowitcher: In spring plumage with
repair. Excellent paint 4,000.00

Dowitcher: In fall plumage with
outstanding original paint 6,500.00

Black-bellied plover: With some repainting 2,200.00

DODGE DECOY FACTORY: DETROIT, MICHIGAN

Bluebill pair: In original paint with light wear 700.00
Mallard pair: In excellent original paint 1,100.00
Canvasback: Chesapeake Model. Working repaint 450.00

DOWN EAST DECOY FACTORY: FREEPORT, MAINE

Black duck: In swimming mode with
fine original paint 135.00

Another: In near-mint condition 200.00

Another: In worn paint 55.00

DUDLEY, LEE and LEM: KNOTTS ISLAND, NORTH CAROLINA

Redhead drake: Circa 1890 in old paint
with bill repair 7,000.00

Another: With old working repaint and neck repair   . . .   6,250.00

Redhead decoy by Lee and Lem Dudley of Knott's Island, North Carolina. (Courtesy James Julia—Gary Guyette)

ELLISTON, ROBERT: BUREAU, ILLINOIS

Mallard drake: With moderate wear to original paint . .   500.00
Pintail drake: With original paint and overpaint 650.00
Blue-wing teal hen: In fine original paint 7,500.00
Pintail drake: In excellent original paint 7,800.00

EVANS DECOY FACTORY: LADYSMITH, WISCONSIN

Mallard pair: In original paint with minor wear 475.00

Canvasback pair: With touched-up original paint 425.00

Bluebill pair: In original paint with minor wear 400.00

Blue-wing teal pair: In near-mint condition 1,550.00

GARDNER, CLARENCE: LITTLE COMPTON, RHODE ISLAND

Dowitcher: Hollow carved. Turned
head. Outstanding paint 18,000.00

Dowitcher: Hollow carved.
Outstanding original condition 17,000.00

Black-bellied plover: In excellent original paint 1,200.00

Eskimo curlew: In outstanding original paint 3,500.00

Another: As above. With replaced bill and fine paint . . . 1,600.00

Another: As above 1,500.00

GELSTON, THOMAS: QUOGUE, NEW YORK

Yellowlegs: Cork-bodied in original paint 300.00

Curlew: In original paint
with professional restoration 6,500.00

Bluebill drake: In old working repaint 150.00

Canada goose: Made of cork and wood in
restored original paint 175.00

GRAVES, BERT: PEORIA, ILLINOIS

Mallard pair: In original paint by Kathryn Elliston 10,000.00

Mallard drake: In original paint
with varnish overcoating 900.00

Canvasback drake: In near-mint condition 1,900.00

Pintail drake: In outstanding original
paint with varnish 2,800.00

Canvasback drake: With two coats of paint by Graves . .   375.00

Another: With old working repaint 125.00

HAERTEL, HAROLD: DUNDEE, ILLINOIS

Blue-wing teal: In sleeping mode
and near-mint condition 2,400.00

Bluebill hen: Circa 1922. In worn original paint 850.00

MILES HANCOCK: CHINCOTEAGUE, VIRGINIA

Red-breasted merganser pair: In good original paint . . .   2,200.00
Merganser hen: In worn original paint 550.00
Another: As above 650.00
Canvasback drake: In good original paint with wear . . .   400.00
Brant: In fine original paint with minor wear 500.00

HARRIS, KEN: WOODVILLE, NEW YORK

Mallard pair: In original paint with minor wear 550.00
Bluebill pair: In original paint and minor wear 425.00
Bluebill hen: In near-mint condition 145.00
Redhead drake: With working repaint 80.00

HOLLY, JAMES T: HAVRE DE GRACE, MARYLAND

Canvasback pair: In outstanding
condition. Circa 1890 . . . .   6,750.00

Black duck: In original paint with minor damage 3,500.00

Blue-wing teal drake: Repainted in the 1940s
by Bob McGaw 2,500.00

Redhead pair: In original paint with minor wear 5,100.00

Bluebill hen: In restored original paint 1,050.00

Canvasback drake: In old working repainted condition . .   625.00

HOLMES, BEN: STRATFORD, CONNECTICUT

Black duck: With touched-up original paint 2,000.00
Goldeneye drake: With old working repaint 700.00
Goldeneye hen: With old working repaint 700.00
Black duck: Hollow. In old working repaint 2,500.00
Another: As above 950.00

HOLMES, LATHROP: KINGSTON, MASSACHUSETTS

Old squaw: Canvas-covered.
Exceptional original condition 18,000.00

HORNER, ROWLEY: WEST CREEK, NEW JERSEY

Bluebill drake: In near-mint unused condition 12,500.00

Brant: In original paint with minor
flaking and wear 3,250.00

Another: In old working repaint 650.00

Canada goose: In exceptional original
condition. Near-mint 11,500.00

Black duck: In fine original paint with minor wear . . . 2,750.00

HUDSON, IRA: CHINCOTEAGUE, VIRGINIA

Goldeneye drake: In original paint
with moderate wear 3,250.00

Canvasback drake: In original paint
with minor wear 2,000.00

Black duck: In original paint with minor wear 2,000.00

Bluebill drake: In original paint
with moderate wear 1,000.00

Another: As above 1,200.00

Merganser hen: In original paint with wear
and bill repair 2,450.00

Pintail drake: Balsa. In near-mint original paint 6,000.00

Redhead drake: In worn original paint 1,200.00

Canada goose: In hissing mode. Worn
to natural wood 1,550.00

Canada goose: In old working repaint 600.00

Yellowlegs: In fine scratch paint and exceptional
form. Near-mint 21,500.00

JANSON, RICHARD "FRESH AIR DICK": NAPA, CALIFORNIA

Pintail pair: In original paint with minor wear 2,750.00
Canvasback drake: In original paint with minor wear . .   950.00
Another: As above 750.00
Mallard drake: With touched-up original paint 500.00

JESTER, DOUG: CHINCOTEAGUE, VIRGINIA

Pintail drake: Oversize in original paint
with minor wear 1,700.00

Black duck: In original paint with minor wear 700.00

Merganser hen: In near-mint condition 1,750.00

JOHNSON, LLOYD: BAYHEAD, NEW JERSEY

Brant: In near-mint original paint and condition 425.00
Another: As above 650.00
Widgeon drake: In excellent original condition 1,400.00

LAING, ALBERT: STRATFORD, CONNECTICUT

Canvasback drake: In fine original paint 29,000.00

Bluebill drake: Turned head. Restored original paint . .   12,000.00

Black duck: Turned head. Exceptional
form and condition 67,500.00

LINCOLN, JOSEPH: ACCORD, MASSACHUSETTS

Canada goose: In calling mode. Exceptional
paint and condition 32,500.00

American merganser drake: In
excellent original paint 15,500.00

Brant: Self-bailing. Near-mint condition 14,000.00

Black duck: In touched-up original paint 1,500.00

White-wing scoter: Canvas-covered.
Near-mint condition 1,800.00

Merganser hen: In original paint with minor
wear and repair 2,500.00

Canada goose: In old working repaint 500.00

Yellowlegs: In near-mint original paint 2,500.00

MASON DECOY FACTORY: DETROIT, MICHIGAN

Redhead pair: Challenge grade. Fine original paint . . . 2,500.00

Widgeon pair: Challenge grade. Original
paint with wear 1,850.00

Bluebill pair: Standard grade. Unused.
Some paint flaking 5,500.00

Mallard pair: Standard grade. Worn original paint 600.00

Another: As above 500.00

Goldeneye pair: Challenge grade. Original
paint with wear 4,000.00

Redhead pair: Premier grade. Near-mint condition 5,750.00

Canvasback pair: Premier grade.
Good original paint 2,350.00

Canada goose: Premier grade. Exceptional condition . . .   7,250.00

Blue-wing teal pair: Premier
grade. Exceptional condition 6,000.00

Another: As above. Fine original paint 4,250.00

Another: Standard grade. Retouched original paint   . . .   500.00

Green-wing teal pair: Standard
grade. Working repaint 300.00

Mallard hen: Standard grade. Near-mint 325.00

Sickle-bill curlew: Near-mint with
crazing on back 5,500.00

Yellowlegs: Near-mint condition 1,100.00

Sicklebill curlew stick-up by the Mason Decoy Factory of Detroit, Michigan. (Courtesy Richard A. Bourne Co., Inc.)

Willet: In worn original paint with overwash repaint . .   800.00

Dove: In original paint with average wear 700.00

MITCHELL, MADISON: HAVRE DE GRACE, MARYLAND

Canvasback pair: Rare sleepers. Near-mint condition . .   2,300.00

Green-wing teal pair: Near-mint and signed 1,600.00

Canvasback drake: In excellent signed condition 250.00

Pintail drake: In repainted condition 250.00

Redhead drake: In excellent condition 325.00

Widgeon hen: In excellent original
paint and condition 575.00

PERDEW, CHARLES: HENRY, ILLINOIS

Mallard pair: In mint condition. Original paint 7,600.00

Bluebill pair: In near-mint condition 12,000.00

Green-wing teal drake: In original paint
by Edna Perdew 17,000.00

Redhead drake: Only known example.
In near-mint paint 39,500.00

Crow: In worn original paint 475.00

PETERSON DECOY FACTORY: DETROIT, MICHIGAN

Bluebill drake: In worn original paint 325.00
Mallard drake: In worn original paint 75.00
Blue-wing teal hen: In refinished worn condition 90.00

PIOLOTTI, MARIO: SPRING VALLEY, ILLINOIS

Mallard pair: Oversize. In near-mint condition 1,750.00
Mallard drake: In original paint with moderate wear . .   500.00

A crow decoy by Charles Perdew of Henry, Illinois. (Courtesy Oliver's Auction Galleries)

PRATT DECOY COMPANY: JOLIET, ILLINOIS

Black duck: In fine original paint 50.00

Green-wing teal drake: In original paint
with minor wear 370.00

Six decoys: Mixed species. In excellent condition 225.00

Coots: 3 in original worn paint with missing eyes 110.00

QUILLEN, NATE: ROCKWOOD, MICHIGAN

Bluebill pair: In old working repaint 600.00

RATHMELL, LOUIS: STRATFORD, CONNECTICUT

Mallard hen: In outstanding original scratch paint . . . 11,000.00

Black duck: Sleeper. In excellent original paint 4,500.00

RENNISON, CHET: OLD LYME, CONNECTICUT

Black duck: Swimming. In worn original paint 350.00

SCHMIDT, BEN: CENTERLINE, MICHIGAN

Mallard pair: In mint original condition 1,000.00

Wood-duck pair: In near-mint condition 2,000.00

Coot: In near-mint original condition 650.00

Canvasback pair: In near-mint repaired condition 800.00

Pintail pair: Early. In old original paint
with bill repair 5,000.00

Canada goose: In excellent original paint
with average wear 500.00

Bluebill hen: In worn original paint 150.00

SCHROEDER, TOM: FAIR HAVEN, MICHIGAN

Ringbill drake: In excellent original paint 500.00

Coot: Composition body. Original paint shows wear . . . 200.00

Redhead pair: Composition bodies. In
fine original paint 450.00

SHOURDS, HARRY V.: TUCKERTON, NEW JERSEY

Yellowlegs: In fine original paint with minor wear 1,500.00

Goldeneye pair: In old working repaint 1,000.00

Old squaw pair: In fine old repaint 4,600.00

Goldeneye drake: Taken down to original paint 1,000.00

Bluebill drake: In original paint with minor wear 1,600.00

Brant: In old working repaint 550.00

Canada goose: In old worn repaint 350.00

As above: Swimming mode. With
old working repaint 1,600.00

Canada goose: In outstanding
original condition. Swimmer 55,000.00

Bluebill pair: In excellent original
paint with restoration 3,500.00

STEVENS DECOY FACTORY: WEEDSPORT, NEW YORK

Bluebill drake: In old working repaint 400.00
Redhead pair: In good original paint with wear 950.00
Canvasback drake: With old working overpaint 250.00
Goldeneye drake: In old repaint with brand showing . . . 325.00

STRATIER and SOHIER: BOSTON, MASSACHUSETTS

Six folding-tin plovers: In original flaking paint 450.00
Six folding-tin golden plovers: In old repaint 325.00
Six folding-tin yellowlegs: In varying condition 375.00
Two folding-tin dowitchers: In original paint 300.00
Folding-tin "peep": In average original paint 160.00
Folding-tin ruddy turnstone: In original paint 160.00

TAX, JOHN: OSAKIS, MINNESOTA

Canada goose: Stick-up. In original paint
with minor wear 9,000.00

THENGS, HARALD: BABYLON, NEW YORK

Merganser pair: In original paint with minor wear 7,500.00
Surf scoter pair: In old repaint 975.00

VERITY FAMILY: SEAFORD, NEW YORK

Ruddy turnstone: In feeding mode in fine old paint . . 21,000.00
Black-bellied plover: In old worn paint 650.00
Yellowlegs: Semi-flatty. In touched-up original paint . . 325.00

WALKER, CHARLES: PRINCETON, ILLINOIS

Pintail drake: In exceptional paint and
condition. "His best" 25,500.00

As above: Early-style in discolored original paint 1,450.00

Mallard drake: In preening mode with
old Walker repaint 8,000.00

Mallard drake: Early-style in original paint
with minor wear 6,250.00

As above: Later flat-bottom style 4,500.00

WARD BROTHERS (Len and Steve): CHRISFIELD, MARYLAND

Canvasback drake: Sleeper. In mint condition 3,450.00

Widgeon drake: Signed and dated 1948 . . . . 5,000.00

Goldeneye drake: In retouched original paint 4,750.00

Goldeneye hen: In retouched original paint 6,250.00

Canvasback pair: Circa 1936. In near-mint condition . . 32,000.00

Bluebill drake: Circa 1936. In
touched-up original paint 2,500.00

As above: In cedar. Circa 1936.
In near-mint condition 3,200.00

Black duck stick-up: Circa 1928 in worn
paint and condition 2,250.00

Pintail drake: Circa 1920s in outstanding condition . . . 16,500.00

Pintail hen: Circa 1920s in worn original paint 12,500.00

Black duck: Circa 1921 in
exceptional original condition 21,000.00

Canada goose: Circa 1950. Signed and near-mint 2,450.00

High-head and low-head hollow-carved black ducks by Charles "Shang" Wheeler of Stratford, Connecticut. (Courtesy James Julia—Gary Guyette)

WHEELER, CHARLES "SHANG": STRATFORD, CONNECTICUT

Blue goose: Circa 1935 in near-mint condition 14,500.00

Surf scoter: Cork-bodied. In
outstanding original paint 5,500.00

Black duck: Cork-bodied. With
original scratch painting 1,200.00

Black duck: High head. In original paint
with minor wear 3,000.00

Black duck: Low head. In original paint on
head. Body repainted. 6,500.00

WHEELER, CHAUNCEY: ALEXANDRIA BAY, NEW YORK

Canvasback drake: In near-mint original paint 1,300.00

Bluebill hen: In fine subtle original paint. Near-mint . . 1,100.00

> ### REPAINTED DECOYS
>
> *Collectors don't like decoys that have "old working repaint" or "in-use touch-up paint" no matter who did the work. As a long-time duck hunter in New England waters, I know that my decoys were touched up each year and repainted time and time again. Rare indeed is the true working decoy that found its way to a mantlepiece before it was ever wet.*

As above: With touched-up original paint 400.00

Bluebill drake: In original paint with very slight wear . .   800.00

As above: With original head paint
and repainted body 800.00

Black duck: In original paint with restoration to bill . . .   375.00

Black duck: In excellent original paint
with bill restoration 700.00

Plover: In fall plumage. Circa 1918.
In near-mint condition 3,000.00

WILDFOWLER DECOY COMPANY: VARIOUS LOCATIONS

Old Saybrook, Connecticut

    Eider pair: In near-mint condition 1,000.00

    Green-wing teal pair: In near-mint condition 575.00

    Bluebill drake: Balsa-bodied. In original paint 105.00

    Mallard drake: In original touched-up paint 135.00

    Pintail drake: Worn repaint 70.00

    Mallard hen: In excellent original paint 200.00

Quogue, New York

    Green-wing teal pair: In near-mint condition 375.00

PROFESSIONALLY RESTORED

Professionally restored decoys are those that have been restored by a professional, not by an amateur or gunner. If a given decoy has been restored by a professional, it is mandatory that you know who that person was before you consider buying. Your receipt should reflect this information.

Blue-wing teal pair: In near-mint condition 400.00
Six mallards: In mint condition (4 drakes, 2 hens) . . .   1,300.00

Point Pleasant, New Jersey

Brant: "Harry Shourds" model in near-mint condition . .   325.00
Black duck: Sleeper in near-mint condition 275.00

WILSON, GUS: SOUTH PORTLAND, MAINE

Rocking-head black duck: In calling mode
in original paint 3,500.00

Rocking-head merganser: In
outstanding original paint 4,750.00

Red-breasted merganser: In excellent original paint . . .   4,750.00

Goldeneye pair: In good original paint
with minor cracking 600.00

Surf scoter: High head. In old repaint 800.00

Rocking-head surf scoter: In old working repaint 800.00

ZACHMANN, JOHN: DETROIT, MICHIGAN

Canvasback pair: Cork-bodied. In
old working repaint 200.00

Canvasback pair: First-place winners
in 1967 contest 3,250.00

SUGGESTED READING

There are more decoy books and booklets available to the decoy collector than there are good decoys, and many of them are misleading and often written, it seems to me, to prove a point or enhance a given collection. But even the worst decoy book serves a purpose if it introduces this wonderful Americana to new collectors and enthusiasts. Fortunately, the great majority of the available decoy books are informative and interesting and of real value to both beginning and advanced collectors; unfortunately, there are so many books it is often impossible to know which to buy. For the beginning collector I suggest the three books mentioned earlier. Add the superb *American Factory Decoys* by Henry Fleckenstein, and other titles as desire and need for knowledge demand. Additionally, I recommend that the collector obtain the auction catalogs of recent auctions, which are available from various galleries. They are priceless.

BOOKS

Wild Fowl Decoys by Joel Barber.
American Bird Decoys by William Mackey.
The Art of the Decoy by Adele Earnest.
American Factory Decoys by Henry Fleckenstein.

DECOY AUCTION CATALOGS

Richard A. Bourne Co., Box 141, Hyannisport, Maine 02647
Julia/Guyette, Box 830, Fairfield, Maine 04937
Oliver's Auction Gallery, Route 1, Kennebunk, Maine 04043
Decoy's Unlimited, 2320 Main St., West Barnstable, Maine 02668

FISH DECOYS

Fish decoys are the most controversial of all sporting "antiques," and fine fakes and born-yesterday specimens far outnumber the real thing. Were you to back me into a corner and ask, I'd tell you that I wouldn't touch a fish decoy that cost more than fifty bucks with a ten-foot pole. I know these wooden wonders continue to thrive in the face of controversy, but if the stories about auctioneers with fresh fish on their hands and shills running up prices to enhance a $250,000 collection are true, it is only a question of time until the controversy kills the market and fish decoy collectors are left with empty nets. In my opinion, fish decoys are an "iffy" collectible and a poor choice for the long term. With the exception of rigged auctions, fish-decoy prices dropped in 1990 from the late-1980s values.

There *are* some fine old fish decoys hiding among the fakery, and if my words regarding the "fishy factor" fail to deter you I suggest you traffic only with honest dealers who guarantee what they sell in writing. Fish decoys have been touted as the next six-figure item of Americana by one or more collectors, but that is not going to happen in your or my lifetime. Fish decoys are nonetheless attractive and collectable; they may or may not increase in value as the market continues to rise and fall.

The following fish decoys were sold at auction or offered for sale in 1990.

KENNETH BRUNING: ROGER CITY, MICHIGAN

7" brook trout: Painted in green, orange, and yellow
with one small chip 1,300.00

6" trout decoy: In shades of red, orange, and yellow in excellent condition 900.00

14" whitefish: In pearlescent bronze and silver with a white belly. In excellent condition 1,150.00

VARIOUS MAKERS: LAKE CHAUTAUQUA, NEW YORK

Blended green-bodied fish: With leather tail 2,200.00

Blended black-and-grey fish: With red details 1,100.00

Brown fish with black and white spots 2,700.00

Circa 1870–80 perch: In brown and brown-red 3,750.00

Early 8" trout: In greens and brown 2,250.00

7" brook trout: Attributed to Harry Seymour. Circa 1880s 2,100.00

$7\frac{1}{4}$" trout: In red, black, and yellow 3,250.00

9" shiner: In shades of beige 1,100.00

7" trout: Attributed to Seymour 1,750.00

8" rainbow trout: Attributed to Marvin Willard. Circa 1880s 2,100.00

Circa-1890 "Mr X" bass: In green and maroon 1,300.00

Early fish decoy from Lake Chautauqua, New York. (Courtesy Oliver's Auction Galleries)

6½" chub: In blended shades of brown 900.00

6" steelhead: From Maple Springs, NY 1,000.00

7¼" perch: With carving details and leather tail 1,600.00

8" trout: In brown, red, yellow, and white 600.00

Trout: With "happy smiling face" 300.00

6" brown trout: In brown, black, and white 550.00

Another: Same carver 550.00

7¼" river chub: Reportedly from Mayville, NY 500.00

6½" fish: In natural wood with replaced tail 350.00

8" fish: In natural wood and black 500.00

6" chub: With "small pinched face" 250.00

ISAAC GOULETTE: NEW BALTIMORE, MICHIGAN

9" perch: With unusual paint pattern
and minor chipping 600.00

6½" herring: In green and silver. Excellent 400.00

4½" white shiner: In all-white paint 150.00

OSCAR PETERSON: CADILLAC, MICHIGAN

7½" trout: With iridescent gold sides 2,300.00

8½" sucker: In beige with original "$1.25"
price on belly 1,200.00

7" brook trout: In tan with red and black accents 1,300.00

5" sucker: In green with golden sides and belly 1,600.00

5½" perch: In green and yellow with black stripes 1,250.00

7" perch: With tack eyes. Worn. 250.00

A nine-inch brown trout decoy by Oscar Peterson, circa 1910–20. (Courtesy Oliver's Auction Galleries)

9" brown trout: In unusual paint pattern 5,500.00

7" perch: Showing considerable wear 550.00

Shiner: With in-use wear 650.00

8" rainbow trout: With tack eyes and minor flaking . . . 2,500.00

6" brook trout: With minor chipping 1,800.00

JESS RAMEY: CADILLAC, MICHIGAN

6" fish decoy: In olive brown and
with original "$1.50" 450.00

7" sucker: With carved eyes in shades of brown 500.00

Other carvers of note include Otto Bishop, Leroy Howell, and so many others that the serious fish-decoy collector will benefit greatly from the Kimball family's fine books: *The Fish Decoy,* volumes I and II. These two books comprise the "bible" for fish-decoy collectors, and if you look closely in volume II, you might even see this author's name there.

SINK OR SWIM

Almost ten years ago I wrote an article about fish decoys wherein I suggested serious collectors of these things always take a pail of water with them when contemplating purchasing a fish decoy. If one puts it in the water and it floats, it's a fake, I wrote. It's true. Fish decoys are supposed to sink, and if they don't . . . caveat emptor piscator.

SPORTING FIREARMS

We are concerned here with "sporting" firearms—those rifles and shotguns used in the pursuit of sport afield, on the target range, and on skeet and trap fields. Pistols can properly fit the target-shooting guidelines, but they are not truly sporting firearms and are therefore not included.

Sporting firearms fall into two general categories and each of these divides further into many more. Basically, there are either breech-loading or muzzle-loading firearms. Each then is classified as a shotgun or fowling piece, or a small-bore or large-bore rifle. Add to this the five types of ignition that have been used over the years, from matchlock and wheel-lock to today's self-contained cartridges and shot shells, and you begin to see what a vast number of possibilities are available to the beginning collector. Let's begin with the famous American Kentucky rifle: A sporting firearm that goes hand in hand with our nation's history from our earliest Colonial days to the years just before the Civil War.

The finest Kentucky rifles were made not in Kentucky, but in Pennsylvania, and the name derives from their use on the then-frontier of Kentucky and Tennessee. A classic Kentucky rifle will be a flintlock, full-stocked in fancy tiger or curly maple with fine brass fittings, including a fancy brass patchbox in the stock. The cost for an example such as this can run to six figures but goes down quickly for those that have been converted from flintlock to percussion and have less than full-length stocks. The Kentucky style

---

BEWARE THOSE LOVELY DAMASCUS BARRELS

All too many collectors purchase breech-loading double-barrel shotguns with Damascus or twist-steel barrels, then decide to fire them with modern ammunition. You can get hurt doing this and, even more painful, you can ruin a fine firearm. Don't do it!

---

rifle of the mid-1800s is often called a "plains rifle," because these were the guns that went West with the early settlers. Examples of these later firearms are far less costly than are true early-type Kentucky rifles, but still command top dollar, particularly if made by a famous maker or if they have historic significance.

The development of the breech-loading rifle and shotgun and the coming of the Civil War combined to change firearms forever. The war issued in mass-produced American firearms, and the breech-loader opened the way for all that followed, including the lever action, pump or slide action, and the semiautomatics we know and use today.

It goes without saying that these developments also opened up an entire field of sporting firearms for today's collectors. Names like A. H. Fox, Baker, Ballard, Lefever, and L. C. Smith competed for attention in a time of plenty, and American sporting firearms were plentiful and available at prices to fit all pocketbooks. It is fair to say that these and other American and European firearms makers set the table that we savor to this day. Prices are up and the pickings increasingly meager, but the table is far from bare and it is still possible to pick up a fine morsel if you persevere.

Collecting sporting firearms is a costly proposition and no one should approach it lightly. Before you purchase even one gun, learn all you can about whatever it is you have elected to collect. Read one or more of the many fine books on gun collecting in general, and everything you can find about your specific area of interest. Talk to other collectors and go to gun shows. Visit a gun collection in a museum if possible, and arm yourself for competition in every way you can.

There are a variety of ways to purchase collectable sporting firearms.

FEDERAL AND STATE FIREARMS REGULATIONS

Laws regarding the interstate sale of firearms can pose problems for collectors, as can those imposed by state and local governments. Interstate laws are enforced by the federal government, state and municipal regulations by those governing bodies respectively. Learn the law before you buy. You may want to consider a dealer's license. Information may be obtained from the National Rifle Association, local gun clubs, and law enforcement agencies.

The safest way is by working with reliable and trustworthy dealers who stand behind what they sell. Guns are also sold through mail-order advertisements and at numerous firearms auctions. It is a good rule never to buy a mail-order gun unless the right to return it in a reasonable length of time is clearly guaranteed. Buying firearms at auction is a common practice, but unless you have seen the merchandise or have some one in attendance who faithfully represents your best interests, I suggest you pass.

After you have decided what you are going to collect, how to go about acquiring whatever that is, and made certain you are in compliance with federal and all other laws, your two remaining concerns are security and insurance. No one in his or her right mind is going to spend the money it costs to put a decent collection of sporting firearms together only to have it stolen or destroyed. Insurance is relatively simple. Security, which almost all of today's insurance companies will require, can cost more than you think; both these matters deserve serious consideration before you begin to amass a collection. What you are after in the way of insurance is a "fine arts floater policy" that not only covers what you have on hand, but will protect anything you add as well. If your agent cannot provide this, find one that can. Also find out from your agent just what kind of home security is required, so as to make absolutely certain your policy fully covers your collection. This will vary greatly from one part of the country to another, but whatever is required is what you gotta have—so get it. (This type of insurance applies to fine art, decoys, and other sporting collectibles, as well. As I said, you gotta have it.)

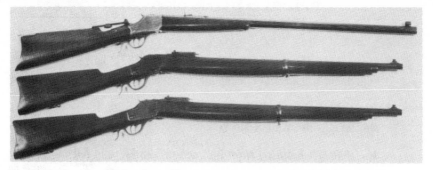

Top, Winchester single-shot rifle, and two single-shot muskets. (Courtesy James Julia)

One last thought regarding a collection of fine firearms is to keep your guns locked up and your lip buttoned. It is human nature to want to show off your collection, but if you want to keep it, the fewer people who know about it, the better.

Two things about the following listing of values should be noted: First, the list, with some exceptions, includes only sporting firearms made in this century; and second, the values given are either actual "for sale" prices or a compilation of selling prices from a wide variety of sources. Antique sporting firearms will be given full treatment in the next edition of this guide. When referring to the prices listed, always remember that values of sporting firearms vary greatly from one part of the country to another and from one season to another, but the most important consideration is the overall condition of any given example. The prices that follow here are for fine firearms in excellent condition; those in lesser condition are worth proportionately less and those with exceptional engraving, fancy wood, or historic significance are often worth considerably more. It is impossible to properly evaluate a given firearm without seeing it, and, with this in mind, I trust you will use the list as it is intended—as an estimate of retail price.

Sporting Rifles

ANSCHUTZ

Model 54: Caliber .22 LR, hardwood stock, checkered.
Tapped for scope 750.00

Model 1411 Match rifle: Bolt action, .22 LR, 27½″ barrel, adjustable trigger and cheekplate 700.00

Model 1418 Sporter: Bolt action, .22 LR with 5- or 10-shot magazine. Walnut stock 300.00

Model 1427B Biathlon rifle: Bolt action, .22 LR, clip fed with two-stage trigger 750.00

Model 1433: Bolt-action sporter in .22-Hornet with a 5-shot magazine. Walnut stock. Light pitting 450.00

Another: As above. Fine overall condition 725.00

Model 1813 Super Match: Single-shot bolt action with 27¼″ barrel, adjustable trigger and cheekplate, select walnut stock 1,200.00

Browning rifles were made for import in three locations: Belgium, Finland, and Japan. Several models were made in both Belgium and Japan, and these locations are noted in the following listings because they do affect value.

BROWNING

.22 automatic rifle: Grade I made in Belgium 300.00

Another: As above, but made in Japan 200.00

.22 automatic rifle: Grade II made in Belgium 450.00

Another: As above, but made in Japan 250.00

.22 automatic rifle: Grade III made in Belgium 1,000.00

Another: As above, but made in Japan 600.00

BAR automatic rifle: Grade I. Various calibers, French walnut stock and forearm. Excellent 500.00

Another: As above, but Grade II. Excellent 1,050.00

Another: As above. Fine condition 650.00

Another: As above, but Grade III. As-new 995.00

BLR lever-action rifle: .308 caliber. Mint 325.00

BPR .22 caliber pump rifle: Fine 175.00

High-power bolt-action rifle, Safari grade:
  Short action (various calibers) Finland 650.00
  Medium action (various calibers) Finland 700.00
  Standard action (various calibers) Belgium 750.00

CHARTER ARMS

AR-7 Explorer survival rifle: Plastic stock is hollow to
contain 16″ stainless barrel. 8-shot .22 LR 85.00

COLT INDUSTRIES

Lightning magazine rifle: .22 caliber made with round
barrel and three-size frames.
Mfg. 1887–1904. Excellent 750.00

As above: Various calibers. Round and octagon barrels.
Discontinued in 1902. Excellent 1,000.00

Lightning carbine: As above. 20″ barrel. Excellent 1,500.00

Lightning Baby carbine: As above with lighter frame . . .   2,500.00

Coltsman bolt-action sporting rifle:
  Deluxe model with Mauser action
  and various calibers 350.00
  Custom model with Mauser action
  and various calibers 400.00
  Standard model with Mauser action
  and various calibers 300.00

Note: 1957 and 1961 models with actions by Sako are priced as the above by
grade.

COLT-SAUER RIFLES

Colt-Sauer rifles were made for Colt by J. P. Sauer and imported for sale by Colt Industries beginning in 1973. The Standard, Short-Action, and Magnum models were sold without sights. The listed prices are for firearms in excellent condition.

Colt-Sauer sporting rifle:

Standard model with Sauer non-rotating bolt action,
various calibers, with walnut cheekpiece stock 800.00

Short-Action model in various calibers 800.00

Magnum model in various magnum calibers 900.00

Grand Alaskan model in 375 H&H caliber 1,000.00

Grand African model in 458 Win. Mag. caliber 1,000.00

HARRINGTON & RICHARDSON

Model 60 Reising semiautomatic rifle: 45 automatic
caliber with 12- and/or 20-shot magazine. Excellent . . .   400.00

Model 65 Military: .22 LR with 10-shot magazine.
Plain stock with "Garand" dimensions.
USMC training rifle 275.00

Model 150 Leatherneck autoloader: Worn 85.00

Model 151 autoloader: With Redfield sights. Excellent . .   150.00

Model 157 single-shot: With
shotgun-type action. Good 50.00

Model 158 Topper Jet: With interchangeable barrels.
Rem Jet barrel interchanges with 30-30, .410,
and 20 gauge barrels 100.00

With extra barrel add 25.00

Model 250 Sportster: Bolt action .22 LR with 5-shot
magazine and open sights 65.00

Model 265 "Reg'lar": Bolt action .22 LR. 10-shot
magazine, Lyman #55 rear sight 75.00

Model 300 "Ultra" bolt-action rifle: Various calibers,
with Mauser-style action. Excellent 400.00

Model 301 Carbine: As above
with Mannlicher stocking 400.00

Model 317 Ultra Wildcat: Bolt-action rifle with
Sako short action. Various "hot" calibers.
Overall very good 350.00

Model 360 Ultra Automatic rifle: Gas-operated
semiautomatic in 243 Win. caliber. Checkered
rollover stock. Fair 150.00

Another: As above. In excellent condition 350.00

Model 422 slide action: .22 repeating rifle. Fine 95.00

Model 700 autoloading rifle: In .22 magnum caliber with
Monte Carlo stocking of walnut 150.00

Model 750: Bolt-action .22 caliber single-shot rifle 75.00

REPLICA RIFLES BY H & R

Harrington and Richardson produced fine replica rifles during the 1970s and early 1980s. All were based on the Springfield Cavalry Carbine and made in 45–70 caliber. Values of the various issues are from $200 to $3,500 in new unfired condition.

Model 751: As above, with
Mannlicher-style stocking 75.00

Targeteer Junior: Bolt-action .22 LR. Scaled down
"junior" size target stocking. Excellent 100.00

Model 5200: Turn-bolt repeater .22 LR. Adjustable
trigger, classic walnut stock, and
peep sights. Excellent 300.00

Model 5200 match rifle: As above with target barrel . . .   300.00

HIGH STANDARD

Flite-King pump action: .22 caliber rifle. Excellent 125.00

Hi-Power field grade bolt-action rifle: Various calibers.
Mauser-type action. Excellent 200.00

Hi-Power Deluxe: As above with Monte Carlo-style
fine walnut stocking 275.00

Sport-King field grade autoloader: .22 caliber rifle 85.00

Sport-King special grade: As above with
Monte Carlo stock 100.00

Sport-King deluxe grade: As above, but checkered stock   125.00

Sport-King carbine: .22 caliber rifle with straight stock
and 18" barrel 125.00

HOLLAND & HOLLAND

Magazine Rifle—Best Quality: Various calibers with
either Mauser or Enfield action and French
walnut stock. As-new 5,500.00

Add for deluxe-grade wood and engraving 500.00

Royal Hammerless Ejector Double Rifle: Various
calibers, side lock, French walnut cheekpiece

stocking. As new 9,500.00

Deluxe model: With exhibition stock and engraving . . . 24,500.00

ITHACA GUN COMPANY

Model 49 Saddlegun: Lever-action rifle. .22 caliber with
western carbine stock 85.00

Six other models are priced from . . . .   75.00 to 200.00

Model 72 saddlegun: .22 caliber rifles priced at 150.00

Model LSA–55 standard grade bolt-action rifle: Various
calibers, checkered walnut stock. Excellent 300.00

Model LSA–55 deluxe grade 375.00

Model LSA–55 heavy barrel 400.00

For Model LSA–65's, see above

Model X5–C Lightning: Autoloading rifle. 7-shot clip. .22
LR with 22″ barrel 125.00

Model X5–T Lightning: Autoloading rifle with 16-shot
tubular magazine. Caliber .22 LR 125.00

IVER JOHNSON

Model X bolt-action .22 caliber rifle 100.00
Model 2X: As above with heavier barrel and stock 125.00

MANNLICHER-SCHOENAUER

Model 1903 bolt-action sporting carbine: Caliber 6.5 ×
53mm with full-length stock. Excellent 1,200.00

Model 1924 carbine: As above, but 30–06 caliber 1,200.00

Model 1950 bolt-action rifle 1,000.00

Model 1950 carbine 850.00

Model 1952 improved carbine: Various calibers 1,000.00

Model 1952 improved sporting rifle: Various calibers . . .   1,200.00

MARLIN FIREARMS COMPANY

Model 18 slide action: Repeater with exposed hammer.
.22 caliber with tubular magazine and plain
stock. Very fine 275.00

Model 20 slide action: Repeater. .22 caliber with 24″
octagon barrel and tubular magazine. Fine 225.00

Model 36 Lever Action: Repeating rifle. Various calibers,
once called "Model 1936." Excellent 300.00

Model 38 slide-action repeating rifle: 24″ octagon bbl.,
.22 caliber tubular magazine. Very good 165.00

Model 39 lever-action repeating rifle: .22 caliber with
tubular magazine. Excellent 400.00

Model 39A 90th Anniversary Rifle:
New unfired condition 500.00

Model 322 bolt-action varmint rifle: Sako short action.
Caliber 222 Rem in 3-shot clip. Excellent 350.00

Model 336 sporting carbine: Various calibers with a 20″
barrel. Very good 150.00

Model 336 Micro Grove Zipper: Chambered for the 219
Zipper cartridge. Excellent 500.00

Other 336 models are priced from 150.00 to 250.00

Model 444 lever-action repeating rifle 200.00

Model 455 bolt-action Sporter: Mauser action, Sako
trigger, various calibers, Monte Carlo stocking 375.00

Marlin-Glenfield models priced from 50.00 to 150.00

MAUSER SPORTING RIFLES

Bolt-action sporting carbine: Pre-WWI. Various calibers, full stocking to muzzle. Excellent 750.00

Bolt-action sporting rifle: Pre-WWI. As above 900.00

The following .22 caliber rifles are pre-WWII: Prices are for rifles in excellent condition.

Model DSM34 . . . . 400.00
Model EL320 . . . . 250.00
Model ES340 . . . . 300.00
Model ES340B 325.00
Model ES350 . . . . 400.00
Model ES350B 350.00
Model KKW 400.00
Model M410 . . . . 350.00
Model MM410B 400.00
Model MS420B 400.00

Type "A" bolt-action sporting rifle: Various calibers. Many options and variations available at that time. Pre-WWII 650.00

Type "B" bolt-action sporting rifle: As above 700.00

Type "M" bolt-action sporting carbine: As above 600.00

Type "S" bolt-action sporting carbine: As above 700.00

Post-WWII Mauser models:

Model 66S standard bolt-action sporting rifle: Various calibers, Monte Carlo cheekpiece stock. Excellent condition 1,000.00

Model 66S Ultra: As above but with 20.9" barrel. Excellent 1,250.00

Extra barrels for above, each 225.00

Model 2000 bolt-action sporting rifle: Various calibers in 5-shot magazine. Checkered walnut stock. As new 300.00

Model 3000 bolt-action sporting rifle: Various calibers, 5-shot magazine, Monte Carlo stocking. Excellent . . .   450.00

Model 3000 Magnum: As above with 3-shot magazine. As new 600.00

O. F. MOSSBERG & SONS

Model 10: single-shot bolt-action .22	75.00
Model 14	60.00
Model 20	75.00
Model 25	50.00
Model 35 target grade: single-shot .22	125.00
Model 40 bolt-action repeater: Tubular feed	50.00
Model 42 bolt-action repeater: 7-shot box magazine . . .	50.00
Model 43	80.00
Model 44	60.00
Model 44B Target Model: .22	125.00
Model 45	60.00
Model 46 bolt-action repeater: Tubular feed .22	65.00
Model 50 autoloading .22 LR: Tubular feed	85.00
Model 51	100.00
Model 140B bolt-action sporter: Target .22 rifle	75.00
Model 142	75.00
Model 144. 22 target rifle	135.00
Model 151K autoloading .22 rifle	125.00
Model 152	110.00
Model 320B	85.00
Model 321	75.00
Model 333	85.00
Model 340K: Hammerless bolt-action .22 rifle	65.00
Model 341	65.00
Model 346K	75.00

PEDERSEN-MOSSBERG

A division of O. F. Mossberg, Pedersen Custom Guns produced three models of their Model 3000 based on the Mossberg 810 action during the mid-1970s. These richly enhanced rifles command prices from $500 to $800 and the Pedersen Model 4700 (Mossberg 472) lever-action rifle goes for about $225.

Model 350K autoloading .22 rifle	85.00
Model 351K	75.00
Model 352K	75.00
Model 353	75.00
Model 377	75.00
Model 380	80.00
Model 400: Palomino lever-action .22 Rifle	90.00
Model 402: As above. Carbine	110.00
Model 430: Automatic .22 Rifle	65.00
Model 432	60.00
Model 472 brush gun: 30-30 caliber	175.00
Model 472: Lever-action rifle. Various calibers	150.00
As above: Carbine	150.00
Model 640K: Hammerless bolt-action .22 RF magnum . .	75.00
Model 800 bolt-action centerfire rifle: Various calibers . .	200.00
Model 810: Various calibers	200.00
As above: Magnum calibers	225.00

PARKER-HALE LTD

Model 1200 super bolt-action rifle: Various calibers. 24″ barrel, European walnut stock with Monte Carlo cheekpiece. As-new	300.00
Model 1200 super magnum	350.00
Model 1200V	350.00

JAMES PURDY and SONS LTD

Purdy Single Rifle: With Mauser-type action, 3-shot magazine, 24″ barrel, and cheekpiece stock.
Various calibers. Excellent 4,500.00

Purdy double rifle: With side-lock action, ejectors, cheekpiece stocking in various calibers. Excellent 20,000.00

REMINGTON ARMS COMPANY

Number 2 sporting rifle: Single shot, rolling block action, with various calibers and barrel lengths 350.00

Number 3 sporting rifle: Single shot, Hepburn falling block action in various calibers and barrel lengths . . .   750.00

Number 3 high power 1,500.00

Number 4 single-shot rifle: Rolling block. Various calibers 225.00

Number 4 military: .22 caliber single-shot rifle also known as the "Boy Scout Rifle" 400.00

Number 5 special rifle: Rolling block action, various calibers and barrel lengths. Made for export 250.00

ANTIQUE VS. MODERN

Firearms made before 1898 are, for the most part, considered antique and free from the rules and regulations placed on modern firearms by the federal government. Lacking a better delineation between antique and modern firearms, I have used that date for the purposes of this book. Modern firearms are included here, and antique American firearms will be featured in the next edition of this guide. There are exceptions to all things and you will discover mine quite easily, but don't leave yourself open to penalty when it comes to local, state, and federal regulations. Check them out before you buy any firearms.

WHAT'S IN A NUMBER?

Early Remington firearms were designated by number, whereas modern guns carry the designation "model," and this can lead to considerable confusion if you're not on your toes. The Remington Number 4 was a single-shot rifle made from 1890 to 1933, while the Remington Model 4 is an autoloading rifle that went into production in 1981. The same applies to other number or model Remington firearms as well.

As above: Sporting model 300.00

Number 6 takedown rifle 150.00

Number 7 target and sporting rifle: Single shot. Rolling
block action, various calibers. Army
pistol frame. Excellent 600.00

Model 4 autoloading rifle: Various calibers, 22″ barrel,
open sights, and Monte Carlo stocking. As-new 375.00

As above: Peerless grade 1,250.00

As above: Premier grade 3,500.00

Remington Model 6: Slide-action repeating rifle. Various
calibers. Checkered Monte Carlo stocking 350.00

As above: Peerless grade 1,250.00

As above: Premier grade 3,500.00

Model 7 bolt-action repeating rifle 325.00

Model 12A: Slide-action .22
hammerless repeating rifle 250.00

Model 12B: .22 short only 250.00

Model 12CS: .22 WRF 225.00

Model 14A high-power slide-action repeating rifle: 22″
barrel, plain walnut stock. Excellent 350.00

Model 14R: As above, but 18½″ barrel carbine 350.00

Model 14½ rifle 600.00

Model 14½ carbine 700.00

Model 16 autoloading rifle: Various .22 calibers. Tubular
magazine and plain straight-grip walnut
stock. Very good 200.00

Model 24A autoloading rifle: Tubular magazine for .22
short and long only. Open sights,
straight-grip stock. Excellent 300.00

Model 25A: Slide-action repeating rifle 350.00

Model 25R: As above, but 18″ barrel carbine 400.00

Model 30A bolt-action Express: Standard grade 550.00

Model 30R carbine 600.00

Model 30S sporting rifle 650.00

Model 33: Single shot .22 rifle 100.00

Model 33NRA target rifle 150.00

Model 34 bolt-action repeating .22 rifle 150.00

Model 34NRA target rifle 165.00

Model 37 Rangemaster bolt-action target rifle: .22 caliber
with magazine and single-shot adapter.
Target stock. Excellent 450.00

As above: With "Miracle trigger/Randle stock" 450.00

Model 40X centerfire rifle: Various calibers, adjustable
trigger, high comb stock. With Redfield sights 450.00

Model 40X heavyweight	300.00
Model 40X standard	300.00
Model 40XB	600.00
Model 40XB match rifle	650.00
Model XB Rangemaster .22 caliber rifle	400.00
Model XB Varmint Special: Various calibers	775.00
Model XBBR Bench Rest rifle: Various calibers	700.00
Model XC National Match Course rifle	700.00

Model 40–XR Custom Sporter rifle:

Grade I	850.00
Grade II	1,550.00
Grade III	2,500.00
Grade IV	3,750.00

Model 41A Targetmaster: Bolt-action .22 single-shot rifle	125.00
Other models to	150.00
Model 81A Woodmaster: Autoloading rifle. Various calibers, 5-shot magazine, open sights, plain walnut stock. Excellent	375.00
Model 121A	250.00
Model 121S	300.00
Model 121SB: Smoothbore	350.00
Model 141A Gamemaster: Slide-action repeating rifle. 5-shot magazine, various calibers, open sights. Excellent	350.00
Model 241A Speedmaster: .22 caliber autoloading rifle . .	275.00
Model 341 Sportsmaster: Models to	125.00

Model 510 Targetmaster: Models to 125.00

Model 511 Scoremaster: Models to 125.00

Model 512 Sportsmaster: Models to 140.00

Model 513S Sporting: .22 bolt-action rifle 225.00

Model 513TR Matchmaster 240.00

Model 514 bolt action: .22 caliber rifles to 125.00

Model 521 TL Target: Bolt-action .22 LR 135.00

Model 540X: Models to 250.00

Model 541S Custom Sporter: .22 caliber bolt action, 24″
barrel, and checkered walnut stocking 350.00

Model 541–T 250.00

Model 550A: .22 caliber autoloading rifle 125.00

Other models to 150.00

Model 552: .22 caliber autoloaders to 150.00

Model 572: .22 caliber slide actions to 150.00

Model 580: .22 caliber single-shot rifles to 100.00

Model 581: .22 caliber bolt-action repeating rifles to . . .   140.00

Model 582: Tubular .22 caliber bolt-action repeater . . .   125.00

Model 591 . . . .   200.00

Model 592 . . . .   200.00

Model 600: Bolt-action carbine. Various calibers,
$18\frac{1}{2}″$ barrel, open sights, and Monte
Carlo stocking. As-new 400.00

As above: Magnum model 575.00

CENTENNIAL AND COMMEMORATIVE MODELS

Many firearms manufacturers have issued both centennial and commemorative models in limited editions. These firearms are not listed here, but will be featured in a future issue of this guide if the demand is forthcoming from readers. Let me hear from you about this.

Model 660 bolt-action carbine: Various calibers, 20″ barrel, walnut Monte Carlo stocking. Excellent 455.00

As above: Magnum model 525.00

Model 700ADL centerfire bolt-action rifle: Various calibers, checkered walnut stocking. Excellent 300.00

As above: 7mm Rem magnum 325.00

As above: Classic 300.00

As above: Classic magnum 350.00

Model 700 custom bolt-action rifle:
  Grade I 900.00
  Grade II 1,500.00
  Grade III 2,500.00
  Grade IV 4,000.00

Other Model 700s priced from . . . .   350.00 to 2,250.00

Model 721A: Bolt-action high-power rifle. Excellent . . .   250.00

As above: Magnum 400.00

Other Model 721s priced from . . . .   300.00 to 500.00

Model 722 bolt-action sporting rifles: Various calibers. . . . .   250.00 to 375.00

*Model 725 ADL bolt-action repeating
rifle:* Various calibers 350.00

Model 725 Kodiak Magnum 700.00

Model 740A Woodmaster autoloading rifle: Either 30–06
or 308 caliber. Gas-operated, 22″ barrel. Excellent 250.00

As above: Deluxe grade 300.00

As above: Deluxe special grade 325.00

Model 742 Woodmaster automatic big-game rifle: Various
calibers, 22″ barrel, checkered stock,
4-shot clip. Excellent 300.00

As above: Custom grade 335.00

As above: Peerless grade 850.00

As above: Premier grade 2,250.00

Model 742 carbine 350.00

Model 760 Gamemaster slide-action repeating rifle:
  Standard grade 275.00
  Deluxe grade 300.00
  Custom grade 300.00
  Peerless grade 1,250.00
  Premier grade 2,500.00
  Carbine 300.00

Model 788 centerfire bolt-action rifle: Various calibers,
22″ and 24″ barrels, plain walnut stock. Excellent 200.00

As above: Left-hand model 225.00

Model 7400 autoloader 300.00

Model 7600 rifle 275.00

As above: Carbine 300.00

International Free rifle: Various rim
and centerfire calibers 650.00

International Match Free rifle 700.00
Nylon rifles priced from . . . .   50.00 to 100.00

RUGER

Number One standard rifle: Various calibers, 26" barrel,
checkered stocking. Excellent 300.00

Number One Light Sporter 375.00

Number One Special Varminter 375.00

Number One Medium Sporter 400.00

Number One Tropical rifle 450.00

Model 44 standard autoloading carbine 250.00

Model 44–RS carbine 275.00

Model 44 Sporter 325.00

Model 44 International 500.00

Model 77 bolt-action rifle: Various calibers and action
stroke, scope-mount or round-top receiver,
checkered walnut stock:
  Model R5 . . . .   300.00
  Model 338 Win. magnum 325.00
  Model RS from . . . .   350.00 to 500.00
  Model ST from . . . .   300.00 to 350.00

Model M–77 Ultra Light rifle 350.00

As above: Carbine 325.00

Model 77V Varmint Rifle 325.00

Model 77/22R bolt-action rifle 275.00

Model 10/22 standard autoloading carbine: 10-shot rotary magazine, 18½″ barrel. Excellent 150.00

Model 10/22 Sporter 175.00

Model 10/22 Deluxe Sporter 185.00

Model 10/22 International 375.00

SAKO

Classic bolt-action rifle: Various calibers, walnut stock, and A-II bolt action. Excellent 650.00

Deluxe (Grade A–I) 675.00

Deluxe (Grade A–II) 700.00

Deluxe (Grade A–III) 750.00

Deluxe lightweight bolt-action rifle 850.00

Fiberglass bolt action rifle 800.00

Finnbear Sporter: Long Mauser-type bolt action, various calibers, Monte Carlo cheekpiece stocking 550.00

Finnbear Carbine 700.00

Finnwolf lever-action rifle: Various calibers, 23″ barrel, Monte Carlo stocking. Very good 600.00

Forester Sporter: Medium Mauser-type bolt action, various calibers, Monte Carlo cheekpiece stock 575.00

Forester carbine 575.00

Forester heavy barrel 575.00

High-Power Mauser sporting rifle: FN Mauser action, various calibers, Monte Carlo cheekpiece stock. Excellent 450.00

Hunter lightweight bolt-action rifle:
Short action . . . .   550.00 to 600.00
Medium action 600.00
Long action . . . .   600.00 to 800.00
Left-handed models add . . . .   300.00 to 400.00

Magnum Mauser 625.00

Standard grade bolt-action rifle:
Short action 500.00
Medium action 600.00
Long action 600.00
Deluxe grade of any of the above 1,500.00

Vixen Sporter: Short Mauser-type action, various
calibers, Monte Carlo cheekpiece stocking. Excellent . .   550.00

As above: Carbine 700.00

As above: Heavy barrel 575.00

Model 72 . . . .   500.00

Model 73 lever-action rifle 550.00

Model 74 bolt-action carbine: With Mannlicher stocking   575.00

Other Model 74 rifles . . . .   550.00 to 625.00

Model 78 Super Hornet Sporter 400.00

Model 78 Super Rimfire Sporter 350.00

J. P. SAUER & SON

Sauer-Mauser bolt-action sporting rifle: Various calibers,
half-octagon barrel, walnut
cheekpiece stock. Excellent 900.00

SAVAGE

Model 3 bolt-action single-shot .22 rifle 100.00

Model 3–S 125.00

Model 3–ST 100.00

Model 4 bolt-action repeating .22 rifle 100.00

Model 4–S 120.00

Model 5 bolt-action repeating .22 rifle 75.00

Model 5–S 90.00

Model 6 autoloading .22 rifle 125.00

Model 7 autoloading .22 rifle 100.00

Model 19 bolt-action .22 target rifle 200.00

Other Model 19 .22 rifles . . . .   200.00 to 350.00

Model 23 bolt-action sporting
rifles: Various calibers . . . .   175.00 to 300.00

Model 25 slide-action repeating .22 rifle 250.00

Model 29 slide-action .22 rifle 275.00

Model 40 bolt-action sporting rifle: Various calibers,
22/24″ barrel by caliber, plain walnut stocking 275.00

Model 45 Super Sporter: As above with checkering and
with Lyman sight 350.00

SAVAGE-ANSCHUTZ/SAVAGE-STEVENS

Beginning in 1965, Savage began importing .22 caliber rifles made by J. G. Anschutz of West Germany, and beginning in 1969 they added the Stevens name on another line of .22 caliber rifles. Fine Savage-Anschutz rifles are valued from $250 to $500, and those with the Savage-Stevens designation run from $65 to $85 in fine condition.

Model 60 autoloading .22 rifle 75.00

Model 63–K: Single-shot .22 rifle. Trigger
lock and key 75.00

As above: Magnum .22 rimfire 75.00

Model 90 autoloading .22 carbine 85.00

Model 99 lever-action repeating rifle:
Various calibers, styles and stockings,
in production since 1899 in one form or another.
This popular rifle is priced from . . . .   250.00 to 1,200.00

Model 110 Sporter bolt-action repeating rifle: Various
calibers, stockings, and sights. Introduced in the 1950s,
these rifles are priced from . . . .   200.00 to 750.00

Model 111 Chieftan bolt-action rifle 275.00

Model 112V varmint rifle: Various calibers 250.00

Model 170 centerfire pump-action rifle:
Various calibers 150.00

As above: Carbine 150.00

Model 219 single-shot rifle: Top-lever shotgun action . .   75.00

Model 219–L: As above with side-lever 85.00

Model 221 utility gun: 30/30. Action as 219–L 100.00

Model 340 bolt-action repeater: Various calibers, 22/24″
barrels, plain and checkered stockings . . . . .   150.00 to 200.00

Model 340C: As above, but carbine 165.00

Model 340S: As above, but Deluxe 185.00

Model 1903 slide-action .22 repeater 200.00

1904 bolt-action single-shot .22 rifle 100.00

1905 bolt-action single-shot .22 rifle 100.00

1909 slide-action .22 repeater 175.00

Model 1912 autoloading .22-LR rifle 350.00

Model 1914 slide-action .22 repeater 235.00

Model 1920 hi-power bolt-action rifle: Various calibers,
open sights, and checkered stocking 425.00

SMITH and WESSON

Model 1500 bolt action: Made by Husqvarna
for S&W. Various calibers, open sight,
American-walnut stock. Excellent 250.00

Model 1500 Deluxe 265.00

Model A bolt-action sporting rifle: Various
calibers, folding-leaf sight, checkered
Monte Carlo stock. Excellent 350.00

Model B 325.00

Model C 325.00

Model D 375.00

Model E 375.00

J. STEVENS ARMS CO

Number 12 Marksman single-shot rifle: Various calibers   135.00

Number 14$\frac{1}{2}$ Little Scout: .22 single-shot rifle 125.00

Model 15 . . . .   100.00

Model 15Y 100.00

Number 44 Ideal single-shot rifle: Lever action, rolling
block action. Various calibers 425.00

Number 44½: Falling block 475.00

Number 45 through 54: From . . . . 500.00 to 5,000.00

The above Stevens models included both rolling and falling block single-shot rifles, and refinements such as the Schuetzens and Pope barrels. They are very expensive and must be judged individually by knowledgeable experts.

Number 66 bolt-action repeating rifle 75.00

Number 70 visable loading slide-action repeating rifle . . 200.00

Model 87 autoloading rifle 125.00

Model 322 hi-power bolt-action carbine 175.00

Model 322S 200.00

Model 325 hi-power bolt-action 30-30 rifle 125.00

Model 325S 135.00

Number 414 Armory Model .22 single-shot rifle 375.00

Model 416 bolt-action .22 target rifle 175.00

Number 419 junior target model: Single-shot .22 rifle . . 75.00

Buckhorn Model .22 bolt-action rifles . . . . 75.00 to 125.00

Number 26 Crack Shot: Single-shot .22/32RF rifles . . . 125.00

Number 26¼ 135.00

Favorite #17 . . . . 150.00

Favorite #18 . . . . 200.00

Favorite #19 . . . . 200.00

Favorite #20 . . . . 150.00

Favorite #27 . . . . 185.00

Favorite #28 . . . . 225.00

Favorite #29 . . . . 225.00

Walnut Hill Number 417–18: Single-shot rifles in various
.22 and .25 calibers from . . . . 475.00 to 800.00

Stevens-Springfield: .22 caliber rifles from . . . . 100.00 to 135.00

WALTHER

Model 1 autoloading rifle: Light model. Excellent 425.00
Model 2 autoloading rifle 400.00
Olympic bolt-action .22 single-shot match rifle 975.00
Model V bolt-action: Single-shot rifle 350.00
Model V Champion rifle: Meisterbuchse 425.00
Model GX–1 Free .22 LR rifle 800.00
Model KKJ Sporter .22 LR rifle 500.00
Model KKM International Match rifle 775.00
Model KKM–S 800.00
Model UIT Super Match rifle 650.00
Moving Target match rifle 550.00
Model 400 target rifle 550.00
Model SSV varmint rifle: .22 LR and 22-hornet 500.00

WEATHERBY

Deluxe rifle: Various calibers 850.00

Deluxe magnum rifle 900.00

Deluxe 378 magnum rifle 1,100.00

Vanguard bolt-action sporting rifle 350.00

Vanguard VGL 300.00

Mark V deluxe bolt-action sporting rifle: Various calibers,
right/left hand, Monte Carlo stocking from . . 600.00 to 1,750.00

Mark XXII Deluxe .22 automatic sporter 275.00

Mark XXII tubular magazine sporter 275.00

WESTLEY RICHARDS & CO, LTD

Best Quality magazine rifle: Various
calibers, 22/24" barrels, Mauser action,
French walnut stock. Excellent 4,500.00

Best Quality double rifle: Various calibers,
detachable box locks, French walnut stock
with cheekpiece. Excellent 18,500.00

WINCHESTER

Single-shot rifle: 3 models, various calibers, and 5 barrel weights.
Multitudinous options priced from . . . . . .   250.00 to 10,000.00

High-wall/Thick-wall 38 Express 2,400.00

Take-down high-wall musket .22LR 900.00

High-wall .22 short-musket 450.00

*Model 1885 Deluxe take-down high-wall .22 Target
Rifle:* With full Schutzen butt stock, Winchester A–5
scope in deluxe XXX wood. Excellent 6,600.00

Model 02 bolt-action single-shot .22 rifle 250.00

Model 02 Thumb Trigger .22 rifle 375.00

Model 03 self-loading .22 Win rim-fire rifle 275.00

**Winchester Deluxe take-down high-wall target rifle. (Courtesy James
Julia)**

WHAT'S IN A NAME?

What's in a name? A great deal if the name happens to be Winchester. All of the rifles, shotguns, knives, fishing tackle, roller skates (yes, roller skates and ice skates, too), and other "Winchester"-marked paraphernalia are in great demand and often overpriced and reproduced.

Model 04 bolt-action single-shot .22 rifle 200.00

Model 05 self-loading rifle: Various calibers 225.00

Model 06 slide-action repeating rifle 425.00

Model 07 self-loading rifle: 351 Win SL caliber 350.00

Model 10 self-loading rifle: 401 Win SL caliber 425.00

Model 43 bolt-action sporting rifle: Various calibers . . .   475.00

Model 43 special grade 675.00

Model 47 bolt-action single-shot .22 rifle 150.00

*Model 52 bolt-action .22 target
rifle:* Various models . . . .   400.00 to 600.00

Model 52 heavy barrel 600.00

Model 52 International Match 750.00

Other Model 52 .22 rifles . . . .   600.00 to 1,750.00

Model 53 lever-action repeater: Various calibers 975.00

Model 54 bolt-action high-power rifles . . . . .   500.00 to 1,200.00

Model 55 "Automatic" single-shot .22 rifle 100.00

Model 55 lever-action repeater:
Straight grip 700.00
Pistol grip 1,350.00

Model 56 bolt-action .22 sporting rifle 350.00

Model 57 bolt-action .22 target rifle 500.00

Model 58 bolt-action single-shot .22 rifle 250.00

Model 59 bolt-action single-shot .22 rifle 425.00

Model 60 bolt-action single-shot .22 rifle 125.00

Model 60A 500.00

Model 61 hammerless slide-action repeating .22 rifle . . . 475.00

Model 61 magnum 550.00

Model 62 visable hammer slide-action
repeating .22 rifle 400.00

Model 63 self-loading .22 rifle 550.00

Model 64 deer rifle: 30–30 Win special calibers 825.00

Model 64 lever-action repeater:
   Pre-1956 . . . . 525.00
   1970s models 275.00
   219 Zipper (1937–47) 1,500.00

Model 65 lever-action repeater: 25–20
and 32–20 calibers 1,250.00

As above: 218 Bee caliber 1,500.00

Model 67 bolt-action single-shot .22
rifle: Smooth-bore 95.00

As above: Boy's rifle 175.00

Model 68 bolt-action single-shot .22 rifle 150.00

Model 69 bolt-action repeating .22 rifle 175.00

As above: Match rifle 325.00

As above: Target rifle 150.00

DEMAND FOR WINCHESTER'S MODEL 70

Writing in the April 1937 issue of The Sportsman, *Colonel H. P. Sheldon announced: "The Winchester 70 is proving so in demand that the factory is miles behind in production . . . trying hard to catch up on the production of the .30/06 which seems to be the best seller." The demand goes on: Pre-1964 Model 70s are hard to come by.*

Pre-1964 Winchester Model 70s:

Standard grade (various calibers)	700.00
Super grade	1,500.00
Super grade (Featherweight)	1,500.00
Featherweight sporter	700.00
Target rifle	900.00
Varmint rifle	850.00
Westerner	900.00
Bull gun	650.00
Alaskan rifle	1,250.00
African rifle	2,500.00

Post-1964 Winchester Model 70s:

Standard grade	400.00
Deluxe grade	400.00
International match	650.00
Magnum . . . . 275.00 to	400.00
African	600.00
Target model	550.00
Varmint	450.00
Mannlicher stocking	500.00

1972-type Winchester Model 70s:

Standard	325.00
Other models . . . . 325.00 to	500.00

Model 70A: Various calibers 225.00

As above: Magnum 250.00

Model 71 lever-action repeater: Caliber 348 Win
   Standard grade 750.00
   Special grade 1,000.00

Model 72 bolt-action .22 repeater 175.00

Model 73 lever-action repeater: Various calibers and
magazine capacities. Plain stock. Excellent 6,000.00

Another 850.00

Another 1,000.00

Model 73: "One of One-thousand" . . . . ± 50,000.00

Model 74 self-loading .22 rifle 175.00

Model 75 bolt-action .22 target rifle 400.00

As above: Sporting rifle 450.00

Model 77 semiautomatic clip-type .22 rifle 150.00

Model 77 semiautomatic tubular-feed .22 rifle 150.00

Model 86 lever-action repeater: Various calibers 1,250.00

As above: Carbine 5,000.00

Model 88 lever-action rifle 425.00

As above: Carbine 475.00

Model 90 slide-action .22 repeater 500.00

Model 92 lever-action repeater: Various calibers 900.00

As above: Carbine 1,200.00

Model 94 carbines and rifles:
   Pre-WWII . . . . 350.00 to 1,000.00
   Pre-1964 . . . . 250.00 to 350.00

Current models . . . .   100.00 to 200.00

Commemorative models . . . .   400.00 to 2,000.00

Model 95 lever-action repeater: Various calibers 1,000.00

As above: Carbine 1,200.00

Model 100 autoloading rifle: Various calibers 425.00

As above: Carbine 475.00

Model 121 bolt-action single-shot .22 rifles . . . . .   75.00 to 85.00

Model 131 bolt-action repeating .22 rifle 85.00

Model 135 . . . .   100.00

Model 141 . . . .   100.00

Model 145 . . . .   100.00

Model 150 lever-action .22 carbine 85.00

Model 190 . . . .   85.00

As above: Carbine 100.00

Model 250 standard lever-action .22 rifle 100.00

*Model 255 standard lever-action .22
Win magnum rifle* 125.00

Model 270 standard slide-action .22 rifle 115.00

As above: Deluxe model 135.00

Model 275 standard .22 Win magnum rifle 125.00

As above: Deluxe model 145.00

Model 290 semiautomatic .22 rifle 135.00

As above: Deluxe model 135.00

Model 310 bolt-action .22 single-shot rifle 125.00

Model 320 bolt-action repeating .22 rifle 150.00

Model 490 semiautomatic .22 LR rifle 200.00

Model 670 bolt-action sporting rifle: Various calibers . .   200.00

As above: Carbine 220.00

As above: Magnum calibers 240.00

Model 770 sporting rifle 275.00

As above: Magnum calibers 300.00

Model 1900 bolt-action single-shot .22 rifle 125.00

Model 9422 lever-action .22 carbine 225.00

Model 9422M 250.00

Model 9422 Win-Cam 250.00

Model 9422 XTR 225.00

Ranger bolt-action carbine: Various calibers 250.00

As above: "Youth" model 250.00

*Ranger "Angle Eject" lever-action
carbine:* 30–30 caliber 200.00

Double Xpress rifle: 30–06 caliber. Over and under
double rifle made for Winchester in Japan 2,000.00

SHOTGUNS

BAKER SHOTGUNS

Batavia Leader hammerless double (various gauges and
barrels):
Plain ejectors 375.00

Automatic ejectors 450.00
Special model (plain wood, ejectors) 275.00
Ejector model (fancy wood, automatic ejectors) 725.00

Black Beauty Special (various gauges/barrels):
Plain ejectors 625.00
Automatic ejectors 725.00

Grade "S" (various gauges and barrels):
Plain ejectors 750.00
Automatic ejectors 850.00

Grade "R" (various gauges and barrels):
Plain ejectors 1,000.00
Automatic ejectors 1,250.00
Paragon grade: Various gauges and barrels . . . . . . to 1,750.00
Expert grade: Various gauges and barrels . . . . to 3,250.00
Deluxe grade: Various gauges and barrels . . . . to 5,000.00

THOSE LOVELY TWIST-STEEL BARRELS

Many early shotguns were made with twist steel, or Damascus, barrels and will not handle today's shot shells. In fact, they can blow up if modern shells are used. Designed for black-powder shells, these lovely barrels are far safer in the den on a wall than in the field on your shoulder.

BERETTA

Model 409BP: Over and under. Various gauges and
barrel lengths, plain ejectors, straight
or pistol-grip stocking 750.00

Model 410E 775.00

Model 410 magnum 950.00

Model 411E 1,200.00

Model 424 hammerless double: Box lock, 20 and 12
gauges, plain ejectors, straight-grip stock 700.00

Model 426E 875.00

Model 626 S/S hammerless double: 12 and 20 gauges . .   775.00

Model 682 O/U sporting shotgun: 12 gauge 1,500.00

Model A–301 autoloading shotgun:
Field gun 350.00
Magnum 375.00
Slug gun 350.00
Skeet gun 350.00
Trap gun 350.00

Model A–302 autoloading shotgun:
Fixed choke 375.00
Multichoke model 475.00
Custom grade (Super Lusso) 1,850.00

Model A–303 autoloading shotgun 525.00

Model AL–1 autoloading shotgun (12 and 20 gauges):
Field gun 300.00
Magnum 350.00
Skeet gun 375.00
Trap gun 350.00

Model AL–3 autoloading shotgun: 12
and 20 gauges . . . . 350.00 to 425.00

As above: Deluxe model 750.00

Model Asei over and under shotgun 1,000.00

Model "BL" over and under shotguns . . . . . 350.00 to 1,500.00

Model FS–1 folding single-shot shotgun 125.00

Silver Snipe over and under shotgun 400.00

Golden Snipe over and under shotgun 650.00

Model GR–2 hammerless double-barrel shotgun 600.00

As above: Model GR–3 . . . .   700.00

As above: Model GR–4 . . . .   800.00

Grade 100 over and under shotgun: 12 gauge 1,750.00

As above: Grade 200 . . . .   2,250.00

Model S55 over and under shotguns:
S55B 500.00
S56E 600.00
S58 (skeet) 750.00
S58 (trap) 700.00

Model SL–2 12 gauge pump gun 265.00

Model "SO" over and under shotguns (12 gauge):
SS–2 . . . .   3,250.00
SS–3 . . . .   5,250.00
SS–4 . . . .   6,500.00
SS–5 . . . .   8,250.00

Model "SO" hammerless double-barrel shotguns:
SO–6 . . . .   8,250.00
SO–7 . . . .   9,500.00

Model TR–1 single-barrel trap gun 225.00

BERNARDELLI

Brescia hammer double 700.00

Elio hammerless double 1,000.00

Uberto 1 hammerless double-barrel shotgun 700.00

> ### CREAM-OF-THE-CROP PRICES
>
> *The prices listed throughout this section of this book are for fine firearms in excellent condition. Any flaw will reduce the value.*

Uberto 2 . . . .   1,000.00

Italia double 1,000.00

Roma double-barrel shotguns:
Roma 3 . . . .   1,000.00
Roma 4 . . . .   975.00
Roma 6 . . . .   1,275.00

V.B. Liscio deluxe double-barrel shotgun: With Holland
and Holland-type side-lock, various barrels and stocks . .   5,000.00

BOSS & COMPANY
Hammerless double-barrel shotguns:
Double-trigger or nonselective single trigger . . . .   ± 17,500.00
Selective single trigger . . . .   ± 20,000.00

Hammerless over and under shotgun . . . .   ± 20,000.00

BROWNING
A–500 semiautomatic shotgun 425.00

Browning autoloading shotguns (various gauges):
Grade I (New York) 500.00
Special (New York) 600.00
Utility field (New York) 425.00
Skeet (New York) 500.00

Browning Automatic–5 shotguns (various gauges):
Standard (Made in Belgium) . . . .   500.00 to 600.00
Light 12 (Belgium) . . . .   650.00 to 700.00

BROWNING SHOTGUNS

Browning shotguns were made in Belgium and Japan, and during WWII at the Remington factory in Ilion, New York. These designations are of great interest and importance and are noted where there may be confusion.

Light 12 (Japan)	450.00
Light 20 (Belgium)	650.00 to 700.00
Light 20 (Japan)	475.00
Magnum 12 (Belgium)	650.00 to 750.00
Magnum 12 (Japan)	475.00
Magnum 20 (Belgium)	700.00 to 750.00
Magnum 20 (Japan)	475.00
Skeet model (Belgium)	650.00 to 750.00
Skeet model (Japan)	450.00
Buck Special (Belgium)	600.00
Buck Special (Japan)	475.00
Trap model	650.00
Sweet 16	650.00 to 800.00
Sweet 16 (new model)	475.00

Model B–80 gas-operated automatic:

Standard	425.00
Magnum	450.00
Superlight	425.00
Upland Special	450.00

Model BPS pump shotguns: All models	300.00 to 325.00
Model B–SS double-barrel shotgun:	
Standard (various gauges)	600.00
Side-lock model	1,500.00
20 gauge sporter	600.00

Model BT–99 single-barrel trap gun 625.00

As above: Competition grade 625.00

Superposed shotguns: hunting models:
Grade I standard 1,200.00
Grade I Lightning (pre-WWII models
are worth more): 1,500.00
Grade II Pigeon 1,850.00
Grade III Pointer 2,800.00
Grade IV Diana 3,000.00
Grade V Midas 4,800.00
Magnum 1,500.00
Skeet 12 and 20 gauge 1,500.00
Skeet 28 and .410 gauge 1,750.00
4-barrel skeet set 4,500.00

Superposed (reissue) . . . . 3,000.00 to 5,500.00

Superposed (presentation) . . . . 3,250.00 to 7,500.00

Twelvette double automatic 450.00

Twenty-weight double automatic 450.00

E. J. CHURCHILL, LTD.

Utility model hammerless
double-barrel shotgun . . . . 3,500.00 to 5,000.00

Premier hammerless double . . . . ± 12,500.00

Premier over and under shotgun . . . . ± 12,500.00

Modern "Churchill" shotguns: Are made
in Italy and Spain in a variety of models
and are priced from . . . . 400.00 to 10,000.00

COLT

Colt auto shotgun:
Ultra Light standard (12 and 20 gauges) 250.00

Ultra Light custom 300.00
Magnum 250.00
Magnum custom 450.00

Custom hammerless double 375.00

Standard pump shotgun 200.00

Custom pump 250.00

Colt-Sauer drilling: Box lock, set trigger, barrel selector,
12 gauge over 30–06 or 243 rifle barrel.
Made by Sauer 2,750.00

CHARLES DALY

Hammerless double-barrel shotgun: Various gauges, and
barrels. Box lock. Discontinued mid-1930s:
Superior grade 1,500.00
Empire grade 3,000.00
Diamond grade 5,000.00
Regent grade 7,500.00

Hammerless drilling: Many gauges
and barrel combinations . . . .   to 7,500.00

Over and under shotgun (various gauges)
pre-WWII . . . .   to 6,500.00
post-WWII . . . .   to 850.00

Commander over and under shotgun (various gauges):
Model 100 . . . .   550.00
Model 200 . . . .   750.00

*Empire grade hammerless double-barrel
shotgun:* Various gauges 600.00

Novamatic autoloading shotguns . . . .   300.00 to 350.00

Single-barrel trap gun:
Standard grade 5,000.00

Empire grade 6,000.00
Diamond grade 7,500.00
Superior grade (post-1968) 600.00

Field semiauto shotgun 265.00

Field III over and under shotgun 350.00

Multi-XII self-loading shotgun 375.00

Presentation grade over and under shotgun 750.00

Superior II grade over and under shotgun 450.00

Empire grade hammerless double-barrel shotgun 625.00

FOX SHOTGUNS

Sterlingworth hammerless shotguns: 12, 16, and 20
gauges. Many barrel and choke choices,
checkered pistol-grip stock:
  Plain ejectors 850.00
  Automatic ejectors 1,000.00
  Selective single trigger add 225.00
Sterlingworth Deluxe model:
  Plain ejectors 850.00
  Automatic ejectors 1,000.00
Sterlingworth skeet and upland game gun:
  Plain ejectors 800.00
  Automatic ejectors 900.00
Hammerless double-barrel shotguns:
  Grade A 950.00
  Grade AE 1,500.00
  Grade BE 2,100.00
  Grade CE 2,250.00
  Grade DE 6,000.00
  Grade FE 15,000.00
  Grade XE 4,000.00
  Grade HE (Super Fox) 1,750.00

Single-barrel trap guns (12 gauge only):
  Grade JE 1,500.00
  Grade KE 2,250.00
  Grade LE 3,000.00
  Grade ME 7,500.00
Model B hammerless double 225.00
Model B–DE 275.00
Model B–DL 300.00
Model B–SE 275.00
Model B–ST 235.00

FRANCHI SHOTGUNS

Model 48/AL ultra light shotgun: Autoloader . . . 375.00 to 425.00
Model 500 standard autoloader 325.00
Model 520 Deluxe 350.00
Model 520 Eldorado Gold 975.00
Model 2003 over and under trap gun 1,200.00
Model 2004: single-barrel trap gun 1,200.00
Model 2005: 2 barrels 1,400.00
Model 2005: 3 barrels 2,100.00
Model 3000: Combination trap gun 2,500.00
Airone hammerless double-barrel shotgun 1,200.00
Alcione over and under shotgun 600.00
Aristocrat over and under shotgun:
  Field model 550.00
  Deluxe grade 1,000.00
  Supreme grade 1,500.00
  Imperial grade 2,500.00
  Monte Carlo grade 3,000.00
  Other grade Aristocrat models . . . . 500.00 to 750.00
Astore hammerless double-barrel shotgun:
  Standard grade 1,000.00
  Grade II 1,250.00
  Grade "S" 2,250.00

Falconet over and under shotguns:
Field grade . . . . 550.00 to 600.00
Standard skeet 900.00
International skeet 1,000.00
Standard trap 950.00
International trap 1,000.00
Hammerless side-lock double-barrel shotguns: Various
gauges, barrels, chokes. Made to order:
Condor grade 7,500.00
Imperiale 9,500.00
Monte Carlo 15,000.00
Monte Carlo extra grade 16,500.00
Standard model autoloader . . . . 300.00 to 350.00
As above: Hunter model 335.00
As above: Magnum model 400.00
As above: Skeet model 400.00
As above: Slug gun 350.00
As above: Turkey gun 400.00
Peregrin model 451 over and under shotgun 550.00
As above: Steel receiver 600.00
PG–80 gas-operated semiautomatic shotgun:
Prestige model 425.00
Elite model 475.00
Box-lock hammerless double-barrel shotguns: All gauges,
barrel lengths, chokes:
Model 6886 . . . . 2,000.00
Model 8446 . . . . 2,500.00
Model 6930 . . . . 2,500.00
Model 4996 . . . . 2,500.00
Model 11/18E 3,000.00
Model 8457 . . . . 3,000.00
Model 9261 . . . . 3,000.00
Model 10/18E/628 . . . . 4,250.00
Abercrombie & Fitch designations:
Knockabout 3,000.00

Jubilee	3,750.00
Number 14	3,750.00
Number 20	4,250.00
Number 25	4,750.00
Number 30	5,250.00
Number 45	6,500.00
Half-Fine over and under shotgun	6,500.00
Fine over and under shotgun	8,750.00
Box-lock hammerless sideplate shotguns	3,200.00 to 4,250.00

W. W. GREENER, LTD

Empire model hammerless double-barrel shotgun	1,500.00 to 2,000.00
Far Killer hammerless double-barrel shotgun	2,250.00 to 3,250.00
General purpose "GP" single-barrel shotgun	325.00

Hammerless ejector double-barrel shotguns:

Grade DH35	2,250.00
Grade DH40	2,500.00
Grade DH55	3,000.00
Grade DH75	4,000.00

HARRINGTON & RICHARDSON

Number 3, 5, 6, 7, 8, and 9 hammer shotguns	100.00
Number 348 Gamester bolt-action shotgun	100.00
As above: Deluxe model	110.00
Model 351	125.00
Model 400 pump shotgun: Various gauges	185.00
Model 401	185.00
Model 402	200.00
Model 403 autoloading .410	200.00
Model 404 double-barrel shotgun: Various gauges	185.00
Model 404C	200.00
Model 440 pump shotgun: Various gauges	150.00

BUYING AND SELLING FIREARMS

The prices listed here are retail or auction selling prices, or average selling prices. If you are selling, you must know that buying and selling prices vary greatly. If you have a fine rare firearm, you can expect to get close to the listed prices, but don't be surprised to find you can only get a fraction of that for a common firearm.

Model 442	175.00
Model 12/12 over and under field gun	350.00
As above: Waterfowl gun	400.00
H & R "Folding Gun": Various gauges	125.00
Model 159 Golden Squire hammer shotgun	110.00
Model 459 Golden Squire Jr.	100.00
Number 1 single-barrel trap gun	2,250.00
Number 48 single-barrel hammer shotgun	75.00
Model "Topper" shotguns	75.00 to 100.00

HIGH STANDARD

Flite-King pump-action shotguns	225.00 to 350.00
Supermatic gas-operated autoloading shotguns	225.00 to 750.00

HOLLAND & HOLLAND

Hammerless double-barrel shotguns: Various gauges, barrels, stocking:

Dominion	5,000.00
Northwood	3,500.00
Badminton	8,000.00 to 8,500.00
Pigeon Gun	$\pm$ 10,000.00
Royal	$\pm$ 12,500.00
Deluxe	$\pm$ 17,500.00

Royal Model over and under shotguns: Various gauges, barrels, stocking:

Old model double trigger	$\pm$ 12,500.00

Old model single trigger . . . .   ± 13,500.00
New model double trigger . . . .   ± 16,000.00
New model single trigger . . . .   ± 18,000.00
Single-barrel trap gun . . . .   9,000.00 to 12,000.00

ITHACA GUN COMPANY

Model 37 standard grade slide-action shotgun: Various
grades, barrel lengths, chokes . . . .   250.00 to 600.00

As above: "$5,000 Grade" 6,000.00

Model 51 automatic shotgun:
Standard 250.00
Magnum 250.00
Turkey gun 400.00
Deerslayer 275.00
Skeet 300.00
Trap 275.00

Model 66 single-shot lever-action . . . .   95.00 to 135.00

Hammerless double-barrel shotguns: Various gauges,
barrels, chokes. Models made before 1925 are worth
less. Final production was in 1948.
Field grade 625.00
Number 1 grade 800.00
Number 2 grade 1,750.00
Number 3 grade 2,250.00
Number 4–E grade 3,250.00
Number 5–E grade 4,250.00
Number 7–E grade . . . .   7,500.00 to 12,500.00

Hammerless single-barrel trap gun: 12 gauge only,
various barrel lengths. Models made before
1921 are worth less . . . .   1,250.00 to 7,500.00

Mag-10 automatic shotgun . . . .   550.00 to 850.00

Ithaca-Perazzi single-barrel trap gun . . . . to 1,750.00

Ithaca-Perazzi over and under shotguns . . . 1,500.00 to 3,850.00

Ithaca-SKB side-by-side shotguns . . . . 350.00 to 675.00

Ithaca-SKB automatic shotgun . . . . to 275.00

Ithaca-SKB over and under shotguns . . . . 550.00 to 750.00

IVER JOHNSON'S ARMS

Champion grade single-barrel hammer shotgun 135.00

Hercules grade hammerless double-barrel shotgun: Various
gauges, barrel lengths, chokes, and extras . . . 650.00 to 800.00

Skeeter models . . . . 800.00 to 995.00

Special trap single-barrel hammer shotgun 250.00

Super trap hammerless double-barrel shotgun 900.00 to 1,200.00

LEFEVER ARMS COMPANY

Side-lock hammerless double-barrel shotguns: Various
gauges, barrel lengths, chokes, and extras:
H grade	1,500.00
HE grade	1,500.00
G grade	1,600.00
GE grade	1,800.00
F grade	1,500.00
FE grade	2,000.00
E grade	1,750.00
EE grade	2,250.00
D grade	2,250.00
DE grade	2,500.00
DS grade	1,000.00
DSE grade	1,200.00
C grade	3,250.00

ITHACA AND "UNCLE DAN"

In 1915, Lefever was sold to the Ithaca Gun Company, which continued making Lefever shotguns until 1942. These shotguns in various styles and gauges are priced from $500 to $1,250, while the shotguns made by the D. M. Lefever Company in 1904–06 are priced at $1,500 to $12,500. "Uncle Dan," who was the founder of both companies, died in 1906.

CE grade	5,000.00
B grade	5,000.00
BE grade	7,500.00
A grade	10,000.00
AA grade	15,000.00
Optimus grade	20,000.00
"Thousand Dollar" grade	±25,000.00
Box-lock models	300.00 to 1,250.00

MARLIN FIREARMS COMPANY

Model 16 visable-hammer slide-action shotgun	350.00 to 1,250.00
Model 17 brush gun	450.00
Model 17 standard	450.00
Model 19 visable-hammer slide-action shotgun	375.00 to 1,250.00
Model 21: Trap	375.00 to 1,250.00
Model 24	350.00 to 1,450.00
Model 26	to 350.00
Model 28	375.00 to 1,500.00
Model 30	375.00 to 1,250.00

Model 31 hammerless slide-action repeater . . 400.00 to 1,250.00

Model 42A: Visable hammer 250.00

Model 43 hammerless slide-action repeater . . . 250.00 to 500.00

Model 44 . . . . 350.00 to 450.00

Model 49 . . . . 400.00

Model 53 . . . . 350.00

Model 55 bolt-action repeater . . . . 85.00 to 125.00

Model 59 . . . . 75.00

Model 60 single-barrel shotgun 225.00

Model 63 hammerless slide-action repeater . . . 250.00 to 375.00

Model 90 standard over and under shotgun: Various
gauges, barrel lengths, chokes . . . . 450.00 to 675.00

Model 120 slide-action magnum 250.00

Model 410 lever-action .410 repeater 475.00

*Model 1898 visable-hammer
slide-action repeater* . . . . 600.00 to 1,800.00

Model 5510 . . . . 200.00

Premier Mark slide-action repeaters . . . . 200.00 to 350.00

MERKEL SHOTGUNS

Model 100 over and under shotgun: Box-lock, plain
extractor, various gauges, barrels, chokes . . . . . . ± 1,000.00

Model 101 . . . . 1,350.00 to 1,500.00

Model 127 hammerless side-lock double-barrel shotgun:
Wide variety of gauges, barrels, chokes, extras . . . ± 15,000.00

Model 130 . . . . ± 7,500.00

Model 147E: Post-WWII 1,250.00

As above: Other models . . . .   to 3,500.00

Model 200 over and under shotguns . . . . .   1,200.00 to 5,000.00

Model 300 over and under shotguns . . . . .   2,500.00 to 6,000.00

Model 303E . . . .   ± 10,000.00

Model 304E . . . .   ± 15,000.00

Model 400 over and under shotguns . . . .   to 1,800.00

Combination guns: Rifle, shotgun,
over and under . . . .   1,200.00 to 5,000.00

Drillings . . . .   5,000.00 to 7,500.00

MOSSBERG

Model 83D bolt-action shotgun	85.00
Model 85D	85.00
Model 183K–185K	85.00
Model 190D	85.00
Model 190K	100.00
Model 195D–195K	100.00
Model 200D	110.00
Model 200K slide-action repeating shotgun	175.00
Model 385K bolt-action repeater	100.00
Model 390K–395K	100.00
Model 395S "Slugster"	110.00
Model 500 "Accu-steel" pump-action shotgun	250.00
As above: "Bullpup" model	325.00
Pre-1977 Model 500 pump-action shotguns:	
Field grade	200.00 to 300.00
"L" model	200.00 to 250.00
Pigeon grade	325.00 to 400.00
Other Model 500 designations	200.00 to 300.00
Model 590 military models	275.00

Model 595 . . . . 125.00
Model 712 autoloading shotgun 425.00
Model 1000 . . . . 325.00 to 500.00
Model 5500 autoloading shotgun 200.00

PARKER BROTHERS

Hammerless double-barrel shotguns: Various gauges,
barrel lengths, chokes. Value differences reflect the very
considerable differences in price between 12 and 16
gauge shotguns and .28 and .410 models—less is more.
Prices are for shotguns in excellent original condition.

Trojan grade . . . . 1,500.00 to 2,500.00
VHE grade . . . . 2,000.00 to 5,000.00
GHE grade . . . . 2,500.00 to 9,500.00
DHE grade . . . . 3,500.00 to 15,000.00
CHE grade . . . . 6,500.00 to 30,000.00
BHE grade . . . . 7,500.00 to 30,000.00
AHE grade . . . . 6,500.00 to 15,000.00
AAHE grade . . . . 10,000.00 to 50,000.00
A–1 Special grade . . . . 25,000.00 to 150,000.00

Single-barrel trap guns:
SC grade . . . . to 2,500.00
SB grade . . . . to 3,000.00
SA grade . . . . to 4,500.00

Parker Brothers Deluxe AHW Grade 12-gauge shotgun with twenty-six-inch barrels chambered full and improved. This exceptional shotgun was sold in 1990 by James Julia of Fairfield, Maine, for $12,650. (Photograph by David Beane for James Julia)

THE OLD MAN'S PARKER

Parker shotguns are special beyond almost all reason, and today's prices reflect the ever-increasing popularity of these wonderful firearms that went out of production before Lucky Strike Green went to war. My father owned two shotguns: a Francotte A & F Knockabout for upland gunning, and a Parker Trojan with thirty-inch barrels for ducks and geese. There came a day in my youth when I outgrew my single-shot 20 gauge Stevens and started shooting the Parker with the old man's fond approval. I got so I could fire it at everything, from ducks to skeet targets, with great success back in my salad days, and I was forty years old before I discovered the fool thing weighed nine pounds. Yes, Parker shotguns are special, and the following list of monetary values cannot begin to reflect the reasons why.

SAA grade . . . .　to 6,500.00

SA–1 Special grade . . . .　to 10,000.00

JAMES PURDEY & SONS LTD.

Hammerless double-barrel shotgun: Side-lock, various gauges, barrel lengths, chokes, and extras:

Double triggers . . . .　to 25,000.00

Single selective trigger . . . .　to 30,000.00

Over and under shotgun: Various gauges, barrel lengths, chokes, extras, and action options . . . . .　to 30,000.00

Single-barrel trap gun . . . .　to 18,000.00

REMINGTON ARMS

Model 10A slide-action shotgun . . . .　300.00

Model 11A standard grade automatic shotgun . . . .　250.00

As above: Solid rib . . . .　325.00

As above: Vent rib 350.00

Model 11B 425.00

Model 11D 800.00

Model 11E 1,250.00

Model 11F 2,000.00

Model 11A . . . . 250.00 to 350.00

Model 11–87 premier autoloader . . . . 375.00 to 450.00

Model 17A standard grade slide-action shotgun 250.00

Model 29A 300.00

Model 29T: Trap 350.00

Model 31 slide-action repeater:
Model 31A . . . . 275.00 to 375.00
Model 31B 400.00
Model 31D 800.00
Model 31E 1,200.00
Model 31F 1,800.00
Model 31H 400.00
Model 31S 450.00
Model 31TC 650.00

Model 32 over and under shotgun: Hammerless, 12
gauge only, auto ejectors, various barrel lengths and
chokes:
Model 32A . . . . 1,000.00 to 1,500.00
Model 32–Skeet . . . . 1,250.00 to 1,750.00
Model 32TC–Trap . . . . 1,500.00 to 1,750.00
Model 32D–Tournament 2,000.00
Model 32E–Expert 2,500.00
Model 32F–Premier 5,000.00

Model 870 slide-action repeating shotguns . . . . 250.00 to 350.00

GETTING THE LEAD OUT

I cannot write about Remington firearms without a fond thought or two about the many happy days I spent at their Lordship Skeet and Trap Field, and I cannot write about that wonderful spot without thinking about the advent of steel shot and how it has changed so much. Never, I repeat, never, shoot steel shot in a valuable old shotgun.

As above: Tournament and Premier grades . . . . . .   to 4,500.00

Model 1100 automatic shotgun: Various barrel lengths, chokes, and in 12, 16, and 20 gauges: . . . . .   300.00 to 450.00

As above: Tournament and Premier grades . . . . . .   to 4,500.00

Model 1900 hammerless double-barrel shotgun . . . . .   to 600.00

Model 3200 over and under shotgun: 12 gauge with various chokes and barrel lengths . . . .   900.00 to 2,250.00

As above: 4-barrel skeet set . . . .   to 4,500.00

Sportsman–48A autoloader:
Standard grade . . . .   250.00 to 300.00
Skeet gun . . . .   250.00 to 300.00
Extra grade models . . . .   to 1,500.00

DANGER!

The Remington Model 1900 shotgun and earlier models such as the Model 1894 and Model 1889 were made with both steel and twist-steel (Damascus) barrels, and it is unsafe to shoot modern ammunition in many of these fine old shotguns. If you have questions, talk to a gunsmith.

Model 58 Autoloaders:

Model 58ADL . . . .   250.00 to 300.00
Model BDL . . . .   300.00 to 350.00
Model SA 325.00
Other models . . . .   450.00 to 1,300.00

RUGER SHOTGUNS

Red Label over and under shotguns: 12
and 20 gauge . . . .   650.00 to 750.00

J. P. SAUER & SON

Model 66 over and under field gun . . . . . .   1,500.00 to 2,800.00
Model 66 over and under skeet gun . . . . .   1,500.00 to 3,000.00
Model 66 over and under trap gun . . . . . .   1,500.00 to 3,000.00
Royal double-barrel shotgun . . . .   to 1,500.00
Artemis double-barrel shotgun . . . .   to 5,500.00

SAVAGE ARMS

Model 24 combination shotgun/rifles . . . .   125.00 to 175.00
Model 28A standard grade slide-action shotgun 225.00
Model 28B 250.00
Model 28D 300.00
Model 30 slide-action shotgun . . . .   125.00 to 200.00
Model 60RXL slide-action shotgun 150.00
Model 220 single-barrel shotgun . . . .   85.00 to 100.00
Model 242 over and under shotgun 150.00
Model 330 over and under shotgun 425.00
Model 333 over and under shotgun . . . .   500.00 to 550.00
Model 420 over and under shotgun:
Double trigger . . . .   to 500.00
Single trigger . . . .   to 600.00
Model 430 over and under shotgun:
Double trigger . . . .   to 550.00
Single trigger . . . .   to 650.00
Model 440 . . . .   to 500.00

Model 444 . . . . to 525.00
Model 550 hammerless double-barrel shotgun 250.00
Model 720 autoloading shotgun 250.00
Model 726 Upland Sporter autoloading shotgun 250.00
Model 740C skeet gun 300.00
Model 750 automatic shotgun 225.00
Model 750–AC 275.00
Model 750–SC 275.00
Model 755 autoloader 200.00
Model 775 . . . . 225.00
Model 2400 over and under rifle/shotgun 600.00

SEARS, ROEBUCK & CO

Sears shotguns: Also marketed as Ted Williams and
J. C. Higgins, are many and varied.
Prices range from . . . .   50.00 to 250.00

SKB ARMS CO

SKB automatic shotguns . . . . 250.00 to 350.00
SKB single-barrel trap gun . . . . 500.00 to 600.00
SKB double-barrel shotguns . . . . 400.00 to 550.00
SKB over and under shotguns . . . . 550.00 to 2,000.00

L. C. SMITH SHOTGUNS

Hammerless double-barrel shotguns: Various gauges,
barrel lengths, chokes, and stocking by Hunter Arms
Company.
00 grade . . . . ± 1,000.00
0 grade . . . . ± 1,250.00
1 grade . . . . ± 1,500.00
2 grade . . . . ± 1,500.00
3 grade . . . . ± 1,500.00
Pigeon grade . . . . ± 4,000.00
4 grade . . . . ± 5,000.00
5 grade . . . . ± 6,000.00

Monogram grade	± 9,000.00
A1 grade	± 6,000.00
A2 grade	± 9,000.00
A3 grade	15,000.00 to 20,000.00
Field grade	to 1,200.00
Ideal grade	to 1,800.00
Olympic grade	to 1,800.00
Skeet special	to 1,800.00
Skeet special (410)	to 10,000.00
Trap grade	to 1,200.00
Crown grade	to 4,500.00
Monogram grade	to 7,500.00
Premier grade	to 12,000.00
Deluxe grade	to 12,500.00

Hammerless double-barrel shotguns made by the Marlin Firearms Company are worth from 30% to 50% less than the above prices. These were made from 1946 to 1951 and again from 1968 to 1973. Hunter Arms Company manufactured the L. C. Smith shotgun from 1890 to 1945 and used numerical markings until 1913, when they changed to the name designations as shown above. Marlin continued the name designation.

Single-barrel trap guns (Hunter Arms Company):

Olympic grade	to 1,000.00
Specialty grade	to 2,000.00
Crown grade	to 3,500.00
Monogram grade	to 4,000.00
Premier grade	to 6,500.00
Deluxe grade	to 10,000.00
1968 model hammerless double-barrel shotgun	400.00
As above: Deluxe model	500.00

SMITH & WESSON

Model 916 slide-action repeating shotguns . . . . 125.00 to 175.00
Model 1000 autoloader . . . . 335.00 to 400.00
Model 3000 slide-action shotgun 200.00

J. STEVENS ARMS CO

Number 22–410 combination over and under gun 125.00
Model 51 bolt-action shotgun 65.00
Model 58 . . . . 75.00
Model 59 . . . . 100.00
Model 67 pump shotgun . . . . 125.00 to 225.00
Model 77 slide-action repeater 150.00
Model 94 single-barrel shotgun . . . . 75.00 to 85.00
Model 95 . . . . 85.00
Model 107 . . . . 75.00
Model 124 cross-bolt repeater 125.00
Model 240 over and under shotgun 325.00
Model 258 bolt-action repeater 75.00
Model 311–R hammerless double-barrel shotgun 165.00
Model 530 . . . . 175.00
Model 620 hammerless slide-action shotgun 165.00
Model 621 . . . . 200.00
Model 820 hammerless slide-action shotgun 150.00
Model 940 single-barrel shotgun 85.00
Model 9478 . . . . 85.00
Stevens/Springfield hammerless double . . . . to 200.00

WEATHERBY

Model 82 autoloading shotgun 375.00
Model 92 slide-action shotgun 350.00
Athena over and under shotgun 1,100.00
Field grade automatic shotgun 350.00
  Trap gun 350.00
  Deluxe model 375.00
Orion over and under shotgun 700.00

ALL GUNS ARE ALWAYS LOADED

In our home when I was growing up, our guns were kept unloaded under lock and key, and the ammunition was kept in a separate locked cupboard. I was allowed access with two separate keys. A constant reminder was hanging in both cupboards in block letters: All Guns Are Always Loaded.

Patrician slide-action shotgun	325.00
Trap gun	350.00
Deluxe model	400.00
Regency over and under shotgun	1,000.00

WESTLEY RICHARDS & CO., LTD

Model E hammerless double-barrel shotgun	3,000.00 to 3,500.00
Box-lock hammerless double-barrel shotgun	7,000.00 to 8,500.00
Side-lock hammerless double-barrel shotgun	12,000.00 to 20,000.00
Box-lock over and under shotgun	10,000.00 to 15,000.00

WINCHESTER SHOTGUNS

Model 1887 lever-action shotgun	600.00
Model 1901 lever-action shotgun	750.00
Model 1911 autoloading shotgun	500.00
Model 12 slide-action repeater:	
Standard grade	500.00 to 600.00
Standard grade .28 gauge	2,000.00
Skeet gun	700.00 to 1,000.00
Trap gun	800.00 to 1,000.00
Featherweight	600.00
Duck gun	800.00

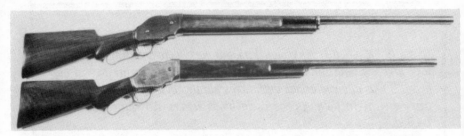

Top: Winchester Model 1901 lever-action 10-gauge shotgun. *Bottom:* Winchester Deluxe Model 1887 lever-action 10-gauge shotgun with Damascus barrels. (Courtesy James Julia)

Pigeon grade . . . .   1,000.00 to 1,800.00

Model 21 double-barrel shotgun: Box-lock, various chokes, barrel lengths, gauges, stocking:

Field gun . . . .   2,250.00 to 3,500.00
Duck gun . . . .   3,000.00 to 3,500.00
Skeet gun . . . .   3,250.00 to 4,500.00
Trap gun . . . .   3,500.00 to 4,500.00
Custom grade . . . .   6,000.00 to 8,000.00
Pigeon grade . . . .   8,000.00 to 10,000.00
Grand American . . . . 10,000.00 to 12,500.00
Model 23 side-by-side shotgun . . . .   1,200.00 to 3,500.00
Model 24 hammerless double-barrel shotgun 350.00
Model 25 slide-action repeater 350.00
Model 36 single-shot bolt-action 250.00
Model 37 single-barrel shotgun . . . .   150.00 to 225.00
As above: .28 gauge 700.00
Model 37A single-barrel shotgun . . . .   to 90.00
Model 40 standard autoloader 500.00
As above: Skeet gun 650.00
Model 41 single-shot bolt-action shotgun 275.00
Model 42 slide-action repeating shotgun:
Standard grade 650.00

As above with solid matted rib 1,250.00
Skeet gun 1,500.00
Deluxe grade 1,500.00
Model 50 autoloader . . . . 300.00 to 550.00
Model 59 autoloading shotgun 375.00
Model 97 visable-hammer slide-action repeating shotgun:
Standard grade 500.00
Trench gun (with bayonet) 750.00
Trap gun 750.00
Tournament grade 850.00
Pigeon grade . . . . to 1,250.00
Model 101 over and under shotgun . . . . 650.00 to 1,250.00
Model 370 single-barrel shotgun 85.00
Model 1200 slide-action shotgun . . . . 150.00 to 250.00
Model 1300 slide-action shotgun . . . . 225.00 to 300.00
Model 1400 automatic shotgun . . . . 225.00 to 350.00
Model 1500 XTR semiautomatic shotgun 300.00
Ranger semiautomatic shotgun . . . . 150.00 to 200.00
Super-X model shotguns . . . . 375.00 to 450.00
Xpert Model 96 over and under shotguns . . . . to 650.00

Selected Bibliography

There are probably as many gun books as there are gun makers, but there are a few books beginning collectors will find invaluable, such as the annual *Gun Trader's Guide,* published by Stoeger Publishing of Hackensack, New Jersey; *The Shooter's Bible,* from the same publisher; and *Gun Digest,* from DBI in Northfield, Illinois. Auction catalogs are an excellent source of information and up-to-date selling prices, and the 1990 catalogs of both the James Julia gun auctions in Fairfield, Maine, and Richard Bourne gun auctions in Hyannis, Massachusetts, are available at affordable prices.

A new publication, *The Double Gun Journal,* and an old one, *Shotgun News,* can prove beneficial to collectors and are worthly of your consideration. The first is based in East Jordan, Michigan, the latter in Sidney, Nebraska.

CARTRIDGES, SHOT SHELLS, AND SHOT-SHELL BOXES

C artridges have probably been collected since the time when women on the frontier were admonished to "Save the last one for yourself" in the event of Indian raids, and serious collectors have been at it since the time of the Civil War. Shot shells, on the other hand, have gained popularity with collectors slowly, and it was not until the introduction of the plastic shot shell that the brass and paper varieties were truly appreciated. Collectors can still find a wide variety of paper shot shells, both in and out of their original containers, but brass shells are now hard to come by. Strange as it may seem, many paper shells are worth much more than are the brass shells, but the latter have caught on with noncollectors, and the always present law of supply and demand creates the market.

Shot-shell boxes are eagerly sought by many collectors and are in demand both with and without their contents; in many cases, the box itself is the objective of the collector. Cartridge boxes are collected also, but here the primary object is the cartridge and not the container, although .22 caliber boxes are collected in themselves, and for many are the only boxes of interest.

Cartridges, shot shells, and shot-shell boxes are all specialized collectibles, and books have been written about each. Some of these guides are listed at the end of this chapter, and I recommend that prospective collectors learn more before buying.

Cartridge collectors tend to specialize, and it is impossible in the limited space here to even begin to list more than a handful of the thousands of

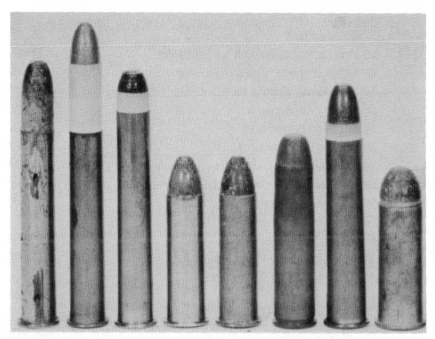

Black powder cartridges. *From left to right:* .45–100 Sharps; .45–100 Remington Creedmore; .45–100 Sharps; .50–70 U.S. Springfield; .50–70 U.S. Springfield; .50–115 Ballard; .50–90 Sharps; .58 musket. (Courtesy James Tillinghast)

rimfire, pinfire, centerfire, and other possibilities. A collector I know recently bought an antique dentist's cabinet with many narrow drawers just to house his vast collection of more than two thousand different 30–06 caliber cartridges, and he is looking for another cabinet for the rest of his collection. This man knows more than I do about cartridges, but the following list of recent sale prices should prove interesting to seasoned and beginning collectors.

CARTRIDGES

.45 Adams Patent (1852) with Eley headstamp 275.00
.307 Triangular (rarity) 1,687.00

.31 Crispin (rare) 1,274.00
.50 Crispin Short 551.00
.36 Thuer's Patent for Colt pocket model 220.00
.40 Logan & Hart 206.00
.50–70 Rodman-Crispin Patent 115.00
.58 Morse tinned case 420.00
.54 Burnside tinned case 193.00
.50 Ball Carbine (rimfire) 242.00
.50 Warner Rimfire 302.00
.40–90 Peabody Martini "What Cheer" 298.00
.50 3¾″ Sharps paper patched bullet 205.00
.50–140 Winchester Express 521.00
.58 Danderfield & LeFever 260.00
.41 Roper Revolving Rifle (brass) 175.00
.41 Roper Revolving Rifle (steel) 185.00
.44 Henry flat rimfire 178.00
.56–46 Long Spencer Sporting Cartridge 200.00
.40–60 Colt 160.00
.42 Russian Gattling 500.00
.43–77 Hollow Bullet—Brass Dummy 315.00
.45 Van Choate 150.00
.50–70 with Orcott primer 165.00
.40–70 Remington Reloadable 200.00
.50 Maynard Model 1865 Logan & Hart 850.00
.32 Long Rimfire (Merwin's cone base) 110.00
.46 Short Ethan Allen Rimfire 120.00

EXPLOSIVE

Cartridges and shot shells were intended to be shot and not collected, and collectors need to keep this in mind. Even empty cases with the primer unfired can be hazardous and should be handled and stored with respect for the explosives they are. Keep them under lock and key.

.50 Remington Pistol	260.00
.54 Star Rimfire	200.00
.58 Rimfire	155.00
.58 Musket Rimfire	125.00

FOR THOSE OF YOU WHO FEEL CARTRIDGE COLLECTING IS ONLY FOR LOADED COLLECTORS . . .

.30 Cup Fire	5.00
.42 Cup Fire	10.00
.50 Remington Army	7.50
.50 Remington Navy	30.00
.50–70 U.S. Government	10.00
.58 Musket (short case)	17.50
.25 Short Stevens Rimfire	.50
.25 Stevens	.60
.30 Short Blank	1.25
.30 Long	3.50
.310 Remington (shot)	1.50
.32 Extra Short	2.50
.41 Short Rimfire	1.00
.41 Long	1.00
.41 Swiss Rimfire	2.50
.42 Forehand & Wadsworth #64	3.50
.44 Short	1.00
.44 Henry Flat—long case	5.00
.44 Long	2.50
.44 Extra Long	10.00
.46 Carbine	5.00
.56–46 Spencer	8.50
.56–50 Spencer	3.50
.56–56 Spencer	4.50
.32 Winchester Special	1.25
.32–20 W.C.F.	1.50
.32–35 Stevens	4.50
.32–40 Ballard & Marlin	7.50

.338 Winchester 2.00
.340 Weatherby 3.00
.35 Whelen 1.50

SHOT SHELLS

Note: The following shot shells are identified by their headstamps.

.410–12mm Climax brass shot shell 35.00

U.S. No. 32–14mm Climax black paper 15.00

Kynoch Perfect—cutaway brass shot shell 14.00

No. 28 U.S. New Rapid black paper 50.00

Peters League no. 20 brown paper 3.00

Peters Target no. 20 red paper 4.00

Rem-UMC No. 20 Nitro club tan paper "SKEET" 30.00

Western Field no. 20 red paper 4.00

Patent—Zund no. 20 "H" brass 20 gauge shot shell . .   25.00

P.C. Co. Quick Shot 16 purple paper 16
gauge shot shell 8.00

Peters Premier no. 16 orange paper 60.00

Peters Victor 16 gauge black paper 25.00

UMC Co. no. 16 Walstrobe purple paper 75.00

No. 16 U.S. Rapid black paper 50.00

Everlasting no. 12 brass shot shell (rare) 250.00

A.C. Co. 12 gauge rust color paper 4.00

Red Devil no. 12 red paper shot shell: devil on side . . .   181.00

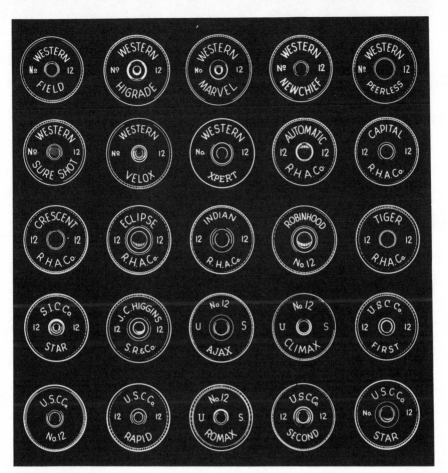

Shot-shell headstamps.

A.C. Co. 12 gauge Alert brown paper	15.00
Austin 12 gauge Ct'ge Co. brown paper	55.00
A.C. Co. 12 gauge Bang red paper shot shell	34.00
A.C. Co. 12 gauge Invincible red paper	75.00
A.C. Co. 12 gauge Crack Shot brown paper	125.00
Mallard C.C. Co. 12 gauge: duck on side	127.00
Federal Hi Power No. 12	45.00
Gambles no. 12 Tiger	45.00

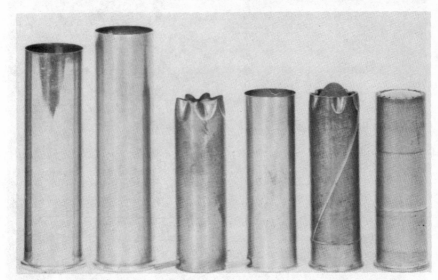

Brass shot shells. *From left to right:* Two Winchester 8-gauge shells; Des & Etienne 12-gauge pin-fire shell; Kynoch 12-gauge pin fire; brass-wrapped Ely 12-gauge shell; two-piece Standard 12-gauge shell. (Courtesy James Tillinghast)

Hudson's Bay no. 12 company brown lacquered paper shell	90.00
Liberty Bulk no. 12 red paper	15.00
Peters Premier no. 12 orange paper	50.00
P.C. Co. Prize 12 gauge brown paper shot shell	10.00
P.C. Co. 12 gauge Victor: red and white striped	157.00
Peters Target no. 12 red paper	3.00
J. Purdy & Sons 12 brass shot shell	32.00
Robin Hood no. 12 1903 red paper	24.00
Robin Hood 12–12 R.H.P. Co.	24.00
Capital 12–12 R.H.A. Co. brown paper	20.00

Clipper 12–12 R.H.A. Co. salmon-colored paper 30.00

Robin Hood no. 12 red paper 11.00

L. C. Smith 12 A brass shot shell 242.00

Squires N.Y. no. 12 blue paper shot shell 12.00

No. 12 U.S. Defiance yellow paper 32.00

No. 12 U.S. Climax green paper 21.00

USC Co. no. 12 Climax black paper shot shell 3.00

No. 12 U.S. New Rapid 35.00

W.C. Co. no. 12 orange paper 15.00

W.C. Co. no. 12 Velox green paper 75.00

Use Winchester Primers no. 2 no. 12 brass shot shell   20.00

Winchester no. 12 WINCO green paper shot shell: rare   412.00

Parker Bros. 12A Meridan Ct. brass shot shell 20.00

Note: Parker Bros 12B and West Meridan address are worth more.

1901 no. 12 metal-lined green paper (Winchester) . . .   50.00

Winchester Leader no. 12 buff colored paper 75.00

W.R.A. Rival no. 12 brown paper shot shell 3.00

1901 Pigeon no. 12 green paper: Winchester 125.00

BLACK POWDER

Black powder, the explosive in early cartridges and shot shells, is very unstable and therefore much more dangerous than modern smokeless varieties.

A. L. Howard no. 10 New Haven, Ct. brown
paper shot shell 20.00

Austin 10 gauge Ct'ge Co. blue paper 43.00

C.C.C. no. 10 Mandan blue paper 15.00

C.A. Co. no. 10 grey paper 31.00

Cassidy no. 10 grey paper shot shell 187.00

Robin Hood no. 10 red paper 20.00

UMC Co. Bridgeport, Ct. nickel-plated
brass shot shell 20.00

UMC Club no. 10 brass 6.00

U.S. Second Quality no. 10 black paper shot shell 4.00

No. 10 U.S. Climax green paper 45.00

No. 10 U.S. New Climax black paper 20.00

V.L. & A. no. 10 Chicago orange paper 25.00

W.R.A. Co. no. 10 brass shot shell 84.00

Winchester no. 10 grey paper 8.00

Winchester Pigeon no. 10 green paper 8.00

Eley's no. 8 Ejector London-brass shot shell 48.00

UMC Co. no. 8 brass 16.00

UMC Co. no. 8 Trap green paper shot shell 21.00

Winchester no. 8 black paper 20.00

Remington-UMC no. 4 brass shot shell 75.00

UMC Co. no. 4 brown paper shot shell 35.00

Winchester no. 4 black paper: reloaded 40.00

Winchester no. 4 metal-lined green paper shot shell . .   180.00

Winchester no. 4 red paper shot shell 188.00

UMC Co. no. 2 paper yacht cannon shell 275.00

SHOT-SHELL BOXES

Winchester 9mm Long Shot (box of 50) red label 43.00

USC Co. 2-piece box (empty) .410 shot shells 42.00

USC Co. sealed 2-piece box .410 brass 90.00

Red Head 2-piece box (empty) .410 with duck on box . .   78.00

Winchester 32 gauge 2-piece box (empty) 30.00

USC Co. Climax 28 gauge box (empty) 20.00

UMC Nitro Club 28 gauge box of mixed shells 55.00

Winchester Leader 20 gauge 2-piece box 20.00

Winchester Repeater 20 gauge (full box) 56.00

Western Super-X 20 gauge (full sealed box) 55.00

As above (partial contents) 11.00

Western Field 20 gauge (full 2-piece box) 31.00

As above (partial contents) 13.00

One-piece boxes with unusual artwork or scarcity are collectible, but most 1-piece boxes are not. All the boxes listed here are 2-piece unless otherwise noted.

Collectible shot-shell boxes. *Clockwise from upper left:* 20-gauge Pointer shells by the Clinton Cartridge Company of Chicago; 28-gauge Pointer shells by Clinton Cartridge Company; 10-gauge Nublack Winchester shot shells; .410-gauge Climax Heavies by the U.S. Cartridge Company; 12-gauge Ajax Heavies by U.S. Cartridge Company.

Montgomery Ward Red Head 20 gauge 1-piece box with duck	25.00
USC Co. Defiance 20 gauge (empty) with setter and hunter	35.00
USC Co. Climax Heavies 20 gauge 1-piece box with gunner	44.00
USC Co. Ajax 20 gauge full 2-piece box	80.00

Remington Nitro Club Game Loads 20 gauge:
Mint with quail 104.00

Remington Shur Shot Shells 20 gauge (full box) 35.00

As above (near-mint) 37.00

Remington "Arrow" 20 gauge (poor) 16.00

Peters 20 gauge Victor Trap 17.00

Peters 20 gauge High Gun 2-piece
box with shorebird 84.00

Winchester Repeater 20 gauge 10-round box 25.00

Winchester Repeater 16 gauge full sealed box 47.00

As above: mixed shells in opened box 21.00

Winchester Repeater 16 gauge 10-round box 7.00

Remington Nitro Club Game Loads 16 gauge 41.00

Remington Kleanbore Shur Shot 16
gauge shells (1-piece) 12.00

Remington Arrow Express 16 gauge shells 37.00

Meridan Fire Arms 16 gauge Pointer
2-piece box (stained) 60.00

American Cartridge Co. 16 gauge American
Eagle 1-piece box 21.00

THE FOLLOWING SHOT SHELL BOXES ARE ALL 12 GAUGE

Winchester Leader (near-mint) 91.00

Winchester Repeater (fair) 20.00

Winchester brass shells (full 2-piece box) 47.00

Winchester Repeater (full box) 21.00

Western Super-X (empty) 3.00

UMC Nitro Club empty with duck in flight 75.00

UMC Nitro Club (later than above) 42.00

UMC Extra Quality Smokeless 47.00

Henry G. Squires empty box with flaws 67.00

Robin Hood Eclipse 2-piece box
in excellent condition 333.00

Remington-UMC Long Range Game Load 30.00

Remington-UMC Nitro Club (full box) 60.00

Remington-UMC Arrow Express (mixed contents/flaw)   24.00

Peters 1-piece Victor Trap shell box 3.00

Mullerite 1-piece box with gunner on label 30.00

Meridan 2-piece Pointer empty box with minor flaw . . .   39.00

Mercury Victoria 1-piece box 11.00

Mercury "new trap load" 1-piece box 11.00

Mallard Sportload empty 1-piece box 21.00

THE FOLLOWING ARE ALL 10 GAUGE SHOT-SHELL BOXES

Winchester New Rival full box 72.00

Winchester Leader full box in good condition 64.00

USC Co. empty 1-piece box with gunner 54.00

UMC Arrow full box with stained label 36.00

UMC Nitro Club in excellent full condition 68.00

Remington-UMC Nitro Club full box
in good condition 72.00

Peters Target empty box in excellent shape 108.00

Peters Referee empty 2-piece box in good condition . . .   78.00

THE FOLLOWING ARE ALL 100-ROUND BOXES

Winchester 16 gauge Repeater shot shells box of 100 . .   72.00

Remington-UMC full box .410 cartridge
cases with soiling 100.00

Winchester 16 gauge Blue Rival full box of 100
with soiled label 60.00

Remington-UMC 16 gauge Nitro Club full box of 100 . .   54.00

Dominion 100-round box with 33 16 gauge shells 21.00

Winchester 12 gauge Leader 100-round empty box 35.00

Remington-UMC Nitro Club Grade full box of
12 gauge shells 78.00

Winchester Repeater 100-round full box of
12 gauge shells 72.00

Winchester New Rival 100-round box full of
12 gauge shells 80.00

UMC Union 100-round box of 12 gauge shells 85.00

Peters League 100-round full box of 12 gauge shells . .   100.00

FOR MORE INFORMATION

A s I said at the start of this section, there is a lot to learn about cartridges, shot shells, and shot-shell boxes, and a variety of books on these subjects. Recent ones include: *The Rimfire Cartridge 1857–1987,* by John Barber; *The*

Shotshell in the United States, by Richard Iverson; *Robin Hood Shot Shells,* by Windy Klinect; and *Shot Shell Box Prices at Auction,* by Bob and Beverly Strauss.

Bob and Beverly Strauss's Circus Promotions and James Tillinghast conduct mail-bid auctions of cartridges, shot shells, and related items. Contact them for more information. Addresses are in the Appendix.

POWDER CANS,
KEGS, AND FLASKS

G unning and shooting were more complex in the days of our ancestors: Between shots they fumbled with powder, patches, and shot, and later often loaded their own brass shot shells and cartridges. The relic tools they used are collected today and often fetch bonus dollars for the scarcer items. Fine, distinctively etched powder horns have become museum pieces, and original brass, copper, and leather shot and powder flasks are eagerly collected. Each of these items have been faked, and collectors should deal only with individuals they can trust in this tricky marketplace. The next issue of this guide will cover powder cans, kegs, and flasks in detail as an accompaniment to antique American sporting firearms, but the limited space here is devoted to the containers that our forebears bought from the suppliers who were often the only store for miles.

For many collectors, powder cans and kegs make up entire collections, and unusual or rare cans can cost hundred of dollars when several enthusiasts go after the same item. On the other hand, many powder cans are nearly worthless because they're in poor condition or are plentiful. The following listing is far from complete, but it does reflect prices paid for these cans, kegs, and flasks at auction.

AMERICAN POWDER COMPANY

   ½ pound can: Minute Man explosives, white label 50.00

American Powder Mills cans, including their famous "Dead Shot" logo
with its stricken mallard. (Courtesy James Tillinghast)

AMERICAN POWDER MILLS

$\frac{1}{2}$ *pound red can:* Dead Shot multicolor lithography . . .   75.00

$\frac{1}{2}$ *pound Dead Shot Rifle Powder:* Pink label 75.00

1 pound red Dead Shot can 92.00

1 pound green Dead Shot can 106.00

6$\frac{1}{2}$ pound keg: "Triple Refined" Dead Shot. Fair 42.00

25 pound keg: Black with green and black label 61.00

AMERICAN "E. C." & SCHULTZE GUNPOWDER COMPANY

1 pound gold and dark green lithographed can 56.00

1 pound orange lithographed can: Scratched 10.00

As above: Fine 55.00

AMERICAN WOOD POWDER COMPANY

1 pound green and black lithographed can: Flaking . . .   22.00

1 pound can: With 1886 patent date. Poor 40.00

AUSTIN POWDER COMPANY

$\frac{1}{2}$ *pound green can with tan paper label:* Rare 75.00

BOSTON POWDER COMPANY

$\frac{1}{4}$ *pound red stenciled can:* Faded 60.00

CANADIAN EXPLOSIVES LIMITED

1 pound black lithographed can with falling duck 32.00

As above: Fine 34.00

*½ pound black can with upside
down falling-duck labels* 89.00

6 pound green keg with red "Snap Shot" lettering 102.00

CURTIS and HARVEY

*1 pound flask of Curtis & Harvey's Gunpowder
on paper labels* 95.00

2 pound yellow can with blue paper Amberlite label . . . 48.00

DITMAR'S POWDER COMPANY

1 pound can of New Sporting powder paper labels 89.00

E. I. du PONT de NEMOURS POWDER COMPANY

*1 pound green keg with black and white labeling
depicting a dog* 54.00

1 pound red keg with deer on top label 30.00

1 pound green keg: "Shot Guns Only" label with dogs . . 51.00

½ pound red can: Indian Rifle Gun Powder label 86.00

As above: Rust spots 50.00

½ pound red can Golden Pheasant Gunpowder 90.00

1 pound dark green Ballistite Smokeless Powder 67.00

As above: Rust spots 46.00

*1 pound red can Eagle Gun Powder
paper label:* scarce 213.00

1 pound Schuetzen Smokeless can 50.00

As above: Good 40.00

EUREKA POWDER WORKS

1 pound can with orange Imperial Gun Powder label . .   30.00

JOHN HALL and SONS

1 pound black can: Tower Proof
Gunpowder label, faded 113.00

1 pound red flask with blue paper "No. 6" label 118.00

HAMILTON POWDER COMPANY

*1 pound lithographed black on grey
Nobel's Empire Powder* 112.00

HAZARD POWDER COMPANY

*½ pound red can with Kentucky Rifle
Powder label:* Torn 38.00

1 pound black can Kentucky Rifle Powder: Label dirty . .   45.00

1 pound red can Kentucky Rifle Powder: Can flaked . . .   20.00

As above: Poor 22.00

1 pound red can Hazard Electric Gunpowder: Poor 30.00

6 pound red keg of Duck Shooting Gun Powder: Fair . . .   75.00

25 pound red can "Cannon" label: Good. Varnished . . .   46.00

HERCULES POWDER COMPANY

1 pound canister (round) Smokeless Rifle Powder 86.00

*1 pound can Black Sporting Powder on orange
and black label* 42.00

1 pound orange lithographed flask:
Black Sporting Powder 70.00

*1 pound can with full label
Infallible Shotgun Smokeless* 12.00

IMPERIAL POWDER COMPANY

1 pound canister with orange and black label 78.00
As above 70.00

IMPERIAL CHEMICAL INDUSTRIES LTD.

3 pound red can with red paper
Sporting Powder label 50.00

KING POWDER COMPANY

1 pound green can with lithographed red
and gold lettering 35.00

1 pound yellow can with lithographed red banner 31.00

6 pound red keg with Quick Shot paper label 50.00

Salesman's sample can: King's Smokeless mint 250.00

LAFLIN & RAND POWDER COMPANY

$\frac{1}{2}$ *pound can Orange Extra Powder* 22.00

$\frac{1}{2}$ *pound can Orange Extra Powder:* Round design 25.00

1 pound black can Orange Rifle Powder paper label . . .   42.00

1 pound black can Orange Ducking Powder label: Good   120.00

1 pound tin can with lithographed Smokeless
Powder in color 10.00

MATHEWSON'S GUN POWDER

1 pound red can with orange and black label 31.00
As above 31.00
And another 20.00

ORIENTAL POWDER COMPANY

1 pound black can with Texas Rifle
Powder label: Fair 126.00

*1 pound maroon can with black and white label
with duck:* Fair 250.00

ROBIN HOOD POWDER COMPANY

1 pound green can with white and red (Robin in red) . .   165.00
As above: Poor 40.00
As above: Crazed paint, but good 60.00

THE SCHULTZE GUNPOWDER COMPANY

*1 pound black tin with Schultze
Gunpowder paper labels* 5.00

Another: Lightning bolt labels 5.00

WARREN POWDER MILLS

1 pound green tin with Snap Shot paper label: Faded . .   96.00
¼ pound tin: Warren Sporting Powder Number 5 label . .   40.00

FURTHER READING

No one with a serious interest in powder cans and kegs can afford to be without the mail-bid auction catalogs of Bob and Beverly Strauss and James Tillinghast. For more information, see the Appendix.

SHOOTING
ACCESSORIES

S hooting accessories include all manner of things: the gunning and hunting odds and ends that, for one reason or another, are not included elsewhere in this book. Virtually everything listed was sold at auction in 1990, and the prices shown are the prices bid and paid by collectors.

Target ball: Deep purple. Plain	100.00
Another: Lavender with raised basket weave and man shooting	115.00
Another: Dark green with man shooting	90.00
Another: Plain amber	36.00

Glass target balls, two inches in diameter. (Courtesy Circus Promotions)

Another: N. B. Glass Works, Perth 60.00

Another: Cobalt blue 154.00

Another: 3-piece mold 110.00

Another: Bogardus's Glass Ball Pat'd April 10, 1877 . . .   247.00

Target ball trap 700.00

Du Pont trap-shooter sterling silver spoon 110.00

Parker Brothers snuff box 102.00

Hercules Powder Company celluloid match safe 110.00

Pocket knife: Remington
gunsmith conference giveaway 48.00

Another: Walnut. 1966 . . . .   26.00

Another: Marked Hibbard, Spencer & Bartlett. $9\frac{1}{2}''$ 85.00

Another: Bullet knife. REM-UMC 7mm 10.00

Another: Russell lock-back 9" overall open 235.00

Sheath knife: 2 marbles with cases 225.00

Another: G. Weil & Co. 800 fire knife 275.00

Another D. B. Randall signed $17\frac{1}{2}''$ fighting knife 725.00

Merrymeeting Bay scull boat 11,000.00

Watch fob: Dead Shot powder. Silver plate 100.00

Another: As above. Bronze and porcelain 158.00

Another: National Sportsman brass 40.00

Another: Sportsman's Digest 25.00

Another: Smith & Wesson. Silver plate 25.00

Pin back: N.Y. License 1934 . . . .   10.00

Another: As above. 1938 . . . .   12.00

Pin back: Austin Powder Company 80.00

Another: Dead Shot Smokeless Powder 45.00

Another: As above. 1" size 75.00

Another: As above. $1\frac{1}{4}''$ size 80.00

Another: Du Pont with quail 21.00

Another: L. C. Smith with setter 60.00
Another: Laflin & Rand "Infallible" 47.00

Pin back: Labrador Retriever Club. Sterling 80.00

Stick pin: Dead Shot duck. Gold 242.00
Another: Du Pont dog 105.00
Another: Hopkins & Allen pistol 90.00
Another: Savage Arms Co. Copper 60.00
Another: As above. Sterling 79.00
Another: Winchester New Rival Hunter's Choice 15.00

Counter felt: Du Pont 80.00
Another: Winchester "They Shoot Where You Aim" . . .   149.00
Another: Dead Shot. Multicolor on black felt 227.00
Another: UMC Cartridges for Game and Gallery 51.00

Cigarette card: Miss Annie Oakley 235.00
Another: Capt. A. H. Bogardus 125.00
Another: Hon. W. F. Cody 125.00
Another: Dr. W. F. Carver 105.00

Game call: Duck call "Duc-em" 19.00
Another: Heidelbauer duck call. Inscribed 100.00
Another: 10 P. S. Olt calls 225.00
Another: 36 mixed game calls 700.00

Note: Game calls will be featured in depth in the next issue of this guide.

Grenfell rug: Of flying mallards. Repaired 600.00

Joel Barber blueprint: For black duck-mallard decoy . . .   650.00

Canvasback paperweight by Joel Barber 500.00

Duck decoy weathervane: Sheet copper 550.00

Flying duck weathervane: Wood 450.00

10 Gauge blank Winchester cannon: Mint in box 1,750.00

Trophy: Sailfish. Mounted 350.00
Another: Elk head and shoulder mount 900.00
Another: Alaskan wolf head mount 300.00
Another: Moose head mount 900.00
Another: As above. Excellent 1,300.00
Another: Black bear on rear legs 1,350.00
Another: Black Bear on four legs 900.00
Another: Black Bear rug. Head and claws 350.00
Another: Deer head from . . . .   90.00 to 350.00
Another: Rattlesnake coiled to strike 125.00
Another: Duck. Various species from . . . .   50.00 to 100.00
Another: Game bird various species . . . .   50.00 to 125.00

And I think I should end this with a bang similar to the one I heard on my very first Christmas in 1929 when my father saluted me, at the ripe old age of 33 days, with a blast from his very first gift to me: a 10 gauge blank Winchester "ship's" cannon just like the one pictured here. Shooting accessories indeed.

Winchester 10-gauge blank salute cannon. (Photograph by David Beane for James Julia)

For more information on pin backs and similar items, contact Bob and Beverly Strauss. The fine books *Knives and Knifemakers,* by Sid Latham, and Brian Mc Grath's *Duck Calls and Other Game Calls* are worthy sources of information on those items. Various auction catalogs are good sources of information.

SPORTING ADVERTISING

Once upon a time in America, fine sporting art hung in nearly every sportsman's and sportswoman's home—and it was replaced each year at no cost to the homeowner. Imagine, pictures by the likes of Carl Rungius, Charles Livingston Bull, N. C. Wyeth, Percival Rosseau, and A. B. Frost for free! What matter if these oldtime freebies carried unobtrusive advertisements; the art was the very finest sporting art of that time, and those long-ago calendars were a very real part of the golden age of American sport. Add to this the many colorful posters of that time, and you have a distinct category of sporting collectibles that is passionately sought today at prices often exceeding four figures. Such collectibles are a good investment if they are in very good or better condition.

Posters—or handbills, as they were once called—have been around for ages, but calendars and advertising as such came into vogue after the Civil War as commerce and mass communication became more a part of American life. Advertising grew beyond individual peddlers, and posters, calendars, and advertising cards and envelopes hawked a wide variety of products. From the last quarter of the nineteenth century until the middle of the twentieth, thousands of sporting posters, calendars, and such were printed, used, and thrown away. What remains is what a lot of collectors seek: the paper remains of a golden time before radio and television.

With few exceptions, such as Bristol fishing tackle and oddball store displays promoting fishing tackle, today's poster and calendar market is con-

A trimmed Smith & Wesson advertising poster. (Private collection)

centrated in firearms and sporting-gun powder. The price listings that follow are arranged in alphabetical order, so it seems logical to begin this brief outline of manufacturers with the Austin Powder Company and Baker Guns.

Both of these companies produced posters before 1900, and those by the Austin Powder Company were distinguished by the art of Edmund Osthaus, who became famous for his bird-dog paintings. Colt was in the poster business by 1910 with a well-armed cowgirl, and Daisy produced a "Happy Daisy Boy" poster in 1913.

Du Pont had calendars and posters before the turn of the century and had advertised before that. Over the years, Du Pont employed some of the nation's finest artists, including Edmund Osthaus, N. C. Wyeth, and Lynn Bogue Hunt. The Hercules Powder Company was an early contender with colorful envelopes and posters, and they, too, used the finest sporting artists of their day. Their posters featuring black hunters were controversial and are collectable.

Hopkins and Allen, the Hazard Powder Company, Harrington and Richardson, and Iver Johnson all turned out calendars or posters together with advertising envelopes.

The Ithaca Gun Company gave us posters by Louis Agassiz Fuertes and Laflin and Rand; Lefever and the Miami Powder Company of Xenia, Ohio, contributed, as well. Marlin Firearms produced posters with art by G. Muss Arnolt and Phillip Goodwin. Parker Brothers calendars, posters, and envelopes are among the most eagerly sought of today's paper collectibles. The Peters Cartridge Company was turning out material before the turn of the century, as were Remington and Union Metallic Cartridge, who merged in the early 1900s. UMC material in itself would make a wonderful and truly historic collection.

Savage Arms, and later Savage-Stevens produced both calendars and posters, and Smith and Wesson gave us the fleeing rider logo, which is often reproduced. U.S. Cartridge contributed both calendars and posters, featuring, among other things, their "black shells."

Finding and authenticating material can take a bit of doing. Next to authenticity, condition is the most important factor in judging any paper collectible, whether it is a calendar, poster, or advertising envelope. Most early posters and calendars were made with metal bands top and bottom, and if these are missing or the material has otherwise been trimmed or altered, value is greatly reduced. Tears, cracks, and heavy creases also can lessen values, as will water or other stains. Badly damaged paper goods are worth next to nothing, and fragments of calendars and posters worth even less. The prices listed are for material in very good or better condition.

One final word before you read on or head out the door with your checkbook, and the word is *reproductions.* The field of sporting advertising probably contains more reproductions than even the most suspicious collector imagines, and caution is well advised. Know what you are buying and who you are buying it from. Deal only with people who stand behind what they sell; demand written guarantees. It is far better to pass up a possibility than to purchase a "hundred-year-old piece" that was produced in Hong Kong last week.

The following list of calendars and posters is restricted to materials issued by major American manufacturers, but this does not imply that adver-

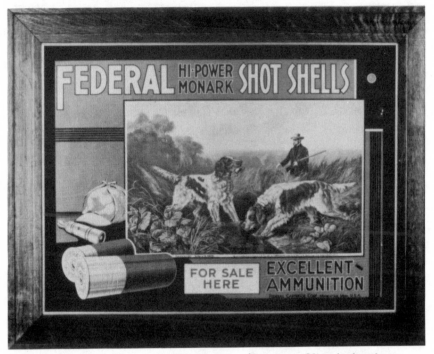

A framed Federal shot shell store poster. (Courtesy Oliver's Auction Galleries)

tising pieces by others are worth less. Posters and calendars by lesser-known firearms and powder manufactures vary greatly in value, but will generally fall within the averages indicated here. Exceptional pieces can be worth much more, as is the case with an early Oriental Powder Mills poster, worth from $1,500 to $2,000.

COLT PATENT FIRE ARMS MGF. CO.

Poster 1910: Depicting a cowgirl with a drawn Colt revolver. Variation #1 with Colt logo $1,000.00

Another: Variation #2. No logo 1,000.00

Another: Variation #3. Spanish without logo 1,000.00

Another: Variation #4. Spanish with logo 1,000.00

Poster 1921: Depicting a girl shooting a clawing jaguar.
Variation #1 in English 1,000.00

Another: Variation #2. Spanish 1,000.00

Poster 1928: Depicting a Texas Ranger by Frank
Schoonover. Variation #1 small type, no logo 800.00

Another: Variation #2. Larger type, no logo 800.00

Another: Variation #3. Logo upper left 800.00

Another: Variation #4. Logo upper right 800.00

Another: Variation #5. No advertising 800.00

Poster WWI: By C. Wilson depicting troops off to do
battle. Horizontal with bands top and bottom 350.00

Poster WWI: Entitled "Colts to the Front" depicting three
servicemen with drawn Colts 300.00

DUPONT POWDER COMPANY

Calendar 1899 . . . .   750.00

Calendar 1900 . . . .   800.00

Calendar 1901: By Edmund Osthaus 350.00

Calendar 1902 . . . .   600.00

Calendar 1905: By Osthaus 750.00

Calendar 1906 . . . .   800.00

Calendar 1907 . . . .   400.00

Calendar 1908 . . . .   300.00

Calendar 1909 . . . .   300.00

Calendar 1910: By N. C. Wyeth 300.00

Calendar 1911: By Osthaus 300.00

Calendar 1913 . . . . 250.00

Poster 1909: By Worth Brehm depicting two boys
hunting in the snow 350.00

Poster by Hy S. Watson: Depicting a woman shooting
trap with others 400.00

Poster by N. C. Wyeth: Depicting man's arrival
at trap field 300.00

Poster 1912 by Lynn Bogue Hunt: Depicting "Broadbills
Here They Come" 750.00

Poster 1913 by G. Ryder: Depicting Green-wing
teal in flight 600.00

Poster 1913 by Lynn Bogue Hunt: Depicting a covey of
bobwhite quail 500.00

Poster 1918? by Lynn Bogue Hunt: Depicting series of
prints available from DuPont 200.00

HERCULES POWDER COMPANY

Calendar 1917 by Charles Livingston Bull: Depicting
black-breasted plover 250.00

Calendar 1919 by Norman Rice: Entitled "Bagged in
France" depicting hunter with German helmet 100.00

Calendar 1920 by Arthur Fuller: Entitled "A Surprise
Party" depicting returning soldier 100.00

Calendar 1921: By Arthur Fuller entitled "Outnumbered"
depicting three boys rabbit hunting 150.00

Calendars 1922 through 1959: In fine condition 100.00

Poster by Lynn Bogue Hunt: Entitled "The Game Bird of
the Future—Chinese Pheasants" 250.00

Poster 1914: Depicting a trap shooter breaking a target   200.00

Poster 1914: Depicting ducks taking off from the water   200.00

Poster 1920 by F. M. Siegle: Entitled "Don't you fool me,
dog" depicting black man and dog 450.00

Poster 1923 by F. M. Siegle: Entitled "I'se lost de lunch"
depicting black man and boy hunting 450.00

Poster 1924 by F. M. Siegle: Entitled "Dah He Goes"
depicting black man and boy hunting 450.00

BLACKS IN SPORTING ART

I am sure that there are those who deplore seeing Black Americans portrayed derisively in sporting and other advertising art. What to like, dislike, or deplore is a matter of taste and experience. I grew up hunting with a black man named Richard who taught me much about many things. He collected black advertising posters and calendars and enjoyed them. Such art can be especially interesting to many people beyond their value as art—as sociology.

ITHACA GUN COMPANY

Poster 1909: "Cross Fox" by Lewis Agassiz Fuertes
depicting a crow escaping from a fox 450.00

Poster 1910: "Snow Shoe Rabbit" by Fuertes 400.00

Poster 1912: "Mallard Ducks" by Fuertes 500.00

Poster 1914: "Wood Cock" by Fuertes 400.00

Poster by Fuertes: Depicting passenger pigeons entitled
"Extinct Passenger Pigeons" 400.00

MARLIN FIREARMS COMPANY

Poster 1904: Entitled "A Great Shot" depicting two
hunters over their campfire 400.00

Poster 1905: Entitled "A Gun For The Man Who Knows"
by Phillip Goodwin 500.00

Poster 1907: By Goodwin depicting a hunter and guide
pushing off a canoe. Title as above 600.00

Poster 1908: By G. Muss Arnolt depicting two mallards
dead in the air 750.00

Poster 1909: By Rosseau entitled "Quail Shooting in
England" 400.00

PARKER BROTHERS GUN COMPANY

Poster 1922: By Bert Sharkey depicting
squirrels in a tree 1,000.00

Calendar 1922: As above, but calendar 1,000.00

Calendar 1929: Depicting "protected" wood ducks with
gunners in the background 1,000.00

Calendar 1930: By C. I. Couse entitled "Sacred Birds
Protected by Our Indians" 1,250.00

PETERS CARTRIDGE COMPANY

Calendar 1903: Entitled "Dawn of a New Era" depicting
an idyllic setting filled with game 500.00

Calendar 1904: Entitled "Protected" depicting a bull
moose in a snow storm 500.00

Calendar 1905: Entitled "Noon Hour" depicting two
gunners with their dogs at noon 500.00

Calendar 1906: Entitled "Coming Out Ahead" depicting a
hunter packing a moose head out of the woods 500.00

Calendar 1907: Entitled "Sun Up and Dad's Finished Milkin'—Reckon I'll get Licked" depicting boy with geese 1,000.00

Calendar 1908: Depicting duck shooter being poled by guide in marsh. Ducks on boat deck 1,000.00

Calendar 1911: By G. Muss Arnolt depicting two setters on point over covey of quail 300.00

Calendar 1912: Entitled "The Tempter" shows gunner in businessman's office 300.00

Calendar 1913: By C. Everett Johnson entitled "Getting Ready" shows man checking gear 300.00

Calendar 1914: By Lynn Bogue Hunt depicts mallard drake jumping from approaching dog 750.00

Calendar 1915: By Arnolt depicts a pair of setters on point at the edge of swale 350.00

Calendar 1916: By Frank Stick depicts mallards flocking to decoys 300.00

Calendar 1917: By Arnolt depicts two dogs on point in a cornfield 300.00

Calendar 1918: Depicting a hunter telling his setter bitch to stay with her pups 350.00

Calendar 1919: Entitled "Hurrah! You Got Him!" showing a woman and guide in the mountains 350.00

Calendar 1920: By Osthaus depicting two pointers in a stubble field 300.00

Calendar 1921: By Phillip Goodwin showing four gunners getting set for a day afield 300.00

Calendar 1922: By C. A. Meurer depicting the relics of WWI, entitled "Lest We Forget" 200.00

Calendar 1923: By Goodwin called "Outpointed" and
depicting hunter, dog, and porcupine 200.00

Calendar 1924: By G. Muss Arnolt depicting setters on
point in overgrown cover 200.00

Calendar 1925: By Joe Burgess showing mallards high
over a gunner's rig of decoys 200.00

Calendar 1926: By Arnolt depicting a covey
of bobwhite quail 200.00

Calendar 1927: By Arnolt shows beagle pack in hot
pursuit in a stubble field 200.00

Calendar 1928: By Arnolt depicts a solitary setter
on a classic point 200.00

Calendar 1929: By Lynn Bogue Hunt depicts five
mallards dropping into a marsh 300.00

Calendar 1930: By Phillip Goodwin depicts a puma eye
to eye with a hunter 200.00

Calendar 1931: By Lynn Bogue Hunt shows a pair of
pheasants in an almost Oriental setting 150.00

METAL BANDS

*Peters calendars had metal bands top and bottom through 1916. After
that the band was at the top only.*

Poster 1903: Depicting a flying mallard in the hole
of a large P 300.00

Poster 1903: Shows a trap shooter being congratulated
in the hole of a large P 300.00

Poster 1911: Depicts a hunter shooting at sharptails
in the large P 300.00

Poster 1911: By Goodwin depicts a grizzly bear with two
cubs in the mountains 400.00

Poster by Goodwin: Showing bugling elk in a
high mountain setting 400.00

Poster by Goodwin: Depicts a caribou in a
typical northern setting 400.00

Poster by G. Muss Arnolt: Depicting mallards in flight
entitled "Steel Where Steel Belongs" 750.00

Poster attributed to Arnolt: Entitled "Steel Where Steel
Belongs" depicts pheasant in flight 500.00

REMINGTON ARMS COMPANY—REMINGTON—UNION METALLIC CARTRIDGE COMPANY

Remington and UMC merged in the early 1900s, and much of their advertising overlaps: Remington for firearms and Remington-UMC for shot shells, cartridges, and general advertising. These calendars and posters are listed together here. UMC materials before the merger are listed under the UMC heading.

REMINGTON and REMINGTON-UMC

Calendar 1912: By Phillip Goodwin entitled "Going In"
shows hunters at railhead 300.00

Calendar 1913: By Carl Rungius depicts moose wading
in lily pads 400.00

Calendar 1917: By Lynn Bogue Hunt depicts covey of
quail in flight 300.00

Calendar 1919: By Hunt depicts diving hawk attacking
flight of Canada geese as they flee 750.00

Calendar 1921: Attributed to Hunt. Depicts fox attacking
two Canada geese 750.00

Calendar 1922: Entitled "Game Loads Get Em!" depicts
sportsmen with purchase of ammunition 300.00

Calendar 1923: Depicts hunter painting decoys with
decoys, shot shells, and 1922 calendar in background ..   600.00

Calendar 1925: Entitled "Let 'Er Rain" depicts old
gunner and decoys in boat 500.00

Calendar 1926: Depicts old gunner cleaning gun on deck
of gunning camp with decoys showing 500.00

Calendar 1928: By Hy S. Watson depicts old-timer with
dog entitled "Old Boy! We Have The Winning—" 200.00

Poster 1901: By F. E. Getty depicts a sassy sportswoman
with a Remington gun 600.00

Poster 1906: Depicts a "well-turned-out" gunner
with autoloading shotguns 300.00

Poster 1907: Shows a hunter and grizzly meeting on
a narrow trail 500.00

Poster by N. C. Wyeth: Depicts hunters approaching
a fishing bear 350.00

Poster 1913: By Hy Watson shows black man directing
hunters and their dogs 300.00

Poster by Carl Rungius: See 1913 calendar 250.00

Poster: Of young boy and dog looking over
a groundhog's digs 150.00

SAVAGE-STEVENS

Calendar 1904 by C. Rungius: Showing hunter with a
downed bull elk 500.00

Poster by Phillip Goodwin: Depicting hunter and guide
in a canoe with guide calling moose 300.00

Poster 1906: Depicting a sportswoman with a gun and a
man showing off a pair of wood ducks 750.00

Poster by Lewis A. Fuertes: Showing a mule deer in
a snowy setting 300.00

Calendar 1921 by Charles Livingston Bull: Showing a
lynx with dead turkey in a live oak 500.00

Calendar 1947: By Richard Bishop entitled "There They
Are" depicting mallards in flight 100.00

UNION METALLIC CARTRIDGE COMPANY

Calendar 1889: Depicts an "Annie Oakley" type woman
loading a shot gun 1,500.00

Calendar 1890: Entitled "The French in Algeria" was
produced for French UMC agent 1,200.00

Calendar 1891: Depicts a young girl dressed for the hunt
surrounded by hounds 750.00

Calendar 1892: Depicts boy in costume of the day with a
gun that is bigger than he is 750.00

Calendar 1893: Depicts black guide poling a boat as
hunter picks up duck from water 1,250.00

Calendar 1896: Depicts Indian mounted on horse in
a desert setting 600.00

Calendar 1897: Entitled "Saving His Scalp" shows rider
escaping from Indians 600.00

Calendar 1898: By Gilbert Gaul entitled "Molly
Pitcher at Monmouth—" 500.00

Calendar 1899: Depicts soldier and sailor and war
scenes of Cuba 400.00

Calendar 1900: Depicts the head of a bison close-up
in grassy setting 500.00

Calendar 1901: Entitled "A Chip Off The Old Block"
shows boy, gun, and game birds bagged 600.00

Poster by Oliver Kemp: Entitled "Calling The Moose"
also illustrates cartridges for big game 300.00

Poster: Illustrates "Shot Gun Ammunition" with shot
shell and window shell illustration 300.00

Poster 1905: By Everett C. Johnson entitled "In A Tight
Place" shows charging bear 300.00

Poster 1906: By Johnson shows mountain lion pursued
by hunter and hounds 350.00

Poster 1907: By Lynn Bogue Hunt depicts pair of
blue-wing teal 500.00

Poster 1908: Depicts a covey of quail in flight headed
toward the viewer 400.00

UNITED STATES CARTRIDGE COMPANY

Poster 1890: Depicts 75 "Popular and Expert Trap
Shooters of America" including Annie Oakley 750.00

Poster 1911: "The Black Shells" depicts man,
dog, and ammunition 400.00

Calendar 1917 by Alexander Pope: Depicts hanging
mallards, shells, and gun 500.00

Calendar 1919: "The Black Shells" shows hunter with
bag of ruffed grouse 300.00

Calendar 1922: Depicts bear with wooden case of "Black Shells" 500.00

Calendar 1925: By H. C. Edwards shows shooter in rigged sink-box 600.00

Calendar 1926: By William Eaton depicts old-timer touching up decoys 400.00

Calendar 1927: Depicts 8 mallards in flight over marsh and rigged decoys 450.00

Calendar 1928: By Joe Burgess shows gunner sitting with setter puppies and bitch 300.00

Calendar 1929: By William H. Foster depicts hunter tugging beagle past hidden rabbit 350.00

Poster: Depicting falcon attacking green-wing teal pair entitled "The Black Shells" 1,750.00

Poster by Burgess: Shows Canada geese huddled in marsh during thunderstorm 500.00

Poster by Burgess: Depicts Canada geese flying through thunderstorm 600.00

WESTERN CARTRIDGE COMPANY

Calendar 1920: By William Eaton depicts card-playing hunters in camp 250.00

Calendar 1921: By Eaton entitled "Devotion" depicts hunter sneaking by church 250.00

Calendars 1922–1934 . . . . 150.00

Poster by A. Russell: Entitled "The Unexpected" depicts an old black man and a boy smoking out a snake 750.00

Poster by A. Russell: Entitled "You Can't Shoot Without Shells" shows black family and dogs 750.00

DETERMINING VALUES

Three factors determine the overall worth of a given poster or calendar and, to a lesser degree, that of envelopes, cards, and other materials considered advertising. Scarcity is, of course the primary factor, but the artist and, more particularly, the subject matter, must be considered as well. People who buy these things want to display them, and the question "How will this look on my wall" cannot be ignored.

Poster by V. K. Murray: Entitled "The Elk Fight"
depicts just that 200.00

Poster: Entitled "Champions of America" shows 200-
target winners Frank Troeh and Bart Lewis
at trap field 250.00

Poster by Norman Hall: Depicts black man napping and
dreaming of rabbits. Entitled "Dreams" 350.00

WINCHESTER ARMS COMPANY

Calendar 1887: Depicts deer, elk, and turkey shooting in
scenes from *Harpers* magazine 2,000.00

Calendar 1888: Depicts moose, bear, and seal shooting
in scenes from *Harpers* magazine 1,200.00

Calendar 1889: By A. B. Frost depicts duck, bear,
and deer shooting 1,200.00

Calendar 1890: Depicts scenes from *Harpers* of moose,
duck, sheep, and deer shooting 1,200.00

Calendar 1891: By Frederick Remington entitled "Shoot
Or You Will Lose Them" 1,200.00

Calendar 1892: By Remington depicts sheep hunting,
plainsman, and deer shooting from canoe 1,200.00

REPRODUCTIONS

In 1960, Winchester reissued their old calendars, and although these are clearly identified, many unsuspecting collectors have paid too much for this modern material. The early reissues are increasing in value, but so far have leveled at the fifty-dollar range: This is far less than the originals, which run to four figures. Remington and Peters materials have also been reissued in clearly identified editions, but a considerable number of Peters calendars are around as unmarked reproductions, and the buyer is advised to use great care with them.

Calendar 1893: By Remington entitled "Hang On To Them" 1,200.00

Calendar 1894: By Remington entitled "A Surprise Party" 1,200.00

Calendar 1895: By A. B. Frost entitled "An Unexpected Chance" 600.00

Calendar 1896: By Frost entitled "A Finishing Touch" . .   600.00

Calendar 1897: By Frost entitled "A Chance Shot" and "An Interrupted Dinner" 600.00

Calendar 1898: By Frost entitled "The 30 Did It" depicts elk and duck hunting 600.00

Calendar 1899: By Frost entitled "We've Got Him Sure" 600.00

Calendar 1900: By Frost entitled "Waiting For A Shot At The Old Ram" 600.00

Calendar 1901: By Frost entitled "Fresh Meat for the Outfit" 600.00

Three panels of a five-part Winchester store display promoting trap, the "Alluring" sport. (Courtesy Oliver's Auction Galleries)

Calendar 1912: By N. C. Wyeth depicts two hunters facing a cornered bear 500.00

Calendar 1913: By Robert Robinson depicting an old hunter with gun and pipe 500.00

Calendar 1914: By George Brehm depicting hunter with dogs on point in cornfield 400.00

Calendar 1915: By Lynn Bogue Hunt depicts eagle attacking Rocky Mountain goats 750.00

Calendar 1916: By Phillip Goodwin shows two hunters on the trail in the mountains 400.00

Calendar 1917: By W. K. Leigh shows hunters trying to load elk on bucking horse 500.00

Calendar 1918: By George Brehm depicts father and son rabbit shooting 300.00

Calendar 1919: By Robert Amick shows farmer plowing and watching waterfowl in flight 450.00

Calendar 1920: Depicts father and son in boat returning with bag of ducks 350.00

Calendar 1921: By Arthur Fuller shows father and son and setter on point 350.00

Calendar 1922: By E. C. Edwards shows cowboy meeting bear on narrow trail 400.00

Calendar 1923: By Goodwin depicts hunter high above a herd of trophy sheep 400.00

Calendar 1924: By G. Ryder depicts gunner in reeds awaiting approaching ducks 300.00

Calendar 1925: By H. R. Poore depicts pointers with setters in background 500.00

Calendar 1926: By Goodwin shows hunter facing bear at point-blank range 350.00

Calendar 1927: By Frank Stick shows hunter on snowshoes approaching deer 400.00

Calendar 1928: By P. F. Elwell depicts hunters in canoe sneaking up on moose 350.00

Calendar 1929: By Lynn Bogue Hunt depicts dog, gunner, and flushing pheasants 400.00

Calendar 1930: Depicts hunter holding calendar pages, which include some fishing scenes 300.00

Store calendars: 1921–1929 . . . . 200.00 to 300.00

Poster 1904: Entitled "The Kind That Gets Them" depicts
hunter with trophy sheep 800.00

Poster 1905: Entitled "Cock of the Woods" depicts a
large turkey in a wooded setting 1,000.00

Poster 1906: Depicts hunter on
snowshoes stalking game 850.00

Poster: Entitled "They Are the Hitters" shows three
mallards in flight 700.00

Poster 1909: Depicts woman with rifle standing near
canoe in wooded setting 1,000.00

Anyone seriously interested in sporting-advertising calendars, posters,
and store displays cannot be without Bob and Beverly Strauss's two-volume
American Sporting Advertising. See Appendix.

Appendix

There are hundreds of reliable dealers. These are some I have dealt with myself and can recommend. I will be adding to these lists in subsequent editons of this book.

Sporting Art and Prints

The Bedford Sportsman: Bedford Hills, NY 10507
Collector's Choice: 10725 Equestrian Drive, Santa Ana, CA 92705
Crossroads of Sport: 36 West 44 Street, New York, NY 10036
Russell A. Fink Gallery: 9843 Gunston Road, Lorton, VA 22079
Ernest Hickok: 382 Springfield Avenue, Summit, NJ 07901
Petersen Galleries: 9433 Wilshire Blvd., Beverly Hills, CA 90212
Sportsman's Edge: 136 East 74 Street, New York, NY 10021
Wild Wings: Lake City, MN 55041

Sporting-Book Auctions

Oinonen Book Auctions: Box 470, Sunderland, MA 01375
Swann Auction Galleries: 104 East 25 Street, New York, NY 10010

Sporting-Book Dealers

Anglers & Shooters Bookshelf: Goshen, CT 06756
Anglers Art: P.O. Box 148, Plainfield, PA 17081
Johnny Appleseed's Books: Route 7A, Manchester, VT 05254
Judith Bowman Books: Pound Ridge Road, Bedford, NY 10506
Callahan & Co.: Box 505, Peterborough, NH 03458
Gary Estabrook: Box 61453, Vancouver, WA 98666
Fin 'N Feather Gallery, Box 13, N. Gramby, CT 06060
David Foley, 76 Bonneville Rd., West Hartford, CT 06107
Game Bag Books, 2704 Ship Rock Rd., Willow Street, PA 17584
Ernest Hickok: 382 Springfield Avenue, Summit, NJ 07901
Highwood Bookshop: Box 1246, Traverse City, MI 49685
Pisces and Capricorn Books: 514 Linden, Albion, MI 49224
Ray Riling Arms Books: Box 18925, Philadelphia, PA 19119
Trophy Room Books: 4858 Dempsey Avenue, Encino, CA 91436

Duck Stamps and Duck-Stamp Prints

Russell A. Fink Gallery: 9843 Gunston Road, Lorton, VA 22079
National Wildlife Philatelics: Box 061397, Fort Meyers, FL 33905
Wild Wings: Lake City, MN 55041

Fishing-Tackle Auctions

Oliver's Auction Galleries: Route 1, Plaza 1, Kennebunk, ME 04043

Fishing Tackle Museum

American Museum of Fly Fishing, Route 7A, Manchester, VT 05254

Fishing Tackle and Accessories

The American Sporting Collector: Arden Drive, Amawalk, NY 10501
Frederick Grafeld: 297 Born Street, Seacaucus, NJ 07094
Martin J. Keane: P.O. Box 288, Ashley Falls, MA 01222
John E. Schoffner: 624 Merritt, Fife Lake, MI 49633
Thomas & Thomas: Turners Falls, MA 01376

Decoy Dealers

Henry Fleckenstein, Box 577, Cambridge, MD 21613
RJG Antiques, P.O. Box 2033, Hampton, N.H. 03842

Decoy Auctions

Richard A. Bourne Co., Inc.: P.O. Box 141, Hyannisport, MA 02647
Ted Harmon: 2320 Main Street, West Barnstable, MA 02668
James Julia—Gary Guyette: P.O. Box 830, Fairfield, ME 04937
Oliver's Auction Galleries: Route 1, Plaza 1, Kennebunk, ME 04043

Fish Decoys at Auction

Oliver's Auction Galleries: Route 1, Plaza 1, Kennebunk, ME 04043

Sporting Firearms

W. M. Bryan & Co.: P.O. Box 12492, Raleigh, NC 27605
Cape Outfitters: Route 3, Box 437, Cape Girardeau, MO 63701
Chadick's Ltd.: Box 100, Terrell, TX 75160
Michael de Chevrieux: P.O. Box 1182, Hailey, ID 83333
Griffin & Howe: 33 Claremont Road, Bernardsville, NJ 07924
New England Arms Co.: Kittery Point, ME 03905

Shooting Accessories

Circus Promotions: 614 Cyprus Wood Drive, Spring, TX 77388
James Tillinghast: P.O. Box 19–C, Hancock, NH 03449

Sporting Advertising

Circus Promotions: 614 Cyprus Wood Drive, Spring, TX 77388
Robert P. Hanafee: 29 Bedford Court, Amherst, MA 01002

ADVERTISING

IN THE

BACK OF BOOK

A tried and true idea that's time has come again!

We trust you share our enthusiasm for the following advertisements that are related to the theme of this book and hope you avail yourself of the services offered. And, if you think that advertising like this is something new, think again. There was a time in this country when most of the books published carried advertising of one kind or another and we plan to continue this service to the trade. Information may be obtained by writing to the Sporting Collectibles Price Guide - Jamaica, Vermont 05343-0251.

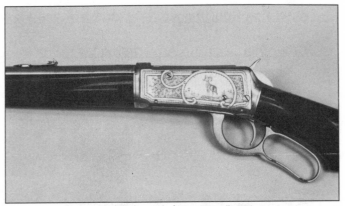

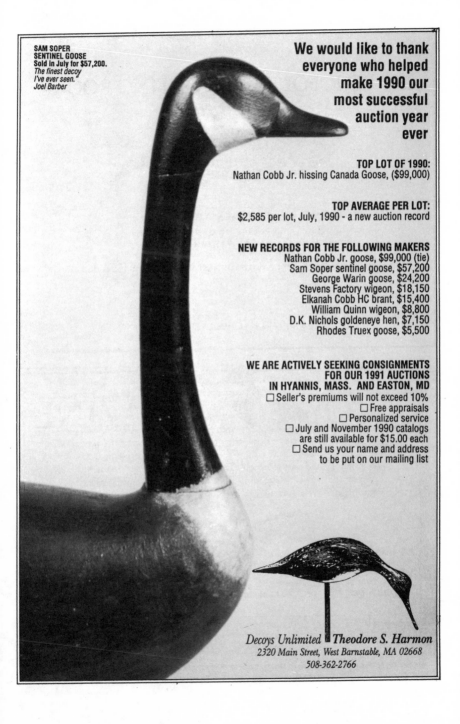

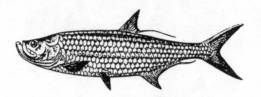

THE HORSE IN LANDSCAPE

FOUR HUNTERS   8¼" × 8¾"

CHRISTINE DALY
Watercolors

6365 E. Arcade Rd.
Arcade, N.Y. 14009
(716) 492-0846

THE DOUBLE GUN JOURNAL

Between gold foil stamped leatherette covers and on the finest gloss enamel stock you will find us to be the first and only periodical in the world that is totally dedicated to double shotguns, rifles and to everything we love to do with them.

Just full of beautiful photos and masterfully written articles by the world's top experts, we are the world's finest quarterly book about the world's best guns.

FOUR BEAUTIFUL BOOKS ★ $35 PER YEAR
Visa, MC, Ck, M.O. Accepted • Send/Call Orders 1-800-447-1658
*U.S. FUNDS • CANADA: Add $8, OVERSEAS: $10, P.O.R. airmail • ADDITIONAL SUBSCRIBER BENEFITS AND DISCOUNTS INCLUDED

Route 1
Box 319 **EAST JORDAN, MICHIGAN** U.S.A.
49727

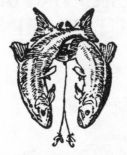
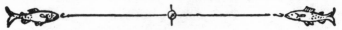

WELCOME 1990s

We are looking forward to continuing
in the next decade as one of your favorite
stores to purchase art work (prints,
reproductions and originals) and other
collectibles. We believe that you will
share our excitement about our plans for
the coming year.

SINCE 1938

36 WEST 44th STREET
NEW YORK, N.Y. 10036

(212) 764-8877

CONFUSION CAN BE COSTLY

This book and subsequent editions can help today's sporting collectors keep abreast of the chaos, costs and changes in the world of sporting antiques and collectibles, but if you want to stay ahead of the game you need more. So, with this in mind, I have decided to publish a bimonthly newsletter devoted to the ins and outs and everyday happenings of this volatile marketplace. You might say it will pick up where this book leaves off. The first issue is at the printers so if you want the latest prices, news and 'insider' gossip, subscribe today.

One year (six issues) - $24.00
Sent by First Class Mail